JULIE BURCHILL
the Guardian Columns 1998–2000

JULIE BURCHILL

the Guardian Columns 1998–2000

ORION

An Orion Paperback Original

First published in Great Britain in 2001 by
Orion, an imprint of the Orion Publishing Group Ltd.

Copyright © Julie Burchill 2001

The right of Julie Burchill to be identified as the
author of this work has been asserted by her in
accordance with the Copyright, Designs and Patents Act 1988

A CIP catalogue record for this book
is available from the British Library

ISBN 0–75284–380-X

Typeset in Great Britain by
Deltatype Ltd, Birkenhead, Wirral
Printed and bound by Clays Ltd, St Ives, plc

The Orion Publishing Group
Orion House
5 Upper St Martin's Lane
London WC2H 9EA

For Susan and Murphy

Acknowledgements

The author would like to thank Ritchie Parrott, Katharine Viner and Alan Rusbridger of the *Guardian* for their considerable patience and good humour.

1998

17 JANUARY 1998

Well, I know that nobody loves them now, but if the Eighties ever want a reference they can certainly come round here. I shall be more than happy to oblige. Because the Eighties were my kind of decade: shallow, shimmering and shifty. I had the biggest, reddest flat in the West End, a baby who looked as though he'd left his wings with the hat-check girl and the ultimate proof of my worth: I was mentioned in soap operas. 'I'll be the next Julie Burchill, just you see!' young Karen Grant would threaten her wet-blanket elders in *Brookside* when they wanted her to get A Sensible Job; 'I'll be the Julie Burchill of Ambridge,' piped Elizabeth Archer less convincingly in *The Archers*. You and a million others, honey, I would smirk knowingly, for by the decade's end New Julie Burchills were about as frequent as sightings of Nessie, the Ab Snowman and Lord Lucan put together. And always greatly exaggerated. I first became a columnist at 24, in 1984, when I left *The Face* to go to Andrew Neil's young, thrusting *Sunday Times*. Them were the days.

A bottle of Bollinger, a gram of coke, dinner at Langan's and you still got change out of 80,000K p.a. I remember the champagne flowed like the Fanta had in my poor, deprived childhood, and often me and my brash, young compadres – Robert Elms, Lesley White, Toby Young, so you can see how long ago it was because it must be ten years since I've exchanged a civil word with any of them – would chuck it on the pot plants because we'd had enough that week and it was still only

Wednesday. To have had so much champagne before you're 30 that you end up watering plants with it is a privilege I believe I was the first generation of the Burchill family to enjoy, *pace* Mr Blair and his fancy education.

I remember my friend at the *Sunday Times* telling me that Bel Mooney had been 'let go' to make way for me because she was 'Seventies' and I was 'Eighties', and – young brute that I was – I just sniggered. Later, at the *Mail on Sunday*, Lady Falkender faced the drop so that I might step up to her mark, and back at the *Sunday Times* a few years later so did that film critic who wrote that turkey with John Cleese – his name escapes me.

I always had the best jobs and the best money; I was always headhunted and never had to go around touting myself, as I was aware some journalists of my age had to. But unbeknownst to me, my salad days were numbered, even if they did have seven sorts of lettuce in them. Because the Nineties were coming up on the inside track, and this dishonest and dull decade required chroniclers as banal and boring as itself. I finally went a bridge too far when, for the sum of £135,000, I followed my original mentor, the bold and brilliant Susan Douglas, to the *Sunday Express*, where she had been made editor. The *Sunday Express*! – house magazine of net-curtain twitchers, doily-fanciers and sex-starved, suburban, self-abusing spouses everywhere. The very boldness and brilliance of Susan set down in this milieu should have given us pause; it was a bit like asking Lucretia Borgia to run a car-boot sale. But it's hard to see straight with those dollar signs clogging up your eyes.

Too bold, too brilliant; this wasn't the Eighties any more, Toto. Finally, we woke up one summer's day in 1995 to find that Susan had been sacked by the new caring, sharing owner of Express Newspapers, Blair's beast Lord Hollick, and we, her 'creatures' – I and a brace of other youngish, stylish journalists –

with her. That was the end of the Eighties, for me: halfway up the Nineties without a paddle.

I'd always known that, like Ruth and Naomi in the Bible, Susan and I would sink or swim together. We had, after all, lived through the vicious rumours that she was the inspiration for my masterpiece *Ambition*, and through the years at the *Sunday Times* when I was rudely called 'Caligula's Horse', after the boy-emperor's mount made a consul by his brash and capricious young owner. But I wasn't prepared for us being sent off without any supper like a pair of naughty schoolgirls and, more than that, I certainly wasn't used to being replaced.

When I read the new editor's sermon, reassuring his readers that this would be a paper that listened to the addlepates thick enough to buy it and that the first thing they'd demanded was that I get the sack, I felt nothing. I laughed. Those things didn't happen to me. My mirth was increased when I read that I could 'Read her exciting new replacement Kate Saunders inside'. I laughed so hard I almost choked on my Triple Sec, and it was only 10 a.m. Kate Saunders! Kate Saunders is many things – blonde, punctual, own teeth – but she is not, was not then and, I can't imagine, ever really was either 'new' or 'exciting'. She was safe; she was going to dispense sensible views in bite-sized, nutritionally balanced spoonfuls over breakfast tables across the nation, and she was not going to cause heartburn to and irritate the hell out of her sex-starved readers with teasers of her own gorgeous, lurid life. Which, it must be admitted, I sometimes couldn't stop myself from doing.

As David St Hubbins says of himself after the departure of Nigel Tufnel in *Spinal Tap*: 'I'd be more upset if I wasn't so heavily sedated!' Some sort of natural sedative must have kicked in that first time I got the sack because I don't remember worrying about it at all. But slowly, as my bank balance dwindled and the phone stayed silent, I realised that the sort of people I had once replaced were now replacing me – I had been exiled to make the world safe for the likes of Tara Palmer-Tomkinson, Tony Parsons and Bridget Jones. In short, the Nattering Classes were taking over the asylum.

I tried to move with the new beat, honest I did.

But somehow, the Holy Trinity of the Nattering Classes Column – I'm A Bloke, Me; I Can't Get A Boyfriend, I Can't; and I'm Dying, I Am – were beyond my frame of reference. The only other alternative for someone my age was what I came to think of as the Sensible Shoes column: obvious opinions expressed in very clear terms by very dull young women who had obviously never turned a stylish sentence in their lives. 'You used to be big,' my faithful retainer at the Sussex Arts Club used to commiserate, à la *Sunset Boulevard*, over one for the road. 'I'm still big,' I'd snarl. 'It's the columns that got small.' Well, I'm still not a man. I'm in rude health, and I haven't been without a boyfriend for more than 24 hours since I was 12. I don't have any sensible shoes, either, but for some reason I seem to have fallen on my feet, and if you'll take my hand, delivered in the spirit of friendship, I'll do my best to take you on a walk on the wildish side every weekend. Hell, I know I've said some evil things about *Guardian* readers in my time, but it's false consciousness and all that. The important thing is that I'm back. BACK, BACK! And I love you all. Trust me – I know we can make it. Whaddya say? Because, after all, even in the touchy-feely Yellow Submariney Technicolor Dreamboat that is Blair's Britain, every medium needs an urchin (admittedly overgrown and over-age, but hey, I was always the oldest juvenile lead in the business since Mickey Rooney) pointing out that something is wrong with this picture. And if not us, then who?

'**No more Mr** Nice Guy,' said Gary Lineker ominously, looking down at Ulrika Jonsson as she lay blondely on the bed. He went to steal her crisps. She tried to grab them back. He drew back his fist and punched her square in the face. I awoke with a start. Gary wouldn't do that, and, of course, no footballer has punched Ulrika. She has dated one though – Stan Collymore, the Aston Villa striker. He's currently awaiting trial for allegedly assaulting his ex, the mother of his children. Was he a man behaving badly? All through the Nineties, football has been famous for four things. People getting killed. Players going out with famous glamour girls: Jamie and Louise, David and Posh, Dani and . . . ah, how much time have you got? And players beating up women.

Oh yes, and anti-racist initiatives. In 1993, the FA and the Commission for Racial Equality launched the hearty-sounding Let's Kick Racism Out of Football campaign. Last year, it was re-launched as the rather more brutalist Kick It Out campaign. It's the difference between Biggles and the Mitchell brothers, this new handle, and came at an unfortunate time: one when women seem to be on the other end of the boot more often than the ball.

The phenomenon of the woman-assaulting sportsman (and every week there is a new, more unexpected one – Boycott, Giggs – to add to the shameful roster of O. J. Simpson, Tyson, Higgins and Gascoigne) is one of the ugliest yet most eerily acceptable of modern times.

Any assault on a woman by a man, unless he acts in self-defence, is contemptible; this is something even hardened criminals have accepted in the past. Controlling your feelings, unless you were nailing the head of a rival gangland pasha to an occasional table, was part of being a man. A sportsman, trained to the peak of his fitness, his body a temple, should have even more regard for his own strength and thus more control of it.

But these are the happy-clappy, touchy-feely Nineties, and not-bottling-it-up is all the rage.

And, unfortunately, rage seems to be the principal emotion that men are unbottling. When they do this, they are treated as though they, not the woman they attacked, was actually the victim of the rage – as though it was a natural phenomenon, like a tornado, that buffeted them about beyond their control. It is not a matter for the police, but for the therapist. And this is why, increasingly, violence against women goes unpunished.

When Paul Gascoigne disgraced himself by beating up his wife Sheryl, there was what amounted to a chorus of approval – from the FA, which excused the incident as a 'domestic' to the 'Christian' Glenn Hoddle, who said it was a private matter and that Sheryl, like Jesus, should turn the other cheek while Paulie got 'help'. On the other hand, Gascoigne's recent miming of playing the flute when he scores a goal for his Protestant team has incensed Catholics and reaped him several death threats.

We can only imagine what the reaction would have been had Gascoigne beaten up an innocent black bystander at that hotel that day. A year later, while out drinking with Chris Evans and Danny Baker, Gascoigne is said to have hit another woman, a complete stranger, in the face. Of this incident, Danny Baker later said, 'It's obvious Gazza has a problem with women, but he's always a lovely bloke around me.' Can we imagine Baker saying of a friend who had beaten up two black men on two separate occasions, 'It's obvious Gazza has a problem with black men, but . . .'? It remains a sad fact that those men who believe in the brotherhood of man do not seem to understand that it should include women. It's as though, these days, if you declare yourself an anti-racist, you can then practise misogyny with impunity. Look at the black/white Prodigy, who sing merrily of smacking their bitch up but would never dream of boasting about doing the same to their Paki or their coon. It's interesting to note that in PC-backlash publications such as *Loaded* no racist jokes raise their heads; it is women, and women alone, who are fair game for ugly humour once more. Imagine what the reaction would have been had Gascoigne hit a black woman – would that have been a man hitting a woman (okay) or a white hitting a black (bad)?

Racism has become a heinous crime, unrelative and total, even if it's just a few thick football fans making monkey noises at black players; sexism is a 'yes, but . . .', even when it ends up with a fist in the face. It's as though racism is a public matter on which the party whips make sure we all go into the NO lobby, while sexism is somehow a 'private' matter, an issue best left to individual conscience, like fox-hunting. But sexism and racism are both social evils; there is simply nothing to choose between them. When Jack Straw put forward plans last year to make racist attacks automatically carry more punishment than other violent assaults, we saw the idiocy of awarding racism a special place in the pecking order of person's inhumanity to person. So beating up a six-two black bouncer is worse than beating up an arthritic 80-year-old white woman? Really?

Of course, everybody's doing it these days. Each morning edition reveals a new luvvie lashing out at his missus, or a vicar doing the hammer-of-God number on his sleeping wife. It would be unfair to cite sportsmen alone as harbouring violent misogynists among their number. What does stick in the craw, though, is the repeated emphasis by the FA, Sports Minister and players on how unacceptable the racist thuggery of their fans is while violent assaults on women continue unpunished by the clubs. Exactly why is a fan who shouts racist abuse doing worse than a player who beats up a woman? Exactly who is bringing the game into disrepute? You'd have thought that people would have got the hang of it by now. If it's wrong to victimise someone because of colour, it's wrong to victimise someone because of gender. There is in sport, though, a woman-loathing strand of homo-eroticism that sees the bodies of men as clean, forever scab-kneed 12-year-old boys, and the bodies of women as honeytraps, not quite nice: 'Stay away from the girls, laddie. They'll drain you before the Big Fight.' As long as footballers are treated like boys, they will think it quite acceptable to knock around soppy girls. It's time they grew up, the crying, screeching, punching lot of them.

It was a great black man, Dick Gregory, who said, 'Woman is the nigger of the world.' The men of the Football Association should spend some time considering this. Until they do, why should any woman care whether Stan Collymore gets a bunch of bananas thrown at him? It beats a bunch of fives any day.

7 FEBRUARY 1998

Once upon a time, 'adultery' spoke in the smoke-roughened voices of James M. Cain's beautiful losers, drifters and grifters. The men and women who schemed their way across the great American thriller-writer's pages had been pushed over the edge by passion, yet they still retained a sort of soiled sanctity. The lips that had lied while a hand rested lightly on the Bible still tasted sweet as they met those of their nemesis one more time, before the condemned lover joined the padre on that last long walk to the gallows . . .

And quite right too. Adultery should be something special. The word is, in its way, onomatopoeic – it sounds like what it is, something that only adults are allowed to do. In the sexual supermarket of party favours, ADULTERY stands out carved in stone among the tawdry kiss-me-quicks of bonking, cheating and two-timing. It is a greater betrayal than any other thing you can do within the bounds of a consensual adult relationship, but it has something dignified about it. You've read about it in the Bible, been told that God thinks it is one of the worst ten things in the world, yet you can dare do it anyway and the sky still doesn't fall upon your head.

But adultery is not what it used to be. And what it actually is now is becoming more and more unclear. The President of the US, apparently, believes that heterosexual oral sex is not adultery. Experts on the constitution of this country have ruled that adultery does not disqualify a man from becoming king or even becoming the head of the Church of England. The law of the land says that lesbian sex is not adultery – but more of that later. An open marriage isn't considered adultery any more, and neither is an 'arrangement' whereby both sides know what's going on. In Ang Lee's new film *The Ice Storm*, we see the ultimate de-caffing of adultery: suburban wife-swapping, something about as sexually arousing as a hostess trolley.

What once were outlaws have now become in-laws, wild as Wednesday, forever working late at the office. More and more, modern adultery seems like just another furtive thing that sad-sack old geezers do, like watching the hotel porn channels and pretending it was an accident, or just another way in which men seek to normalise their own sexual incontinence, like not criminalising kerb-crawlers but still criminalising prostitutes.

Above all, modern adultery is what ugly, middle-aged men have when their wives understand them too well ever to put them on a pedestal again. Cecil Parkinson, David Mellor, Paddy Ashdown, Alan Clark, Robin Cook ... Where adultery once spoke of arcane practices and exotic substances, it now makes me think of trouser presses. Because they make it look so tidy, Robin Cook and his pen-pushing, time-managing ilk – a simple matter of in-trays and out-trays and keeping a neat desk.

Off with the old, on with the new.

But adultery is a messy business, whatever way you slice it. People just know this. According to a recent Mori poll, 79 per cent of people believe that fidelity is more important to marriage than understanding, respect, common interests or even good sex.

Without God or Marx to comfort us, the signs are that we will continue to place ever more importance on the constancy of our Significant Other. 'Have you seen a human heart?' asks a character in Patrick Marber's play about sexual betrayal, *Closer*. 'It looks like a fist covered in blood.' This, not New Labour's prim witterings about 'partners' and press intrusion, is the reality of adultery.

That's why our eyebrows, neck-hair and hackles should rise when we hear some raddled old roué banging on about how civilised they are about these things across the Channel, where that old devil Mitterrand was not less but actually more respected for running two households. Well, *vive la différence*, because the French attitude to adultery fits in very well with the fact that French women didn't get the vote until 1945, that they have fewer female MPs than any other Western European country and that sexual harassment is considered something of a joke there.

On recent showings, tolerance of adultery in public life is not indicative of sexual enlightenment but rather of sexual conservatism. The whole debate continues to be framed in terms which accept that married men can do exactly as they please while married women cannot. The King of Siam believed this, the Victorians believed it, and it looks like the American people believe it. The English ruling class has traditionally believed it – all except Princess Diana, of course, who was obviously a lunatic because she really believed that her husband would be faithful to her. For while Bill Clinton's popularity has apparently gone up since the latest blow by blowjob accounts of his priapism, can we seriously imagine a female leader walking around the White House or Number 10 demanding instant oral gratification from young male researchers and getting away with it?

If we'd found out that Mrs Thatcher had been doing this sort of thing, we wouldn't have thought she was refreshingly upfront. We'd have considered it proof that she was mad, and we'd have chucked her out of office in disgrace.

No matter that being President of the US is a very important job indeed, and presenting a light-entertainment show on television is not quite so responsible. It seems very likely that Clinton will keep his job, while Paula Yates was no longer considered clean enough to be allowed into the nation's living rooms. (What, one wonders, did David Mellor have that Paula Yates didn't – after all, for him adultery spelt the start of a whole new, shiny, big media career. It's true that good looks get you forgiven everything.)

I was divorced by my first husband for adultery, and I was so much in love with my second husband, the co-respondent, that I saw this as a badge of honour; a red, heart-shaped badge of courage in the sex war, perhaps, or a certificate of proficiency in the marital – as opposed to martial – arts. So when I fell in love again three years ago, I asked my lawyer if I might be divorced for adultery a second time.

Imagine my surprise when I was informed that, as the latest

co-respondent was a woman, adultery was out of the question. My failure in this attempt at married life was classed in law, he informed me, as 'unreasonable behaviour'. I couldn't help it, I had to say it: 'Unreasonable behaviour! Have you seen her? It would have been bloody unreasonable behaviour not to sleep with her!'

But unreasonable behaviour it had to be, which put me off the whole idea of divorce altogether. For this, and for many other reasons, adulterer is no longer a label I wish to attach to myself. I've learned my lesson. It's a shame that those even older and uglier than me haven't grasped it yet.

14 FEBRUARY 1998

You'll be reading this column later than usual, of course, because when you woke up this morning you had to wade through a waist-high of love. Then, most likely, you'll have opened a half-split of bubbly and a carton of Tropicana, stuck them on a tray with one perfect croissant and one perfect rosebud, and nipped back upstairs sharpish to make love to the one you desire more than anybody on earth. Afterwards, you'll have had a cigarette and laughed softly to yourself as you perused with ease the optician's chart opposite your bed. And they told you that masturbation would make you go blind!

We've been told to practise safe sex for more than a decade now, and masturbation was always the safest sort there was. But you'll most likely be doing it not because you're scared of catching something but because you're afraid of being caught. They always called it the Sex War, but it seemed a bit of a regional skirmish before. Now it really is a battlefield, and every aisle at Waitrose a potential foxhole. There are books of rules for both sides to refer to when they look like they're about to take a prisoner, sort of a Geneva Convention, and lots of them are written by a man called John Gray.

John Gray is the author of, among others, the bestselling *Men Are from Mars, Women Are from Venus*. I've just seen him on *Richard and Judy*, and what he said sums up the many words he has written: 'Men want sex, women want romance.' Then he advised that, '*Women need regular romance* [my italics] to get them in the mood for sex; men need the promise of sex to make them romantic.'

I suppose it's the word regular that makes me feel queasy, having as it does a whiff of the lavatory about it: keep regular, try ROMANCE! But even before this, I have always been appalled by the idea of romance. I love being in love, but romance strikes me as as much a perversion of the love instinct as prostitution is a perversion of the sex instinct.

Romance started off symbolising the Good Life. Now anyone can have a box of chocs and a bunch of flowers, it's just not the same. We are getting wise to the cheesiness of the whole thing. In the Seventies, the TV heart-throb Gerald Harper had a Sunday morning radio show aimed at housewives, and he was always saying things like 'Champagne, anyone?' and generally being a bit of a David Niven-type smoothie. You couldn't put that out now except as a Steve Coogan character.

We are always being told that Mills & Boon books sell in their hundreds of thousands – and Barbara Cartland's even more so. But if this is so, how come they never get into the bestseller lists? I've had a number-one book in the charts; it's not that difficult. That book was full of sex, though – not romance. Most of its readers were women, as are the readers of the massively successful Black Lace books. The last woman to be more interested in romance than sex was the poor Princess of Wales, her young mind a veritable swamp of Cartlandian mush, and look what happened to her.

Romance is just so damn unsexy; a bit pervy, too, when you come to think of it. The idea that one party has to overcome the 'natural' resistance of the other party to sexual intercourse by a combination of gifts and being economical with the truth takes us perilously near to date-rape territory. In those unfortunate cases where a tragically unappetising young man forces himself upon a young woman at the end of an evening, the man will indignantly list all the lovely romantic stuff he did for the woman during the course of their 'date'. According to John Gray, this should have had her panting for it.

Three years ago, I started seeing a boy of 23 who had no experience of women whatsoever. It shouldn't have worked, but it did. We were easy to please: we drank a lot, played Jenga for literally hours on end and slept together. We were different ages, different genders, different classes, and yet we were exactly the same. Because I was so experienced and he wasn't at all, game-playing – apart from Jenga – would have been not only pointless but impossible. If I said I'd call him and then hadn't, he would simply have presumed I didn't like him any more and didn't want to see him again. The normal, sad, tiring thirty-something minuet of manipulation was beyond us, and it was so refreshing.

Our first Valentine's Day rolled around, and I thought nothing of it. But when he knocked on the door of my hotel room, I opened it and saw not the face I loved, but a bunch of red roses. He thrust them at me; I screamed in shock; he looked dismayed; we both burst out laughing. He hasn't tried anything romantic since, and I couldn't be happier.

Because, by and large, except for a few sad-sob sisters, women don't want romance; they want intimacy, which is the exact opposite. Romance is the booby-prize men give women when they cannot, or will not, give them intimacy. Romance can be bought in the petrol station in the shape of a box of All Gold on the way home after you've been shafting your secretary. But intimacy is impossible to fake. The original meaning of the word 'romance' was to lie. There is a Saki short story from the 1900s called 'The Romancers', about two old men sitting on a park bench telling each other the most extraordinary pack of lies about themselves. And when we see that photograph of Bill and Hill dancing in their swimming costumes, staring into each other's eyes like the waterlogged pair in *From Here to Eternity*, we can see how fitting it is that a word that used to mean lying now means a certain sort of love. It is interesting to note that those few women – such as Barbara Cartland and Jane Seymour – with the bad taste to proclaim their fondness for romance have minds like steel traps, egos as big as Alaska, fast-track careers and husbands we've never heard of. But selling romance is the way they make their living – you can find it in you to forgive them if you try hard.

It is less easy to forgive Bridget Jones and her geeks' chorus of screaming mimis for being apparently so willing to swap their lovely, freed-up lives for a Leisurebreak in York and a man who looks like Mr Darcy. But then, there have always been women who, like mules, are basically sexless. For such women, romance is the curtain that the Victorians used to put over the piano legs.

Roy Raymond was a marketing man who'd had several unsuccessful notions, such as a foam for dabbing on toilet paper before using it (don't ask), when he had the idea of Victoria's Secret: a lingerie store that was demure, upmarket and, above all, romantic. 'Part of the game was to make it more comfortable for men. I aimed it, I guess, at myself,' he told Susan Faludi in *Backlash*. He chose the Victorian theme 'because it seemed like a romantic, happy time'. At the regular brainstorming sessions, managers were called upon to confess their deepest romantic fantasies – that's romantic, mind you, not sexual.

One of the printable ones turned out to be: 'I'm in bed with 18 women.' If that don't say it all – they don't really get it, and we don't really want it. So tonight, don't do anything romantic. Have a good time instead.

21 FEBRUARY 1998

I've lost count of the number of female sex idols who've said, 'If a man has a sense of humour, he doesn't need to be good-looking.' One of them went further, declaring that a man had 'laughed me all the way into bed'. Let's hope she didn't laugh him all the way out of it.

You've only got to look at Woody Allen's mug, and then think all the way back to Charlie Chaplin's legendary pulling power to see that laughter, like power or the physical presence of Robin Cook, is a surefire aphrodisiac. This may be why it is easier to find a lonely heart admitting to being fat, ugly or poor than not in possession of a GSOH.

Laughter is unique to humans, like having sex face-to-face and lying through one's teeth, and it resembles an orgasm in that it is involuntary and can be embarrassing. And like sex, the English have a tricky time with it – liking it more than most, our highly developed reserve can also bring us to grief with it. Laughing aloud in a crowded railway carriage at a book, for instance, is always represented in the blurb for that book as both the most awful and yet the most desirable thing that could happen to you in public without taking your clothes off.

But just as we become sexually jaded, humour wears off too. We need more and more to get off on. And so comedians are everywhere; on comedy quizzes, comedy current affairs programmes, comedy current affairs quizzes, comedy sports shows, writing novels and plays and appearing on *Question Time*. Ben Elton presents prizes: Stephen Fry wins them. Comedians can make the dead walk: look what Vic and Bob did for Ulrika. Look at Ulrika: out there in career Siberia, and then we find out she's got a sense of humour, and next week she's going to get the Nobel Prize! That's the only thing holding back Dani, Anthea and the rest of them from making Ulrika's Lazarus leap: it's not their bodies, it's not their brains, it's because we can see that they don't have any apparent sense of humour. Nothing gets a goodtime girl a bad rap quicker. But all that pre-packaged humour isn't like the real thing, is it? Pump it up all you like, bring out the blondes and the dancing girls and the amyl nitrate and the giggle powder, but when the thrill is gone, it's definitely gone.

I've always thought it was weird that when you bang that thing near your elbow called your funnybone, it hurts like hell and you feel like crying. It's a sad reminder of those long afternoons in double physics when you were meant to be giving your full attention to the Petri dish and the Bunsen burner, but instead you literally ached with laughing, as though you'd been knocked to the tarmac in the playground and kicked by the Hard Girl First Eleven for half an hour. It doesn't seem that remarkable now that the new kid's surname was Smailes; at the time, it affected me the way being sat between Oscar Wilde (not

Stephen Fry) and Alan Partridge (not Steve Coogan) at dinner just might do, on a good night, now.

So what do you do when the thrill is gone or, worse still, you just can't get it in the first place? Traditionally, you end up paying for it. I've always had a theory that paying for laughs eventually becomes as depressing as paying for sex. Because we know in our heart of hearts that consuming comedy isn't the same thing as buying records or books either; it's understood that not all of us have the equipment to move people to tears with words or music, but we've all supposedly got this famous GSOH. Then why do so many of us end up paying for our fun?

In the comedy clubs, the atmosphere is often as sad and sour and seething as that in a strip joint or peepshow; the heckling hides the genuine resentment of the john, while the strumpet up there on the stage can barely disguise their understandable contempt for the paying punter. And just as being a prostitute isn't exactly the best way you'd choose to look after your mental health, professional comedians are notorious for being miserable buggers – the tears of a clown and all that, innit?

A few years ago, I was friends with a comedian; he was rich and famous and orchidaceously handsome, but behind closed doors he couldn't tell a joke to save his life. I got him a date with a woman whom I genuinely believe may be the most beautiful in the Western world – we'll call her Mariella. When they embarked on a tropical idyll a few weeks later, he proceeded to screw it up by waking her up in the middle of the night to tell her he wanted to kill himself. (I wouldn't mention this if Mariella hadn't written about it in detail before, but anyway.) I honestly don't think that any man but a paid fool would have been emotionally inept enough to have done this.

Part of the reason we value intimate relationships is the secret world we create with the Significant Other: a child's secret garden wherein one word, one look can spark a level of hysteria unknown since 5B. We think we want to be in love because it makes us proper adults.

But if it's the best sort of love, it also gives us back our childhood. 'He's having his second childhood,' they say of the man who runs off with a youngster, and they're right. Part of it is sex, but the other equally important part is what the great showman Mike Todd called laffs.

And now they've found the comedy G-spot. Earlier this year at the University of California, doctors looking for the source of a 16-year-old girl's epileptic fits stimulated a part of the left frontal lobe of her brain by using electrodes on her forehead. Whether counting, reading, naming objects or moving her hands and feet, the girl laughed whenever this area was touched.

'Although laughter was evoked by stimulation on several trials, the patient offered a different explanation for it each time, attributing the laughter to whatever external stimulus was present,' one of the team told *Nature* magazine: looking at a picture of a horse, for instance, she would say the horse was funny. So that's the sweet mystery of laughter solved; the supplementary motor area, found in a fold of tissue at the front of the brain, the size of a walnut.

We've been trying to civilise laughter for decades now, make it decent, by saying we're laughing with, not at, people. But all those years, we knew we were faking it. It's a dirty business, and we do get off best when we laugh at; that was the wonder of Alan Partridge. All those years of laughing with nice guys like Alexei Sayle and Lenny Henry because we loved them and didn't want to hurt their feelings, and suddenly here at last was someone we could genuinely despise. And gosh, it felt good. Because it felt like when we were young and hard and cruel.

There's no nice way of saying it; I was at school with what I can only describe, with one or two honourable exceptions, as a bunch of morons. But they made me laugh more than any adult, no matter how witty or wise, ever will. And I really don't think all the clever little neurosurgeons in California could tell me why.

7 MARCH 1998

Don't talk to me about the MandyDome. I've got the Churchill Square Development to worry about. Churchill Square is between Brighton's main shopping thoroughfares, the Western Road and North Street. It was one of the first shopping centres ever built in this country, and retains a sad, thwarted, space-age feel. Over the past decade, however, the traders have been shutting up shop like crazy and now there's not much more there than a Smith's, a Dixon's and a hot-dog cart. Massive renovation has been taking place for the past few years though, and when it's finished it will be the biggest shopping centre in the world. Well, almost.

When I moved down here, it was after 18 years of living in central London; a gradual trajectory from King's Cross to the Angel to Bloomsbury. After such a long time in the epicentre of the capital, the novelty of living in a provincial town delighted me, and with an impish glee I realised that I could severely irritate my then girlfriend, whose family seat lies just outside Brighton and who had then been in London for less than three years, by talking about the Churchill Square Development whenever she tried to talk about something really important, like was Coast as good a restaurant as the Criterion.

She hoped my Sussex mania would soon wear off.

It hasn't. A few months ago, I started listening to local radio. The jingles make me feel especially warm: 'In Brighton – Hove – Shoreham – and Worthing – Southern Counties radio brings you closer to the best part of Britain.' I know it is, too. It's not a nasty, chippy little dormitory to London, but a real county in its own right, from the fleshpots of Brighton to the sumptuousness of the South Downs.

To read our local paper, the *Argus*, is to know the transcendence of provincial tranquillity – especially taken after, say, the neurotic busyness of *Time Out*, which caters for readers who, to judge by its ever-expanding Lonely Hearts column, are so occupied going to the latest exhibition, opera and ballet, they haven't mastered the basics of getting sex yet.

Here, we care about the real stuff of life: School Dinner Lady Retires and Actress Launches Dog Vitamins were recent stories in the *Argus*. Its News in Brief is gorgeous, too: Drinker In Victory Pub Has Handbag Stolen From Under Her Chair. Part of the reason Sussex is such a satisfying place to live is, of course, its possession of Brighton, the town which thinks it's a city. Brighton people are the choicest in England, so cool that this remains the only place in the country to have run a Radio One roadshow out of town because it was so naff.

Brighton makes Swinging London Mark II look peculiarly corny and corporate-led. When I first moved here, I used to go to clubs, and it was always fun to observe how, when a new nightclub opened and bussed down a dozen London celebs for the night (the cast of *EastEnders*, junior league, were par for the course), they would stand sipping their gratis champagne and smiling coyly at the Brighton hipsters, who would have eyes only for each other.

Our self-sufficiency can seem maddening to Londoners. Our

ability to take something and make it work is exemplified by the career of Norman Cook, under whose magic hands Cornershop went to number one in the singles chart a few weeks ago. Urban and ethnic they may be, but 'Brimful of Asha' has become a totally Brighton record: laid-back, playful, sly. When they play it in the pubs here, everyone starts laughing, like children who've gotten away with something again.

The first 45 I ever thought of as a Brighton record was 'Alright' by Supergrass, a hit just after I got here. Though from Oxford, the most important third of Supergrass, Gaz Coombes, passed through Brighton on tour more than a year ago now and never left. The one thing Brighton likes about London is bagging its stars, and when I meet up with my friend Martine we swap names like trading cards.

'Steve Coogan!'

'Alan McGee!'

'Bobby Gillespie!'

The first one to have to say Nick Berry loses.

People live in London because they have to; people live in Sussex because they want to, because they can. In Simon Nye's brilliant new comedy *How Do You Want Me?*, it makes perfect sense that Lisa (Charlotte Coleman) cannot stand London any more and drags her husband, Ian (Dylan Moran), back to her Sussex home, even if it is populated by Neanderthals. So is London, of course: they just talk faster.

I'm not saying that city people are as bad as country people, because no one could be, but the city and the countryside do have quite a lot in common. They are both immensely forbidding places: the country to outsiders, the city to the poor. Provincial towns are generally thought to be narrow-minded, but the Brighton *Argus* recently reported a cheering story that started: 'Squatters have moved into a former baker's, and local traders have welcomed them with open arms.' The café collective, called the Anarchist Teapot, will distribute tea and anarchy and rabble-rousing literature on the site of the old Donut King, and shopkeepers couldn't be happier. 'It doesn't bother me – they are not interfering with anyone. I think they are offering free tea to people,' said one market trader, while the manager of Sofa Workshop said, 'They are not doing any harm. I would like them to pay rent and everything, but it's not a major problem.' Other shopkeepers thought the anarchists might bring in extra trade. I just can't imagine shopkeepers being so relaxed about anarchism in either Oxford Street or any Oxfordshire village.

Proselytisers for both city and country like to think they're living a sort of non-specific epic life: the countryfolk in a blood-and-soil, Lawrentian way and the metropolitans in a cut-and-thrust, Sweet Smell of Success way. I don't know which looks sillier.

I do know which is the one I lived for 18 years, however, and only a city would have accommodated such a silly, shallow, self-regarding kind of life. It took a provincial town to cut me down to size – the right size. For journalists, by their nature, are little people; we are not Mozart or Marie Curie, we do not create but merely comment. We do not cast a giant shadow.

Here I am a humble householder, and I like it. Maybe it's because I did so much so young. For old geezers in their forties who were never teenage queens of the metropolis, I dare say it's quite exciting living in London. But, to my way of thinking, cities are built for the young, and after a certain age you just look silly haring around them with greying hair and gleaming pate and expanding girth – all of which look fine in provincial towns.

These days, I like to go outside and peer into my pond. The koi are coming on a treat and I can see a new baby one. Tenacious as hell, it pushes the big ones out of the way and gets to the foodsticks first, swallowing one of them whole even though it's almost the size of its own body. It swishes off triumphant. I know how it feels. I was like that, once. But this is definitely the only kind of pond life I'm interested in these days.

14 MARCH 1998

In the sunlit, shimmery, early Sixties, when women took the Pill, wore shift-dresses and threatened to take a bigger piece of the pie – as opposed to the late, hippie Sixties when women took the crap, wore kaftans and begged worthless men to 'Take another piece of my heart now, baby!' – Helen Gurley Brown, the founder of *Cosmopolitan*, coined the phrase 'having it all'. She coined it to describe the rather modest desire to combine both career and 'femininity', but as women outside the eternal Prom Night that is American urban society couldn't see what was so difficult about this, it soon came to mean both having a job and children.

Today, a week of programmes on BBC 2 called *Having It All* begins. But that phrase, like its contemporary the Virginia Slims girl, has come a long way, baby. Whereas it used to present itself with an invisible exclamation mark, rigid with anticipation, on the end – Having It All! It Could Happen To You! – it now comes with three dots and a question mark. Having It . . . All? The soundtrack of canned, hollow laughter is almost tangible.

Whenever we use this phrase, we should ask ourselves what we would think if men worried about having it all. It All; you'd think that every woman was walking around reciting a wish list like the one Daryl Hannah reels off to Charlie Sheen in *Wall Street* when he asks her what she wants from life: a perfect ruby, a Picasso, world peace – and that's just for starters. But instead, it means a job and a private life. Wow; next stop, asking for the moon, obviously.

Freud said that love and work were the essentials it took to create happiness in the adult human; then he turned round and asked what women wanted, as though they weren't adult humans. Similarly, certain prominent stupid people still try to put the case that, for women, like children or the handicapped, work can be an optional extra rather than the thing that defines us as adult human beings. We've got too much choice . . . the moaning mantra goes, and on a personal level it makes you feel like gagging them with their own pantyliners, these over-educated female eunuchs who yearn for the stifling sanctuary of the school-run and the single-income household.

On a global level, the way women's rights to education, employment and sexual integrity are being slowly but surely pushed back into the dark ages by religious fundamentalists makes you want to weep, before doing them actual violence. If Ms Thirty-something Singleton really does believe that feminism and its hard-won freedoms have made her a lonely, confused old spinster, and that a life of tending her herb garden and breastfeeding while Mr Darcy brings home the bacon would be preferable, I've got an alternative to Tuscany this year. Perhaps she'd first like to go instead to almost any country in Africa and have her genitalia cut off, and then drop by Afghanistan to have her human rights removed. That should downsize her unwanted options no end.

Though currently posing as a universal dilemma, to have or not to have it all is, in reality, an issue only affecting middle-class Western women. Working-class women have always worked and had children – I was a latchkey kid from the age of six, and loved it, because, as my father explained to me, 'It's like this, love. Women go mad if they don't go to work. You don't want your mum going mad, do you?' Upper-class women, conversely, traditionally found themselves in the strange, though obviously desired, position of having none of it – no job, and children at boarding school as soon as they can walk. In all the current breast-beating about the Family being the basis of society – for the first time coming from Labour as much as the Tories – and about women's responsibility and inherent desire to stay at home with their children, if only the wicked, evil marketplace wasn't forever forcing them down the Job Centre, we never notice that the group of women who could afford to devote all their time to their children – the women of the upper and ruling class – would never dream of looking after their own offspring. Even to a woman as much in love with children as Diana Spencer was, a day-school was not an option.

What is interesting to note, in fact, is that, throughout history, when any group of women has been given the economic nous to do anything, the first thing it does is to buy the chance to get away from their children for sizeable amounts of time, from the aristocracy to Cherie Blair and her besuited sisters. Economic necessity has nothing to do with it; adult humans need to be with other adult humans, or they go spare. In work lies dignity; that's why no man ever grew up dreaming of being a house-husband, and why we consider unemployment a social evil.

And, despite what the loonies on both right and left claim, housework isn't real work; it's just tidying up after yourself. When Denis McShane disgraced himself in the *Daily Mail* recently, he called housewives 'the unsung heroines keeping

Britain together by staying at home'. This is an insult on a par with that clanger that claims the Queen Mother exemplifies all that is best about Britain: the twisting of privilege and passivity into a badge of honour. Because to be a housewife, once one's children are at school, is to be a ponce; women were right to apologise, 'Oh, I'm no one, I'm just a housewife' all those years ago.

Having it all, like sex and shopping and chocolate and everything enjoyable, has been pathologised; under the media-driven influence of middle-class wuss women, it's become Dealing With It All and Worrying About It All. But even as we make a show of frankly addressing the problem, as in this week's programme, *You, Me and the Baby*, one gets the feeling that someone somewhere is not being honest about why women feel so pressured when their lives are actually easier than they have ever been. It is easy to blame employers for making us work long hours, or blame governments for not providing enough child-care, because we don't have to go home and look at their long faces at night. But it may be closer to the truth to say that it is not the obvious suspects of work or children that make women feel harassed and undervalued, but rather their relationships with men who, according to every depressing survey, are doing even less housework than they were ten years ago. In the early days of a relationship, sex and novelty make housework feel like playing house; but add children to the equation and it all falls down.

On a recent *This Morning*, I was fascinated to see Caron Keating interviewing Kate Figes about her book on motherhood; the two of them sat there glorying in the fact that, once you'd had a baby, you could stop having sex for anything up to a year! It was like hearing two teenage girls congratulating themselves on faking a great sick note to get off games. Poor Richard sat there, shaken and stirred; used to the Girlie Show line that women are mad for it. The idea that sleeping with the same person day in, day out for decades might get boring was a new one on him. To the doctors now reporting an epidemic of loss of sexual desire among couples, it wouldn't come as such a shock. 'Not tonight, darling – I'm Having It All in the morning' is well on the way to becoming the modern woman's version of the bedtime headache.

28 MARCH 1998

When I was growing up in the Sixties and Seventies, before video and cable, and when television was a unifying force, as opposed to a never-ending exercise in one-upmanship, there was always some televisual event for which my father saw fit to bring the mattresses downstairs. The fights of Cassius Clay and his alter-ego, Muhammad Ali; the Olympics, if Lillian Board was running; general elections. The Academy Awards, even if they had been broadcast live back then, would never have been allowed the same privileged treatment. And, apparently, most people today feel the same way. The highlights of the Oscars attract around four million viewers in this country; the Eurovision Song Contest, on the other hand, attracts eight and a half million, some 41 per cent of the viewing population.

This lack of interest in watching a lot of rich tossers conduct a well-dressed circle jerk is a rather fine thing, I feel, and seems to reflect public impatience with the silly idea that ordinary people, on top of paying to see films, should actually care about them as well. It is popularly believed within 'the arts community' that

British people should lie awake at nights, weeping into their pillows, because copious amounts of public money are not being spent on engendering even more flickering images. It's okay for a government to spend on entertainment what might otherwise be spent on dialysis machines, goes that impeccable luvvie logic, because, if people don't have a decent film industry to call their own, why, they'd just as soon be dead anyway! But everyone who ever fell in love with the cinema did so because of Hollywood, that conspiracy of frustration and desire. And it is to Hollywood they go when they eventually can. It is hypocrisy to tell British audiences to watch British films when every British director, actor and writer buggers off to Hollywood as soon as is decently possible. (Indeed, who would deny us that great minor pleasure of the Brit-Thesp who flounces off to Hollywood feeding on that Land-of-Opportunity crap, and then stumbles back a decade later having learned the hard way that the Hollywood sign looks best from a distance: Michael Caine, say, who got *Alfie*, *The Ipcress File*, *Get Carter*, *Mona Lisa* and *Educating Rita* out of the allegedly non-existent British film industry – and *Blame It On Rio* and *The Swarm IV* out of Tinseltown.)

The Oscars are not about films, which is why Marilyn Monroe never won one; the Oscars are about Oscars. It's about selling things, as is everything in America, including sex, race and religion. It's about selling dresses, apart from anything else; a quarter of those who watch it claim to tune in only to look at the lovely frocks. And whether it is Jodie and Michelle in their customary, customised Armani, Uma wearing the dress that started Prada on the road to eveningwear, or Sharon showing the style for Valentino that she later reprised on his catwalk, couturiers give the ceremony a glamour that the stars themselves no longer can.

Of course, the ladies still wear long, sparkling dresses; they are still beautiful, and there is even a case for saying that film stars are more beautiful than they used to be; Betty Grable and Jane Russell, for example, were plain-faced girls topping breathtaking structures, while Clark Gable had false teeth for much of his tenure as King of Hollywood. But we are all wise to the fact that glamour, as we knew it – that bitter cocktail of gloom and amour, of which Hedy Lamarr said, 'Any girl can be glamorous: all you have to do is stay still and look stupid' – is only a ghost of what it used to be. A lot of the blame lies with the fact that we know too much about the stars. Despite the received wisdom that the studio system of the past whored its stars to the movie magazines, and that today's stars are very private people, we now have film stars who, as both Winona Ryder and Drew Barrymore have done, actually lend their diaries to journalists writing stories about them. Vulnerable and emotional as they were, we cannot imagine Marilyn, Lena or Judy ever doing this. Whether it is Kate Winslet talking about her burping habits, or Winona and Glenn Close reading poems about vaginas, we are receiving, as Uma Thurman scolded John Travolta in *Pulp Fiction*, 'a little bit more information than I needed to know' about our film stars. But no matter how much they give us, we cannot keep our eyes and hearts from wandering. Right now, despite the united front presented at the Oscars, Hollywood is reeling at the latest changing of the guard. Suddenly, films relying on established stars are stiffing, while movies packed with unknown youngsters – *Starship Troupers*, *Scream* – are cleaning up. 'No one knows anything,' William Goldman famously said of Hollywood, and, as *Vanity Fair* put it this month, 'In the old days – say, last year – studios opted for safety. You went with the star no matter what the cost. Now, it seems, there aren't many names who can absolutely open a picture; Leonardo DiCaprio, maybe Brad Pitt and Will Smith.' But we should have known something, observing the career of, say, Demi Moore alone; her price rising into the stratosphere even as her box office went subterranean, because modern stardom wasn't about how much people loved you, à la Marilyn, James Dean or Charlie Chaplin, but about the deal.

The president of the floundering Planet Hollywood recently announced his intention to hitch his limping wagon to 'newer, more up-and-coming stars'. He'd do well to stay away from the Oscars, then.

Once more this year, mediocrity was rewarded when *Titanic* swept the board, simply for reassuring Hollywood that moving pictures play a big part in people's lives. Just the way they used to in the Twenties, Thirties and Forties, before TV.

This year, mediocrity was rewarded at the expense of Tarantino, *The Full Monty* and the British contingent in general, but nicely personified in the Best Actor triumph of Jack Nicholson, who proved that, while an actress is nothing without youth and beauty, the Hollywood establishment handsomely rewards age, ugliness, misogyny and loss of talent in a man. (In the footsteps of Marilyn, DiCaprio, the world's biggest box-office draw, was nominated for sweet nothing; God forbid people should be given what they want.) Robin Williams finally got his gong ten years after his talent ran out, compere Billy Crystal proved yet again that if he did not exist, nobody would have really felt the need to invent him, while James Cameron served up a classic Oscars cheese-fondue moment by requesting silence for those who died on the *Titanic*, before doing a passable imitation of Neil Kinnock at that Sheffield Rally: 'I'm THE KING OF THE WORLD! Ooo-eee! OOO EEE! RUFF RUFF RUFF RUFF!' Yet there were compensations. In the space of a year, Demi and Bruce and Arnie and Sly have come to look as frozen in the past as the Keystone Cops, only without the laughs. It may have been the *Titanic* that went down so spectacularly this year, but it was these stars of yesteryear who truly appeared to be not waving, but drowning.

4 APRIL 1998

For the purposes of review, let me be quick to assure you – one of the most smug and sickening books I have ever come across (Yes, even more so than *I Knew I Was Right*) was a book about how there are two sides of the brain – one of which is creative and intuitive, the other logical and pragmatic. Women were born with the first half working, went the pretzel logic, and men with the second; no mention was made of why, in that case, the Supreme Director Of All Events had bothered giving both sexes both halves when he could have saved on material and labour by simply giving females the intuitive half and males the logical half.

The book would have struck me as a bunch of sexist, biologically determinist bull under any circumstances, but the fact that it was written by a man and a woman gave it a particularly yucky, coy feel. We're equal but different, you could hear them murmuring reassuringly, and men need women to do certain things, like nurturing them, while women need men to do certain things, like deciding what the money's going to be spent on. The animals went in two by two! A boy for you, a girl for me! I'm a blue toothbrush, you're a pink toothbrush.

No, I'm bloody not, mate, I silently swore, and wished I'd paid more attention in double maths instead of dreaming about writing great novels and owning the complete range of Mary Quant lipsticks, so I didn't still have to take my shoes off in order to do big sums. It was a bitter harvest, for sure: even as I decried such determinism, I was living, goofing-off proof of it. A year later, though, girls were top in the nation's maths exams for the first time ever; and, a few months later, I read that, again for the first time, more young women than men had qualified as accountants, of all the glorious dry, logical things.

I felt like going out and throwing myself under a racehorse, just to prove that, as Helen Reddy predicted, I am invincible, I am woman! My generation may have been creative, Bunsen-burner-shy cretins, but suddenly, out of nowhere, had appeared a generation of babes who were just as at home with a slide-rule and compass as with a blow-dryer and eyelash curler. Take that, Mr and Mrs Toothbrush, with your complacent conviction that gender difference was something we were born with – fish gotta swim, birds gotta fly and teenage girls gotta say, 'Ooh, Gary, what's nine times nine? I can never remember!'

So, what happened that suddenly made teen angels more interested in the statistics on their exam papers than the ones around their T&A? Mr and Mrs Toothbrush might suggest that one dark night, somewhere in the Seventies, a legion of lesbian Martians came down and, à la Midwich Cuckoos, vilely impregnated Earth women with female spawn whose brains, in contradiction of all the laws of nature, function as a whole instead of as men's other half. The more reasonable explanation is that, because real education was so new to girls – we cannot say that girls were educated in the same way as boys before the Sixties (the far greater proportion of boys to girls who went to grammar schools shows that this was true from the Sloane-at-home to the working-class gymslip mother) – they simply tried harder for a long time and finally, in the Eighties, caught and overtook the complacent, confident boys in a classic tortoise-and-hare scenario.

It is the long-time testimony of teachers that girls pay attention in a way that boys will not; and, apparently, this situation has worsened over the past decade.

Lad Culture, while purporting to be pro-male, has, in fact, acted as feminism's Trojan Horse here, helping boys to remain stuck in an infantile, obsessively anti-cerebral state and still feel cool; very much as rap culture has done for large numbers of young black men.

It is not castrating feminism that now sees boys falling behind girls on every educational level, but rather the culmination of centuries of male supremacy, which taught them that, without trying, they will do better than their sisters at school and that the plum pickings of the job market will forever be reserved for them, solely because of the shape of their genitals.

We've been here before, of course: in the Fifties, when even unskilled young whites decided that certain jobs weren't good enough for them. And, again, in the Seventies, when unskilled and skilled white men alike refused to re-train for the 'fiddly' jobs the new technology brought in, because the work was part-time or low-paid or just plain effeminate (sitting around playing with computers all day!), apparently confident that, one glorious day, coal and steel would dominate once more and there would be a tin bath in front of every fire and a woman in a pinny in every kitchen. It is because of this complacency that two out of every three new jobs are taken by women, while two out of every three pinnies are bought by men.

How to get men back on top, where they belong, is the new buzz-phrase. No one can have missed the hysterical shifting of the goalposts now mooted by educationalists: boys are doing badly at school because there are too few male teachers; boys are reading later than girls because they're not interested in poncey old fiction, so they should be given books about practical things like football instead (when did the Latin root of the word 'educate' change from 'lead out' to 'pander to'?); and now, the Labour MP Margaret Hodge has suggested that boys would do better if the teaching of reading was put off until about three years later for both sexes.

I dare say they might. I dare say that boys might do even better if schoolgirls were blindfolded, gagged and had one hand tied behind their backs in the classroom. But who laid it down in stone that boys always had to do better than girls? Girls did worse than boys at school for centuries, and I don't recall any moral panic about this. Similarly, Anglo-Asian, Anglo-Chinese and now Anglo-Irish children are doing better at school than unhyphenated Anglo kids, and it would be a strange, unwholesome person indeed who demanded urgent action to put whites back up there where they belonged.

There is no logical reason on earth why whites, or men, or boys have to be on top. To appropriate the argument of those right-wingers who see 'political correctness' and 'special pleading' everywhere on behalf of women and ethnic minorities, surely it would be highly unfair – and highly insulting to the laggard boys – to bring in social engineering to get them up to par? What sort of respect is a boy going to have for himself if he knows that the whole education system had to be changed to help him back into the ascendancy? No: if boys are to be contenders again, they will get there by feeling oppressed and becoming determined, disciplined and self-reliant, as both girls and ethnic minority children have had to before them.

We never consider that, maybe, boys want to be at the bottom of the class for a bit. Feminism always aimed to take the burden of breadwinning from men and, goodness knows, we women hear enough about how staying at home and bringing up baby is the most valuable, fulfilling job that any human being can do. If this is so, do we women really have the God-given right to deprive men of it for ever?

11 APRIL 1998

In my book, there are few minor walking human tragedies more pitiable than the type who has lived all of his/her life conforming to the norm in every way, sucking up so thoroughly to the boss that they're so far up his fundament that all you can see are the soles of their shoes – yet, somehow, somewhere they get it into their heads that they're wild, crazy, rugged individualists of the type that Steppenwolf wrote 'Born to Be Wild' about.

Born to be mild more like. An early warning of this type – the Mild Thing – was always that heartbreaking sign they'd stick up in their offices: You Don't Have To Be Mad To Work Here But It Helps! When I was 18, I saw one of these signs in a friend's office, and I started crying, spontaneously, out of sheer, they-know-not-what-they-do pity for the whole damned human race. I'd probably just snigger and drop the friend now, but it's nice to feel strongly about stuff when you're young.

The You Don't Have To . . . sign signals, above all, a castrate desperately feeling the loss of his *cojones*. But, in recent years, such mezzobrow Mild Things have found a new way of indicating that, even though they may look like men whose highlight of the week is coming home to find a new copy of the *Radio Times* in its faux-leather case, they are actually just one step removed from their noble savage ancestors who once strode across the plains of the Serengeti with a club in one hand and Raquel Welch's hair extensions in the other. How do they do this? Why, they simply smirk, shrug and say 'I'm not very politically correct, me!'

Well, Mr Walk-On-The-Mild-Side is going to be extra pleased to see his *Radio Times* this week, because on Easter Monday, BBC 2 presents its Politically Incorrect Night, featuring Miss World, the Black and White Minstrels and the Robertson's Golliwog. Yay! Your modern, vibrant Blairist Beeb, first with all the trends!

Political correctness first raised its head on American university campuses in the Eighties. You've got to remember what American university campuses are like before you condemn this so-called New Puritanism. Due to the vast intake of male students on sports scholarships, American colleges are menaced by monstrous regiments of mentally sub-normal young giants who have about as much interest in education as a fish has in physics.

College is, rather, the first chance they have had to carouse ceaselessly and drink themselves blind, during which time they feel like Masters Of The Universe just because they can play that girly rounders game they call their national sport passably. The level of sexual harassment female students receive from these apes – from the 'panty raids' of the Fifties to the date rape of today – is beyond the comprehension of British female students, most of whom think their male classmates are giving them a hard time if they hog the jukebox in the students' union and put 'Three Lions' on twice in a row. As for their attitude to blacks – well, it can't be any coincidence that black-only colleges are currently the choice of a large number of the black intellectual élite.

In such a gung-ho, get-'em-off atmosphere, it was hardly surprising that women and people of colour felt a bit sensitive, and early PC was nothing more than a code of conduct for humanoids – I use that word loosely – who had never really stopped using the word 'nigger' even before Tarantino made it dead fash. It may have become a bit mad and excessive later on, but, then, all things become mad and excessive in America, including eating and driving and religion, and that's no reason for sensible people such as the Brits to abandon said pleasures.

Besides, even when it was mad, there was method in American campus PC madness. I remember once reading the Dating Do's and Don'ts from the university that thought up the whole thing, and it was astoundingly sexy, because every time a person wanted to do something to someone else, they had to say what they wanted to do and ask the other's permission. This might have been a bit boring around the 'I want to take your hat off. Please may I take your hat off?' stage, but imagine how you'd feel by the time they were telling you what they wanted to do with your internal organs! You'd be gagging for it! In my experience, there's nothing much sexier than someone telling you what they're doing as they're doing it (unless it's Anneka Rice running about looking for something), and it may well be that men first turned against PC sex not because they were morally and intellectually opposed to it, but because they're crap in bed ('I'm entering you. I'm shagging you. Oops, it's over.')

But it looks like the wind of change may be about to blow through received notions of what political correctness actually is. The *Daily Mail*, house organ of the Mild Bunch, always identified itself as the most anti-PC paper in Britain; this, while banging on about lack of civility in public and private life!

Having realised that the yob look is the old look, the *Mail* is now attempting to clamber on to the bandwagon by coming on as some sort of Home Counties PC commissar. Bill Clinton is now not a man with a healthy sexual appetite, but, according to a recent *Mail* headline, president of THE NEW AMERICA: THE LAND WHERE POWERFUL MEN ARE NOW FREE TO ABUSE WOMEN. A couple of weeks before this, it led the chorus of disapproval that greeted the gospel according to Newcastle United bosses Shepherd and Hall. It was disgusting that women were called names! How dare they get blind drunk in brothels and charge too much for football shirts! But, if you read publications as diverse as *Viz* and the *Daily Mail*, you couldn't have blamed Shepherd and Hall for believing that such talk was not just acceptable but brave, cocking a snook, as it did, against the Terror. More fool the lot of them for not catching on that, in this country, PC was simply a plea for good manners in a society growing increasingly uncivil.

Anyone who continues to rail against PC reveals themselves to be not a noble maverick, but a truly little man; a bully and a coward, for starters, and the sort of person who will go through life doffing his cap and tugging his foreskin to his betters while being rude to waiters and cleaning ladies. How could we ever have kidded ourselves it was anything else? One clue should have been the sheer scuzziness of the anti-PC heroes. From Jack Nicholson to Bernard Manning – pond-life who want the whole world to be as filthy as them so they don't stick out like a sore thumb.

Contrarily, when Cameron Diaz was asked her opinion of political correctness (she was obviously meant to giggle and say, 'Aw, they're all lesbians!' as she's a tasty blonde), she said something like, 'Political correctness is a good, though occasionally awkward, way of trying to redress great injuries done against various people.' She knows, you know, that being anti-PC is hardly ever more than a mealy-mouthed way of being rude – and what sort of pathetic philosophy can only fully be itself when calling people names? Good manners cost nothing, as our mothers told us. But the social cost of bad manners will bleed us dry, even unto the next generation.

18 APRIL 1998

No one likes a Noel. Noel by name, Know-All by nature: Edmonds, Gallagher and the daddy of them all – if nothing else – Noël Coward, each of them complacent, narcissistic and condescending. Like Gracie Fields, his opposite number, Coward inspired long periods of extreme dislike in his native country for wrapping himself in the flag, rabble-rousing all the way to the bank and then pissing off to Bermuda, Switzerland and Jamaica with the proceeds, while the be-rationed Brits fought each other in the streets for a lick of a butter wrapper. 'I am England and England is me,' said the man who, when David Niven complained that the view in Switzerland was boring, came back, 'No, dear boy. It overlooks a beautiful tax advantage.' Patriotism is not necessarily the last refuge of the scoundrel, but the greedy bastard has often found it a useful string to his bow.

Reactionary, snobbish and fey, Coward was well routed by the youthful energy of the early Sixties, reduced to bleating about the horrible racket the Beatles made and what vile little tarts Christine Keeler and Mandy Rice-Davies were, daring to bring down a giant of a man like John Profumo. Far from being the daring young blade who shocked a nation with the sex and drugs romps of his first play, *The Vortex*, he had become a resentful, tax-dodging old codger, who only cheered up when the Family Addams – sorry, Windsor – allowed him to prance and caper for them. His diaries from the Fifties and Sixties are a scream, full of references to the 'gorgeous' Queen Mother and the 'charming' Queen – 'I was amused to observe the impact of their perfect manners on some of the "pinker" members of the staff!' he notes with glee when the Royals lunch on a film set one day. It's hard to reconcile the 'greatest British wit of the century' with the blushing jelly that appears whenever one of the Windsors so much as sneezes in his direction, and whose witterings read like nothing so much as the servile senilities of the old Jennifer's Diary.

But death is a great beautifier, and this month sees a massive celebration of Coward's ability to cut the custard. The BBC practically wets itself over him, with a three-part *Arena*, a wagonload of his sofa-chewing films and a tribute concert to 'The Master' by a gaggle (giggle?) of Cool Britannia's most mediocre pop moppets and clapped-out old tarts. This is to be made into an album, for our sins, and sold to raise money for Aids.

Well, 'The Master' wouldn't have liked that. He'd have thought the music was a 'racket' and the cause a bloody embarrassment; he'd rather have strolled along with the Jarrow marchers than come out. That hasn't stopped sections of the media from carrying on as though this Windsor-licking Tory was Karl Marx, Marilyn Monroe and Gandhi all rolled together in one Sulka dressing-gown.

Even more insultingly, some halfwits try to draw parallels between Coward and Oscar Wilde; these are the sort of people who can't tell Marilyn from Mansfield, Stork from butter or their ass from their elbow. While Wilde was brave, Coward was craven. Wilde was a humanitarian; Coward was a misanthrope.

Wilde fled the country over love, Coward over money. Wilde was radical. Coward reactionary.

Where Wilde's words still have the diamond-sharp power to make you gasp and laugh a hundred years after they were written, all Coward conjures up is a glazed grin. Wilde is so modern, so hard and true, while Coward is a dusty old thing, equal parts sentiment and snobbery. And last but not least, Wilde gave the world Dorothy Parker and Morrissey; Coward gave the world Richard Stilgoe.

The signs that Coward was a prissy little miss under all that satin and tat were always there: in *The Vortex*, drugs aren't shown simply as a way of having a fun time, but rather as something people take to escape the molten misery of their lives, and which leave them feeling far worse than they did in the first place! Very Blair. And, get this, the reason Nicky in *The Vortex* is miserable is because his mother's got a sex life! With younger men, the shameless hussy! It's only at the end, when Nicky's mum (he's only 28, bless him) agrees never to have sex again, that he cheers up. This is the soap opera the *Daily Mail* editorial collective would write if they could do dialogue. Coward's misogyny gives even his misanthropy a run for its money. Can anyone explain to me why the often-quoted line, 'Certain women should be struck regularly, like gongs', is brimful of wit, while, say, 'Certain homosexuals should be kicked around regularly, like footballs', is offensive? Like a tragic number of gay men, Coward feared and loathed women – unless they were, of course, Queens. What is it about queens and Queens? We've known for ages that the palaces of Britain are full of them, and that the Queen Mother once called down to the pantry, 'I don't know what you old queens are doing down there, but this old queen wants her G&T!'

Another fruit who tries to pass for veg by aping the most

revolting characteristics of the Establishment is Stephen Fry, whose pro-hunting presence on the so-called Save the Countryside March (Save the Countryside – Shoot a Farmer) made a nonsense of his supposed identification with Oscar Wilde, author of the lovely line, 'the unspeakable in pursuit of the uneatable'. In going on that wretched march, Fry cuddled up to the type of people who wouldn't think twice about doing him over if they met him up a dark country lane and didn't know he was famous.

Men are always gloating over the fact that there's no feminist 'movement' any more, but probably the reason that Andrea Dworkin and Catherine MacKinnon and Susan Faludi and, yes, even our sour-sweet old dark star, Germaine Greer, aren't carrying placards down a street near you is that they have been and are working on books and political crusades that will change the way women live.

It is the gay political movement that has become marginalised by its own. The way the gay establishment closed around Ian McKellen in the face of gay dissent when he took his Tory gong was something to see. Sir Elton John and St Gianni Versace have come to epitomise the acceptable face of homosexuality, as Coward did before them – 'creative', rich, cosying up to royalty. I find them far more objectionable than a Peter Tatchell with his finger on the prostate, or a lonely, lovely George Michael looking for some fast love in LotusLand.

Far from being sisters under the skin, Wilde started something that Coward finished: Wilde used the anger of the outsider to fashion lethal critiques of straight society; Coward sold his birthright for a song and a gong. Wilde used his sexuality as a springboard, which linked him with the arguments of socialism and feminism; Coward kept his nicely covered, and disdained any sort of struggle on the part of the disenfranchised as common. Think of the famous gay men of today, and make up your own mind. All I know is that I'd rather be in a toilet with George or up the junction with Peter than on my knees to the powers-that-be with Elton, Ian or Stephen. It may be a dirty job – but it's not obscene.

2 MAY 1998

Last month, a man was convicted of sexually abusing an eight-year-old girl whom he regularly looked after. Nothing unusual there – current levels of abuse by grown men of children are so high that one often feels that this must be something boys are taught by their fathers, like how to shave or urinate standing up. And then you'll be a man, my son!

What made this case different was that 24-year-old John Forrest, a father of three sons – and aren't they lucky children? – was bang to rights when his victim, watching an episode of *The Bill* with her mother, said, 'That's what the babysitter does to me,' when a situation very similar to her own was acted out on screen.

In this instance, the makers of television programmes (and there are very, very many of them these days) who use as the stuff of entertainment those things that cause people the most fear and torment – murder, rape, incest – could claim that they had at least performed some useful social task apart from titillation. But what I want to know is whether that child's mother will ever watch again, in the name of rest and recreation, a drama featuring child abuse.

How does it work, this Atrocitainment? Do people who've been raped watch dramas featuring rape? Can families who have lost a member through murder sit down cosily to watch *The Midsomer Murders* over supper on a tray? Would a survivor of incest have kicked off their shoes after a hard day's work and watched the recent BBC series *The Scold's Bridle* to unwind? Do they watch dramas that feature each other's traumas, but not their own? And what if they don't realise until too late that their own particular terror is coming up?

Taking this further, what about refugees from countries where atrocity is state-sanctioned? Do they watch slasher films, or have they had enough? And how do you explain a club called The Torture Garden to an actual torture victim? I know that murder, rape and violence have always featured in fictionalised entertainment for the screen, stage and page, but the fact that it has to be sought out sets it apart. It is the very cosiness of having atrocitainment piped into your own home that is so singularly strange. We read newspapers full of rape, murder and child abuse each morning, and it breaks our hearts, and then we come home to put our feet up to it every evening. Relax with rape, chill out with child abuse, hang out to homicide.

'What's on the agenda tonight, dear?'

'Well, we've got incest at nine, rape at ten and a serial killer to take us through the witching hour.'

'Lovely! Shall I be Mother?'

It may well be that, as Ian the Manager said in *This Is Spinal Tap*, 'Death Sells!', or even, as cheerful old Baudelaire said, 'To escape from horror, bury yourself in it!' Still, you've got to ask yourself why Jack the Ripper Walks have been such an unremarkable part of Heritage England for so long; and if, in 100 years' time, Hindley/Brady Walks will be. And if not, why not? Because the murders of women are sport and spectacle, while the murders of children are tragedy?

But even the murder of children is not beyond the pale as

prime-time entertainment now. Not a bit of it. Especially if sex is involved. I don't watch violent drama myself – a little hang-up of mine – but I'm fascinated as to how *The Scold's Bridle* was mooted, made and consumed. So you're going to have a casting call at one end – whereupon Mrs Sting turns up, fresh from her most recent pronouncement on positivity and spirituality – and at the other you've got a grown man, a technician, lighting a scene in which a child is dragged across the floor, in flashback, to be raped. Then – just imagine – you're writing the press release for it, trying to attract the viewing public to this thing as a reasonable source of R&R. Just imagine.

And wouldn't you rather crawl on your hands and knees through a warehouse-full of porcine waste than touch this rubbish with a barge-pole?

Apart from the moral angle, that we might become – might! – desensitised, there is simply something pathetic about all this death. We do it because – just as we know 69 ways to have sex with someone and nothing about love – we know of 69 ways to kill a man and nothing about death. Men, who run things, pay lip service to the 'miracle of life', but find both conception and birth obscene; imagine if birth was shown on TV as often as death is! Yet death is so much a staple of home entertainment that even to question it comes across as radical and mad.

Why is death everywhere, propped up by the sort of women who make it their business to celebrate life? Before Mrs Sting was doing her thing, one of the women from the River Café was talking about her perfect evening: 'Supper on a tray, and something exciting like the O. J. trial.' Nicole Brown Simpson, her throat cut; Ronald Goldman, bleeding to death. The only reasonable reaction to people who treat the Simpson trial as a spectator sport is the fervent hope that, if one day they have loved ones slain by jealous cretins, they will still find it in their hearts to forgive and, better yet, to enjoy.

Without doubt, murder is a worse crime than rape. But it is still the crime most used in the name of entertainment, without any apparent scruples; from *Murder She Wrote* to *The Midsomer Murders*, it is the cosiest thing imaginable. You can't imagine a popular prime-time series called *Rape She Wrote* or *The Midsomer Rapes* – yet most of us, male and female, would rather be raped than murdered.

Recently, in *EastEnders*, two actors offered their resignation rather than play a) a rapist, and b) a rape victim. But no actor would shy away from playing a murderer or a corpse. Murder is so clean that it can even be put to work laundering sex – last month, someone wrote approvingly in the *Guardian* of how women were starting to enjoy pornography through the medium of 'erotic thrillers'. Which simply means that if you put in a few killings, the sex will be okay. Gosh, that's really healthy.

9 MAY 1998

I'm getting old. Phew! How did that happen? One minute, I'm younger than springtime, with Johnny Rotten sitting at my feet and me sneering at him that he's too old (him 19, me 17); the next, I'm struggling to get into a size 18 and saying, 'Yes, but it's really great for the garden', when my friends complain about the rain.

I'm 38, my second husband 43, my best friend 58! We're all bloody old! All my life, I was the youngest in any crowd; it seems I've gone from *enfant terrible* to *grande dame*, with nothing in between. And, every day, there's some new reminder. Last month, an American lady phoned, said she was the literary editor of the *Times*, and asked if I'd do a book review for her. Sure, I twinkled, smirking to myself that, though I've been around the block a few times, those fogey old lit eds still know where to come when their pages need a bit of pep! Imagine my surprise, then, when I saw a picture of this woman a week later, in an article about fresh, young talent. She was only 30! I thought I'd been called in to provide youthful vigour, but it was really gravitas she wanted from me! Me – gravitas!

Then, the other day, my young friend brought a boy from a Welsh pop group to my club to meet me. He looked at me and I knew what he wanted. I leaned across and said, 'Do you want me to tell you my punk stories?' 'Please! I've been dying to ask you all night, but I thought it might sound rude.' Why don't I mind that this young person looked up to me, rather than up my skirt? According to the magazines, I should be doing a King Canute in the salons of the south coast, trying to hold back the sea of time. Perhaps the reason I don't give a toss – and I'm guessing here – is because I milked my youth for all I could. Being young was my career for more years than I care to remember. And it got so boring. Most people don't get the number of Young Years I did. No university, no proper job, just straight from school to being rude for a living. I'm not saying it's for everyone, but it sure makes you feel that your youth hasn't been snatched from you, in the way you might if you'd gone straight from college to an office.

Another reason why I might be less than attached to my youthful beauty could be because all it got me was an unprepossessing man six years my senior as a husband. Yet, as I got older, I traded up. And now that I'm old and fat, I've landed up with a tall, calm and lovely 25-year-old who can go three times an hour. Go figure that. This is probably why getting old seems such a scream: you get to sleep with young people! When you're young, you couldn't be less interested in them: they're as gauche and gawky as you, and maturity seems so sexy. But when you're old, the last thing you want to see on the pillow is someone rotting at the same rate as you. You can have too much of a good thing, you know.

It's not just the sex, but the Other of the thing: none of the same boring cultural references that make every thirty-something dinner party such a drag. 'Remember Lift Off with Ayesha? Space Hoppers?' Enough of this incestuous bonding and your contemporaries start to look as sexy as Space Hoppers, too. It's the sour, self-referential world of Hornby Man and Fielding Woman, for whom dating is so dull simply because they're staring over the feuilleté of scallops at a mirror-image of themselves. If you're a stroppy woman, and you know you're smarter than most men, it's almost impossible to go out with someone your own age and be truly happy. Old men will think you're adorable and indulge you, young men will think you're dazzling and devour you, but men your own age will always niggle and compete. Why shouldn't they? You're in the work-force, you're one of the boys. Why on earth shouldn't a man in his thirties or forties – whose first priority is securing his place in the pecking order – treat you with the same back-biting paranoia he dishes out to his male friends? But why on earth would you put up with it?

In the Seventies, someone said to the ever-dreamy Gloria Steinem, 'You don't look 40!' and she quipped right back, 'This is what 40 really looks like!' But it doesn't: that's what Gloria Steinem looks like at 40. Many media women said that her retort was a liberating thing for women, but it wasn't: it meant there was now yet another burden to carry – not only should we be good workers, great mothers and inventive lovers, but we also had to look like tawny-maned lionesses at an age when our mothers were embracing the words 'Elasticated Waist' as the two most beautiful in the English language.

There is very little said about the sensuality of getting old and letting go. One person who understood this was an incandescently beautiful middle-aged lady, whom I met a dozen or so years ago. She was one half of an early Green-aristocracy couple, along with her equally dishy, and very wealthy, husband. She announced her intention to run off with a man who, compared with the rich, dreamy hubby, appeared to have not much going for him. But her logic was immaculate: 'All I want to do is get fat and old and happy. My husband won't let me, but he will.' All I want to do is get old and fat and happy . . . it's gorgeous, that, the very carelessness of it. And it makes any idea of attempting to cling to youth look as common as attempting to cling to, well, to Peter Stringfellow.

A few years ago, when the journalist Michael Vermeulen died, there was an obituary picture of him from sometime in the Eighties. In the background was a very thin, tense brunette. 'Look at that girl!' I said to my friend. 'She's so beautiful! But look at her hands, her arms, how thin she is! How sad she looks! Why would a girl that beautiful look so miserable?' There was a moment's silence, out of respect for my dead memory, before my friend pointed out that the girl was me.

I didn't have to be Desmond Morris to read the body language of that miserable girl, whose youth and beauty proved far less use in a big, bad world than a warm sweater would have. She's dead, and I don't want her back. They say that inside every fat person there is a thin person waiting to get out. But if mine does, I'm going to kill it. And eat it. Because the old, fat me is having the time of her life, and I'm buggered if I'll ever let that skinny little brat get the upper hand again.

6 JUNE 1998

I always hated Frank Sinatra for raising the scummy state of being a class-A bully to a high art, so I was really pleased when he died. In his dealings with waiters, women or anyone less powerful than him, he had the manners of a pig. Confronted with an Italian psychopath, however, he became a genuflecting copy of the girl in *Pulp Fiction* who kept asking, 'What it is like to keel a man.' Besides, Tony Bennett was a better singer.

By anybody's standards, Frank led a turbulent life. Mother an abortionist, father an idler, huge sticky-out ears, married four times, drank like a fish, suicide attempts, career up and down like a yo-yo, lost looks, gained weight, lost mind. Yet when he died, what was the gist of every headline? He did it his way.

Contrarily, the same media lick their lips over the 'decline' of Liza Minnelli and Elizabeth Taylor. Like Sinatra, they have both lived life to the full and so had mandatory brushes with drug and alcohol addiction, marital strife, career doldrums and weight gain. They have also been affected by the amazing fact (amazing to the tabloids, that is) that this thing called 'time' keeps moving forward and people do this thing called 'ageing', which means – and you might want to sit down here – that people do not look at 50 the way they did at 21! Liz and Liza are, in tabloid parlance, 'troubled'. Try naming a female celebrity who isn't: Troubled Farrah, Troubled Kylie and, now, Troubled Geri, Troubled Mel C and all (except Victoria, who's So In Love and therefore won't be Troubled until it wears off).

First you're hot, then you're troubled, then you're a Tragic Heroine; these are the Three Ages Of Woman. When Liza and Liz die, they'll be Tragic Heroines with knobs on. The fact that they produced great works of popular culture will be lost under the gloating roll-call of addictions and marriages. They'll be presented as victims. Above all, the loss of their youthful beauty will be harped on. Yet no one mentioned that Sinatra was once a beauty and at his death was grey, wrinkled and paunchy. It would have been disrespectful.

The point is that you never hear 'tragic' and 'hero' together. Men's lives are always, in the end, portrayed as triumphs; women's as failures. Men have to do extraordinarily little to become heroes these days: in the past, you had to climb Everest; Des Lynam sits behind a desk and twinkles. Neither death nor dishonour can tinge the memory of modern male icons. From Andy Warhol (neurotic queen, rip-off merchant, bully) to James Brown (wife-beater, right-winger, Uncle Tom), the most dysfunctional of lives are rendered triumphant by their hagiographers. Yet a woman, from Piaf to Diana, only ever adds up to the sum of her wounds.

It's obvious why this is happening. As more and more women take it for granted that they deserve everything men get from life, and that Having It All is a bit of a hysterical way to talk about the staples of love and a job, so must the Here Be Dragonnes aspect of modern life be played up. Even glamour girls, who used to be approved of for playing by the rules, are now viewed as not being beautiful for the right reasons, i.e. not to please men, but to advance their careers. This explains the witch-hunt that has accompanied the rise of Emma Noble, whom several papers seem to feel should be made to wear a scarlet A on her flimsy frocks: A for Ambition. When a woman such as the monumentally thick Cher moaned about being 50, what everyone failed to notice was that she is the creature of a society that sees ageing in a woman as a perverse act of rebellion. She is miserable, not because she is getting older, but because she refused to accept that she was getting older and neglected her career to become a living, breathing Barbie Doll. She played to the rules that govern women's behaviour – that their looks are their lives – and has been left with nothing but egg on her expensive face.

As the legion of female suckers-up, the Bridget Joneses and Ally McBeals, are ceaselessly rewarded for reassuring men, the very state of being a woman is a problematic one. The rise of the gimcrack aromatherapy business is a cynical reflection of this neurotic state. What did women do all those years, you wonder, without lavender oil to calm them down and ylang ylang oil to get them in the mood for sex? Went around being frigid and jumping off bridges, I dare say. There are times when so-called modern woman, endlessly soothing and stimulating herself with her little brown bottles, resembles the Victorian lady whiffing away at her smelling salts.

'Pampering' oneself has always been the byword of women's magazines. It used to mean putting your feet up with a box of choccies and watching Lana Turner go to the bad. These days, it means one thing: washing. Keeping the equipment clean for the next time Your Man wants to use it. And aromatherapy performs two tasks at once: keeping women clean and keeping them happy. There's something Stepford Wife-ish about all this, especially as it's not women who run around raping and road-raging people. It's not women who need calming down, but men. Yet you don't see them clutching little brown bottles, unless they've got beer in them.

And there's the rub. When we see modern men pampering themselves, they're not keeping themselves clean and happy for the women in their lives, but getting blind drunk in front of the football and slobbing out on pizza with their mates. Perhaps this is why all men's lives are happy, and no woman's is; why it's so great to be a bloke in the Nineties. This is just the latest example of men wanting their pizza and eating it. It's great to be a bloke, because you can go to the footie and masturbate over pictures of Joanne Guest, but at the same time we're told it's never been harder to be a man, because you don't know what your role is any more.

And that, presumably, is why suicide among young men keeps going up while suicide among young women keeps going down. Hilariously, the media always report this fact with shock and confusion, as if it is the natural state of affairs for women to kill themselves. Never mind: it's probably nothing a few soothing aromatherapy baths won't put right. After all, it would never do for men to become troubled, tragic heroes, would it?

20 JUNE 1998

My boyfriend won't be watching the football, even though he is 25 years old and from exactly the class which, in recent years, has embraced football as they previously embraced the Gormenghast trilogy. For a start, he's got lots of friends called Dominic and Damian and Dorian, which is a sure marker of a tendency towards ball-worship, far more so than having friends called Steve and Paul. (Try calling 'Nicholas' or 'Timothy' at the Arsenal ground, and you'll get trodden to death in the stampede.) But, even though I really like him, if he did prefer to watch 11 men in shorts kick a ball about rather than explore interesting avenues with a sophisticated lady, I'd drop him as if he were a syphilitic with his own sprig of mistletoe. Because it would mean he was a moron. And my mother taught me never to kiss a moron.

What I wouldn't do is lower myself by moaning about his nasty little habit, either to him or to my friends. Because, in a way, a man who vegetates for a month to watch the World Cup has done you a favour: he's shown you his hand. So you can cut your losses and get out early. Let's face it, what are these men doing when they're not slumped on the sofa drinking beer and watching the footie? They're slumped on the sofa drinking beer and watching *TFI Friday*. They're not trotting around lidos and Paula Rego exhibitions with you, are they? Just see football as making them more themselves, not less, and you'll soon see the logic of it. Dump him! Dump him smartish, too, or you could become that most pathetic of modern female types: the Woman Who Loves Football. Remember how we used to laugh at that cheesy, agony-aunt advice about taking an interest in your boyfriend's hobbies if you wanted him to lurrrve you? So what's suddenly made it okay to act like a sad little suck-up merchant, then? 'Oooo, aren't girls boring? I'd far rather hang around with the boys. I love men, me! I'm not a lesbo!' This is nothing less than the female, white equivalent of being an Uncle Tom, a Steppin' Fetchitt, only this time it's a Steppin' Kickitt.

Saddest of all, I know this act so well because I used to be a master of it. 'Just look for a circle of tall dark men wearing suits,' my sarcastic friend once said to someone who was looking for me at a party, 'and she'll be in the middle of it, laughing at their jokes.' It took me a good decade to realise that a woman hangs out with men en masse only by sacrificing her finer feelings – amazingly, during the reign of the *Modern Review* Mark I, I actually laughed like a drain when the magazine's Toby Young told me that he had instituted a casting couch for aspiring female journalists. I should have smashed his face in, except nobody would have noticed the difference.

But, hey, I was being one of the boyzzz.

When Ulrika Jonsson stood by Stan Collymore when the mother of his child accused him of hitting her, she was performing the same stupid step: subservience disguised as sassiness. There's only one good reason to stand by your man, and that's to take the wallet out of his pocket. Anything else, and you're just a little sell-out, no matter how you slice it.

Face it – if you're a woman, there're only ever two good reasons to hang out with men at all: sex and politics. If you're not planning a revolution or a rut, stick with the bitches every time. Even when they have loads of drugs and drink, they're a laugh and, unlike men who consume the same, they won't end up crying on you at four in the morning about their mothers – 'She's dead, and I never told her how much I loved her'; 'One day she'll be dead, and I won't have told her how much I love her.' Men age women – not just by marrying them and making them have children and run around the house with a broom up their backsides, but simply by being in their company. See a bunch of girls out together one night – and the next night, see them all split up, in couples. You'd think they were their own mothers. Just as the presence of boys in the classroom has been proved to make girls silent shadows of their former selves, so the social presence of men renders women into plus-ones.

Leave them to it! You've had a lucky escape. Because I can't help feeling that, with the exception of boys under 20 and gents over 50, the majority of men who would choose watching football with their mates over spending time with the woman they're having sex with are – in their black little heart of hearts – as gay as a Teddy Bears' Picnic.

I call them Jocko Homos: those locker-room lads who spout a lot of cant about the Beautiful Game and silky skills to disguise a burning desire to bend, bugger and blow, but don't have the guts to carry it through, like George Michael did. I wouldn't mind betting that loads of the players are secret swishers, too, and that's why loads of them end up hitting both the bottle and women. It's guilt and disgust and all that, innit? Fantasy Football, I always thought that was a sad little title. What sort of grown man has fantasies about ball games? Wire 'em up to a lie detector, I say, and let's see what their real fantasies are.

It has become, in recent years, cool to say that you find football more exciting than sex. It shows that you can take it or leave it, implying that you've got numerous nooky opportunities whenever you need them, like those nights when rain stops play. Frankly, any man who prefers football to sex is going to be one of the lousiest lays this side of Andy Capp. By the time he's finished, you too will be firmly convinced that a goal-free local kickabout on a wet weekend in Wanstead is more fun than sex with that particular Jocko Homo.

So, as I said, don't moan, and don't join in; just leave them to it, dancing Nobby's dance or sucking Nobby's knob or whatever it is they want to do. Just remember: boxing is a sport where men beat up men, and football is a sport where men beat up women. Which certainly makes it no place for a lady, but very appropriate for a lady-boy.

11 JULY 1998

A lot of people said a lot of thick things in the Eighties, and heck knows I was one of them; 'I do' and 'Isn't Mrs Thatcher brilliant!' come to mind with cruel clarity. But I don't think that even I said that advertising was art, which lots of clever people who should have known better did.

Of course, it went to their heads. Ten years on, ad men don't just think they're art. They think they're religion and politics and the Easter Bunny, too. They think they're the only thing standing between the rest of us and the primeval sludge, but that doesn't quite tally with the fact that an advertising strike would change society in no way except that far fewer people would waste their money on stuff they never really wanted in the first place.

Advertising, like the IRA, may have started with straightforward motives, but has, over the years, become the reason for its own existence – a coven of self-centred zealots with very little regard for what is actually going on in the real world. And, just as the IRA won't be able to stop knee-capping people they claim are child molesters and drug dealers lest they lose face in their own neighbourhoods, so advertising types, were it finally proved that no advert has ever made the slightest bit of difference to the sales of any product, and the lot of them sacked en masse, would still loiter around London WC2, whispering cryptic messages about Pot Noodle and Tango in each other's ears.

More than journalism, more than acting, more than fashion even, advertising is totally parochial, concentrated in a tiny part of each country's capital.

It is entirely possible for everyone in any given city's ad biz to know everybody else in it. They know how parasitical and incestuous they are, and to compensate they really go in a big way for oceanic brotherhood of many storyboards. Coca-Cola's 'I'd Like to Teach the World to Sing' abomination is no longer with us, but it has spawned a school of commercials that are just as corny and twice as patronising. How about the Heinz adverts that show those net-curtain-twitching-type white families having a cosy old nuclear time of it while the township black men croon over the top? You can't help thinking, though, that, however serene the mother looks, gazing at her sleeping child while the unseen Ladysmith choir sing a lullaby, she'd completely lose it if a family of Sudanese refugees moved in next door.

Then there are the new Nestlé adverts which implore us to 'open up your mind' by sharing high-fives and instant coffee with any handy Third Worlder who happens to be passing down your high street. So Nestlé, who in the Eighties were a byword for the exploitation of the developing world, have been reborn in the Nineties as a caring-sharing co-op.

I know that the Eighties are still considered to have been a brash and brutal decade, but the Nineties are far more low and dishonest. In the Nineties, 'respecting' other cultures is what we have instead of politics, instead of seeing what things have always been about – the gap between rich and poor.

The Marxist reading of Third World poverty and deprivation was simply that the West had too much money and others not enough, and that the problem would only be solved when wealth was redistributed. Liberal Whitey, though, got a bit jumpy about this the minute he'd accumulated a few worldly goods, and suddenly it seemed to make a lot more sense that Johnny African was poorer than us because he had a better quality of life than us! Swings and roundabouts? They get sunshine, bare breasts and starvation, we get rain, repression and loadsamoney.

This liberal Western view of Africans in particular as natural and unrepressed goes a long way to explaining why the genital mutilation of women on the continent continues. If any white country took it into its head to go around lopping off women's clitorises and sewing up their vaginas with wire, we would think them, rightly, sadistic sociopaths. Yet it has been so drummed into us by cosmetics pedlars and pop stars that Africans are inherently noble and natural that we think they must have a good reason for torturing their girl children. Well, the reason in Burkina Faso and Mali, for two, is that it is thought a man will die if his penis touches a clitoris.

The bitter irony is that, while Western liberals kid themselves that they are being nice to the Third World by appreciating their 'culture', reformers in those very countries have actually declared certain cultural practices barbaric, and are attempting to get rid of them – only to be told by white liberals that cultural diversity is to be respected, no matter how obscene the results.

Female genital mutilation is the most horrific example; the American health activist Frances Hoskens, who has worked for years to mobilise opinion against it, accused 'international agencies, as well as charitable and church groups and family-planning organisations working in Africa' of engaging in a 'conspiracy of silence – as a result, African women working for change in their own countries have been isolated or ignored'. In Thailand, feminists and health workers are attempting to stop the barbaric tribal habit of fitting metal coils around the necks of women. Weighing up to 11 pounds, these coils eventually crush the collarbone. But the tribes persist – largely due to the six dollars that they make each time a tourist takes a photograph of this cute, ethnic custom.

Accepting cultural differences all too often means letting a cruel bastard off the hook. If I want a little ethnic education, I will turn not to Nestlé's grinning Third Worlders, but to our own pariahs – Orangemen, butt of every racist sneer we can no longer aim abroad, with their 'fancy dress' and 'silly hats'. In those bowlers and rolled umbrellas, I see something far more poignant, fragile and worthy of my respect than a stretched neck, a lower lip the size of a dinner plate or a vagina, slashed and bleeding.

18 JULY 1998

Leonardo DiCaprio's appeal is a simple one: he looks like an angel who could and would fuck you to within an inch of your sanity without once breaking sweat. This combination of divine cleanliness and infernal dirtiness is what makes him the hottest film star in the world.

And, more important, it's also what makes every ugly old geezer we have been force-fed as screen idols for the past two decades suddenly seem like the rancid bits of scrag-end they are. When Gwyneth Paltrow finally stated the obvious last month and said she found it 'creepy' to smooch on screen with Michael Douglas, she was reflecting the widespread distaste young people feel when they take a date to the pictures only to be faced with a 20-foot-high senile delinquent pressing his attentions on a girl young enough to be his granddaughter. Kids are squeamish about old folk having sex at the best of times; when it is with one of their own, it leads to the great sexual turn-off that has resulted in the rejection of vehicles showcasing 60-year-old studs in favour of teen-and-20 ensemble pieces such as *Scream*, in which the only inter-generational kissing is chaste and parental.

Combining, as he does, beauty and righteousness in such singular degrees, it makes total sense that DiCaprio is desperate, at 23, to marry ex-girlfriend Kristen Zang, a young thing only slightly less lovely than Leo himself. She, being more mature for her age, has repeatedly turned him down on the grounds that he isn't ready. But they probably will get married before the year is out, because getting married is very much the thing for beautiful and celebrated young people to do right now – as living in sin was in the Sixties. Louise and Jamie have done the deed; Posh and Beckham, Nicole and Robbie, Winona and Matt are all straining at the leash to follow.

No matter what you think about marriage *per se*, you'd have to be some swell sort of bitter old misanthrope not to want to cheer when you see such perfect specimens, all enjoying their salad days in the sun, promising that they will never want to sleep with anyone else, ever – cross my heart and hope to die! If you are attractive, getting married makes you even more so; further-more, done young, it almost looks like integrity. Whereas, of course, it is simply another, more streamlined sort of sexual greed, with a big helping of need on the side.

But if a white wedding makes the young and lovely seem even more so, how much more sordid does divorce make a couple look who were tawdry already. The legendary Willis–Moore greed, rudeness and conceit, which once made them a unit, binding them tight and making them appear indestructible, will now be turned on each other with all the skill, fury and lawyers that money can buy.

Not only will the divorce be a matter of public interest, it will also be an historical event in that many people will make fortunes from it, and these may well cause certain shifts in the US economy, so massive will the amounts of money involved be. Willis and Moore are also living, spitting proof that, despite their much-vaunted tricks for keeping their marriage 'hot' – the endless saucy faxes and telephone calls on location, the fantasies played out on Demi's perfectly honed Stradivarius of a bod when reunited – they might as well have saved their energy and dignity, and slumped on a sofa together eating pizza and watching soaps.

In the long run, such restorative periods of rest and relaxation might have done a better job of bonding them than flogging a dead horse – or whatever – three times a night. No one who has seen the state of a dinner that one has attempted to keep hot for half an hour would ever want to own a marriage that had been kept artificially hot for upwards of ten years; it would be really shrivelled and dried up and flavourless. Far better to throw it away and get yourself a new one.

Hard though it is for sexual moralists to grasp, it is not that marriage is less popular; just that divorce is seen, covertly, to come with it, like a matching set of bookends. This is what the prenuptial agreements of the stars are about: the assumption that the marriage will collapse. And probably should collapse. I know couples who have seemed perfectly happy, but separated because their relationship 'was getting old'. In the old days, that would have been cause for a celebration; now, an ageing marriage seems a bit depressing, like having to wear the same down-at-heel pair of shoes day in, day out. Marriage is no fun, but being married is great. Once married, you may live the life of the single person with no taint of selfishness; you wear proof on your left hand that you have not been sexually tried and rejected by a generation. Being married is incredibly attractive to the opposite sex, and ensures that you will never go short of proposals. The day I ran off with my second husband, we had dinner with a friend of his who was interested in the fact that I was embarking on my second marriage at 24: common on my side of the tracks, but about as frequent as teenage pregnancy among media girls. He had just read a US survey – cue raised eyebrows all round, but he urged us to stick with it – which proved that the more a woman had been married, the more she would be married.

I thought that this was a good thing, and made a lot of sense; my never-married fiancé and his friend's never-married girl-friend looked decidedly askance. I liked the modernist, feminist angle; the complete contradiction of the idea that saving yourself is the most sexually alluring thing you can do. Virginity stopped being sexy back in the Sixties, but well into the Seventies there was a stupid idea that men would rather sleep with a single woman than a married one.

By the Eighties, we all knew the score.

For the first five years, a marriage is sexy to the people inside it, and after that to the people outside it. Outside every marriage between two attractive people, there is a single person trying to get in.

This may be squalid and amoral, but it is true, and it means you can always do a runner when the walls close in. All you agonising singletons out there, just get married, forget it and get on with your lives. I speak as someone who has not been single since the age of 18. I fully expect to be married until the day I die – to a lot of different people, naturally.

1 AUGUST 1998

The other day, I was in a taxi and we drove past the building I think of as The Place It All Started. Most people can trace their ruin back to an urban crack-house or a suburban brothel, but the place where my long and winding road to nowhere started is a meek, not at all bleak, rather sweet, single-storey, red-brick building in a leafy Bristol suburb called Sandy Park. It looks rather like a Lego house, with a sloping roof and small, high windows, but it is, in fact, a library.

I sort of hissed and drew back from the window, and the driver laughed.

'Old boyfriend, luv?'

'What?'

'An old flame who ruined your life?'

'Something like that.'

I don't read books these days. Correction: I don't read new books that I think I'll love. I can't listen to new music I've been told I'd love, either. I feel I love too much already, and that there's no love left. I feel that the books and music I have loved the most have probably been an extremely bad influence on me; besides, it's depressing to think I won't ever do anything that good again. If I accidentally do stumble on a great new book, like Amy Bloom's *Love Invents Us*, I inevitably end up finishing the last page with the shadow of a smirk, and thinking, 'I could do much better than that, if I ever decide to put my Thinking Head back on.'

I can read books I know I'll hate; for instance, I took on holiday *Intimacy*, by Hanif Kureishi, and *No More Mr Nice Guy*, by Howard Jacobson, and received an almost para-sexual thrill when they were even worse crap than I'd imagined. Sometimes, when I wake up at 6 a.m. with one of my Heads (presumably not the Thinking one), I feel equal to reading my favourite books, *Hangover Square* and *Brighton Rock*, again. I am still able in this half-waking state to enter fully into other people's lives. But mostly, there's me and my big mouth standing between me and the precious page. I knew I had lost the gift of empathy, for such it is, when I finished *Anna Karenina*, threw it down and said, 'Stupid cow!' Obviously, I was missing something.

Only when hungover can I remember what it felt like when my heart was pure enough to be a clean slate that writers could do their magic on. I do think it's an age thing; on this holiday, where I was prostituting my literacy sneering at Howie and Han, my 25-year-old companion was devouring (and this truly is possible at his age) that book by George Perec with no 'e's in it and *Titus Groan*. He would sit there in a rapture, reading every syllable while I speed-read and sneered. I envied him loads.

These days, I flick through magazines and newspapers like a fiend, reading everything, absorbing nothing. I hate magazines, but never feel more relaxed than when I'm reading one. I know they're what you read in waiting rooms, and it seems so appropriate to all of us now, not knowing where we are going or if we should make one last effort to find our Thinking Head and put it on for one last go.

I was not always so. I remember, as a tiny child, embarassing my father because he had bought me the Enid Blyton book, *The Faraway Tree*, which I had coveted for some time. 'Is it mine? Is it really mine, to keep?' I can remember shrieking at the top of my six-year-old lungs. I thought I'd died and gone to Heaven, which was at the end of the book.

'Sssh!' my dad said. Everyone was looking.

I sought out a copy of it last week, seeking to recapture the lost thrill of fiction. Get this, from Chapter One: 'Once upon a time there were three children, Jo, Bessie and Fanny. They lived with their mother and father in a little cottage deep in the country. The girls had to help their mother in the house, and Jo helped his father in the garden.' Sick, sick, sick!

Yet books and me became an item. At home, I made my mother cry as I sat there like Edward Scissorhands, robotically reading four library books at a time, my wrists moving like pistons, reading for my escape and my sanity. At school, I got beaten up for reading in the playground, for being too good for my cawing contemporaries. But it was all worth it; it was books and me against the world.

But now . . . I dunno. It's just that, after a certain age, you feel you should be writing books, not reading them. And then, when you do, so what? 'Books last,' my first husband used to sneer as I laboured over my penny-a-lining in the Eighties, he having temporarily retired from journalism to write books that you might call blockbusters. 'That stuff you're writing will be gone next week, and no one will ever remember it.' Well, have you tried buying a copy of *Platinum Logic* recently? Books are as transient as anything else. Walk into any bookshop, and underneath the top note of sexy sumptuousness of all those paperbacks piled high and overflowing, there's the middle note of sorrow and the bottom note of despair. As well as the thousands of titles that aren't going to sell, so sending their authors back to their day jobs with dashed hopes, which is far worse than having no hope in the first place, there is the ghostly presence of all the books that went before and left no mark on the world whatsoever. The Ghost Books, the majority, growing greater every day.

We never learn, though. Last year, my 12-year-old was reading Goosebumps books, free as a bird; now, his favourites are *Catcher in the Rye, One Flew Over the Cuckoo's Nest* and *Coming Up for Air*, and he worries whether the books he likes are lowbrow. He will be of that class which, on entering adolescence, finds books sexy in the way that the young of other classes find popular music sexy. In the future, he will boast about books he's read to impress a girl who will have read even more than him; together, he and Zoe, or Chloe, will be the young lovers from The Sundays song who mope, 'I never should have said/That the books that you'd read/Were all I loved you for.' Well, good! Let someone else suffer through Book Hell; I've done my bit. When the newspapers rang last week, asking me for my top five, on the occasion of the Top 100 Books of the Century being published by some university with too much time on its hands, I snarled, 'None of them! They're all crap!' I didn't mean it, but I wish I had.

8 AUGUST 1998

It's a funny thing, but the readers who write to me at the *Guardian* tend to be either really silly or really smart. The silly ones plague me with poems about how evil I am – 'Are you a witch?/Or perhaps just a bitch?': move over, Simon Armitage! – but the smart ones make me think; far more, it must be said, than journalists do.

Above all, the people who write to me are honest. Sometimes, they're so honest it breaks your heart; at other times, it breaks you up. Like the young man – I'll call him B – who enclosed his address and phone number to vouch for his reality. A few weeks ago, I argued, apropos the Lords' apoplexy on lowering the age of gay consent, that young men were actually less needful of protection than young women, as they were sex-mad and could have it consensually with practically anyone and suffer no trauma, whereas young girls tended to do it for love or affection, and were then sorely let down.

The basic difference, I concluded, was that while women need to feel at least a modicum of affection for their partner, men will do it with anything, even things that aren't alive. In short, they'll do it with mud. They'll do it to the dinner the family is about to cook, like Portnoy and his piece of liver, thus rendering the concept of vulnerability somewhat farcical; nine times out of ten, it's things that need protection from teenage boys.

Writes B, of mud, 'This is absolutely true, and as a formerly perma-hard adolescent I totally support and endorse your rare insight. About ten years ago, as a teenager, even with the luxury of a real live girlfriend, such was the extent of my sexual desperation . . . I had sex with mud.'

Now, that is just so cool. I can't think of one male journalist who's ever come clean about having had sex with mud, for all that they're so fearlessly frank about sex and what beasts men are, and how they love it that way. To look at them, I imagine quite a few would be well chuffed to find themselves at home of a Saturday night, lying on the sofa with a lump of mud. But they'd never admit to it. They'll confess that they go to prostitutes, that they're pathologically promiscuous, that they hate women – really nasty stuff, as long as it makes them feel like Jack Nicholson. Confessing to having sex with mud, however, doesn't make them feel like that.

It makes them feel like Jack shit.

Journalists lie and preen and put spin on everything, especially when they say they're telling the truth. And, with the advent of Personal Columns ('Woke up this morning/Got a twelve-hundred-word deadline to meet!/Luckily, I'm on Prozac./My man done left me and there's veruccas on my feet!'), this tendency to be economical with the truth has blossomed. It is sobering to reflect that, of all the columnists whose careers would come to an end if the 'I' fell off their keyboard, the one who is telling what could most widely be accepted as the 'truth' is Tara Palmer-Tomkinson. For the rest, searching for that big Bridget Jones-style book contract, the tired post-feminist mantra must be kept up: Sad Woman, Cad Man. Thus, female journalists write about their man dumping them and male journalists write about behaving badly to their girlfriends. It must be true, we reason, because who would make up something that made them look that stupid?

Well, look no further, because I'm here to out the lying creeps. One of those hackettes whose husband left her, well, he left her for a man, which she's never mentioned, because, once mentioned, an element of farce and camp would creep in, and so rob her of her BJ dreams. Another's husband left her for a woman,

and within a month she, too, was gaily playing musical beds –
though, from her column, you'd think she'd walled herself up in
a nunnery. That male journalist who's always writing about his
girlfriend: she dumped him ages ago. None of them dares come
clean, because that would contradict the myth that there are no
spare men around, and that once a woman's got a man, she
holds on to him like grim death. Whoever highlights the truly
surprising fact of modern female life – that a woman can walk
out of one relationship in the morning and into another by mid-
afternoon (like unskilled workers in the Fifties) – makes rubbish
of too many fearful agendas to get a hearing. And so the faux-
lovesick strut their weary stuff, knowing in their heart of hearts
that they will only ever be the journeymen of joylessness. 'Death
is everything,' Spinal Tap's useless manager tried to convince the
band when their album cover came out black by mistake. 'Death
sells.' That is the ludicrousness of our times: Ian from Spinal Tap
foresaw it all. For it is the sick and dying who are the real
aristocrats of the media these days. Not just any old sick and
dying, mind; only our own kind, thank you! To see the space
given to deaths from massacre or famine in faraway countries,
compared with that given to John Diamond, Ruth Picardie and,
before them, Oscar Moore, is to see the modern equivalent of
that surreal Blimpish headline, 'Fog on Channel: Continent
isolated'.

I have witnessed cancer and I have never heard anyone go
into a comic routine about it the way some of my stricken
colleagues do. And why should they? They're dying. We
repressed English were always scolded for keeping death taboo;
what's taboo now, apparently, is feeling unrelieved sadness and
anger about untimely death. Pop stars are not normally known
for their gravitas, but compare The Verve's 'The Drugs Don't
Work', about Richard Ashcroft's father's death from cancer, with

the frantic, fallabout mugging of the media. We are fast reaching a time when some Alan Partridge-type will introduce one of our sick, scribbling brethren with, 'And now, the word on everyone's lips – cancer!' And we'll have only ourselves to blame. But, hey, I'm not a complete killjoy. There is one disease that is barely ever written about, one that sufferers have trouble making sense of. Furthermore, it's one that a great many journalists have – I know, because I know the two people who gave it to most of them! But then, who would buy a book called *Diary of a Herpes Sufferer*?

29 August 1998

'You've Let Yourself Go' was a gorgeous song by Charles Aznavour; a real old *chanson*, in fact, though only the English tongue could have pulled off the pun properly. In it, the narrator is getting ready to go out with his wife to celebrate their 20th wedding anniversary – but when he goes to do up her dress, the zip breaks. Cue song about how she's gone downhill, not the girl he married etc. until, at the end, he has to admit that he's a bit of a slob, too, so – 'Come close to me and . . . let yourself go.'

The phrase came to my mind last week, the week in which those pictures of Kim Wilde were published. Kim was, you'll remember, the toppermost of the poppermost sex sirens in the shimmering, simmering Eighties; the eyes of Monroe, the mouth of Bardot and the sneer of Elvis, all strained through a candy-coloured punky muslin. She was one of those girls – like Louise today – who men like to think of other girls being jealous of, but was actually just so gorgeous that, whenever you saw her, you wanted to stand up and cheer, as though she was a beloved football team. Just by being female, she seemed to reflect well on all of us.

Next to her beauty, the thing that singled out Kim from the other pouting pop strumpets of the Eighties was that she seemed almost eerily well balanced. They say that what makes a star is not that little something extra, but that little something missing – well, Kim obviously had all her bits in fine working order. Because of this, even though she supported Michael Jackson on one of his European tours and was never off *Top of the Pops*, she never quite made it in the style of her screwed-up contemporaries – Jackson, Prince, the Georges Boy and Michael, Madonna. Like her soulmate Sade, who similarly slipped into singing as a convenient way to make big money, she seemed totally undriven, especially by demons, and once she had put aside something for a rainy day and found a suitable candidate to cocoon with, she just slipped away of her own free will. Last week, photographs showed her literally unrecognisable as her former siren self: a 37-year-old mother living in Hertfordshire, happily married and triumphantly overweight.

I say 'triumphantly' because, when a woman known for her beauty lets herself go these days, it looks like triumphalism. It says I Don't Need You: Please Don't Fancy Me; I Don't Want My Dance Card Ticked, Thank You. But we have become so used to a climate in which women strive to be attractive to men right up to and beyond the menopause that it strikes us as the height of weirdness for a 37-year-old woman, once a great beauty, to surrender to gravity in a way that was once totally taken for granted. I blame Demi Moore. Posing naked and pregnant in full make-up and jewellery, Demi was alleged to be celebrating the natural beauty of child-bearing, but actually looked like one of those specialist pregnant prostitutes so beloved of very kinky men. As with most things that American females claim 'empower' women, Moore gave her lazier, less neurotic sisters yet one more jump to fall – or refuse – at. In the past, pregnancy had always been the perfect excuse for a woman to slob out, pig out, get off the treadmill of attractiveness. Now, you had to be bejewelled and painted even as you went into labour, or you were letting the side down.

Within a year, Moore was back on the cover of *Vanity Fair*, naked again but for body paint, her body even buffer than before. Three children; three returns to her fighting weight. Often exercising for four hours a day – a quarter of her waking life – Moore became the logical conclusion of a culture that judges women on their appearance; she spent so much time and energy on her looks that her acting and her marriage – which presumably her hard work on her physical self was meant to secure – fell by the wayside. She lost her credibility to a new generation of film beauties who insisted on no nudity clauses in their contracts, and her husband to a chubby, cheerful waitress whose idea of exercise was to carry two bottles of beer in each hand.

'How could he?' we wail of Bill and Monica, not questioning his right to philander, but his taste. Faced with the blowsy beret-wearer, we all become the judge who was so struck by Mary Archer's 'fragrance' that he could not countenance her husband copping off with a heavy-set hooker.

With slim, groomed Hillary at home? But in our incomprehension we are victims of the modern myth that any thin person is more attractive than any fat person; as Jackie Kennedy and Marilyn Monroe proved a long time ago, it ain't necessarily so. Perhaps the widespread acceptance of this silliness is the reason the thin, less than beautiful columnist Lynda Lee-Potter feels justified in pillorying the big, beautiful actress Kate Winslet over her weight.

I'm not being nasty, but those who write pieces about people losing their looks were never beauties themselves in the first place. And so, naturally, they prize beauty far more than someone who has had it since they were 12. In the recent round of interviews I did this year to publicise my books *I Knew I Was Right* (Heinemann) and *Diana* (Weidenfeld), it was not the attractive people who commented on my physical decline but rather the plug-ugly ones, mostly male; a bigger selection of bum-faces, trolls and chrome-domes you never saw in your life. Often, I feel the pressing question about men is simply this one: don't any of them ever look in the mirror?

It's like what men say about having breasts: 'You'd just lie around playing with yourself all day, wouldn't you?' Of course you don't. It's the same with beauty; often, it just gets boring, not least because of the unwanted attention you get from men. 'I finally did the one thing I knew would put him off me,' Marianne Faithfull has recalled gleefully of Mick Jagger. 'I let myself get fat.'

Easy come, easy go; it is the sheer go-to-hell sensuality of letting oneself go that those not born beautiful will never understand: the fact that beauty, to be enjoyed at its best, must be used, like fuel, not pickled like fruit. Kim Wilde understands, and for achieving wisdom she has received a great gift – the assurance that never again will Chris Evans want to have sex with her. And for that, she must be truly thankful.

5 SEPTEMBER 1998

In the Seventies and Eighties, a particularly loathsome bra advert could be seen on billboards – 'Underneath. They're All Lovable' – over a brassiered babe swooning beseechingly out at the, presumably, male gazer. 'They', of course, were women; and 'underneath' meant underneath the business suit, the briefcase, the flashy battledress of feminism, which, in those days, was called 'Women's Lib'. (By the way, I'd like us to 'reclaim' the phrase Women's Lib as the queers have done for their slur. Feminism is too poncified and slippery, and can end up meaning all sorts; Women's Liberation is extremely bold and crass and to the point. Feminism lends itself to post-feminism, but can you imagine anyone claiming we live in a post-Women's Liberation world?)

Brassieres aren't about reassuring men any more; they're about reassuring women and mocking men, and about time too. But it does seem strange that it is young women in their underwear, nearly naked, who are the one contemporary image of womanhood portrayed in the media as totally bold ('Hello Boys') and utterly contained ('Who Said a Woman Can't Get Pleasure from Something Soft?').

One thing these young women are not is vulnerable. Only them, though: them and the TeleTotties. It's only the girls who show their bras these days who seem to be wearing psychological breastplates; as for the rest of us, underneath, don't worry, we're all still lovable.

Or rather, vulnerable. Because, according to today's popular culture, inside every ball-breaking bitch is a scared little girl just crying out for protection.

Who can forget the Miraculous Weeping All Saints scam at the Brit Awards? These four hardbodies in their combat fatigues blubbing like a quartet of Catholic statues for being so hand-somely rewarded for that filet mignon of maudlin monotony 'Never Ever'. And no wonder they were rewarded: in its opening line, the craze for female vulnerability was taken to a new extreme as a girl in army trousers bleated, 'I need to know what I've done wrong . . .' Not since the days of 'If The Boy's Happy, The Girl's Happy Too' has a pop song shown its female protagonist so dependent on male approval for fulfilment, so close to cracking up if she doesn't get it.

As I said to Emma Forrest as we made vomiting noises at the TV, imagine Geri singing that line! A year later, Geri is doing vulnerable too, trowelling off her slap and slipping about in floaty dresses with self-help manuals under her arm. (At least Marilyn used to pack a history book.) Bridget Jones's middle name is Vulnerability, and Ally McBeal is extremely successful '. . . and falling apart!' Even inside those hard-boiled sweeties you thought you could break your teeth on, the soft centre holds: Anna from *This Life*, Detective Jane Tennison, every leggy lady doctor – no matter how tough they seem to be, you just know that at some point they're going to lock themselves in the john for a good old session with the waterworks.

I don't mind people crying, unless I'm having sex with them at that moment, or unless they're driving a car fast with me in it, but it's one thing to cry out of sorrow, anger or temper, and quite another to blub non-specifically, which is what these women do. Vulnerability, so far as I can see, is a blank cheque to behave like a baby; to hide behind your hair and say 'I'm shy!' and expect the world to pin a medal on you. I should know. I did this act for the entire stretch of my married lives, 17 years in all. My husbands loved it. Everybody loved it: she breaks just like a little girl! Ah! Under all that tough talk, she's so vulnerable! And I stayed that way until I was thirty-fucking-five years old; I was the oldest ingénue in town, and shaping up real good as the thinking man's Baby Jane Hudson. (Not Holzer.) That, or a foul-mouthed Bonnie Langford. But men do love it, and it makes perfect sense that I stopped behaving like a sexy cretin only when I ran off with a woman.

'I wish,' said the brilliantly brittle Tracey Shaw, Maxine from *Coronation Street*, recently, 'she'd leave off that "wounded angel" routine.' 'She' is Anna Friel, the young actress who was dumped first by that smiling human abyss, Darren Day, for the charms of Miss Shaw, and then by Robbie Williams. Throughout it all, while talking a great deal about her life as a dumpee, she has never once blamed either man: she invariably speaks more in sorrow than in anger. Stick thin, tiny, almost pre-adolescent, she has recently had all her hair cut off and looks even more fragile than she did before. Next to Anna, Audrey Hepburn would look like a hod carrier. Interviews centre on the hard knocks life has dealt her; everything in her life is presented as a hurdle she bravely overcame. She's even cited being middle class as a reason she'd been discriminated against in the acting profession. Hmm, I hear that Kate, Emma, Helena say the same, as did Leigh, Ashcroft and Thorndike before them. That Kathy Burke, eh? Cushy cow.

In Friel, we can see that vulnerability is a sort of me-too victimhood, touted mostly by those who've had easy lives. And no one could milk it like the Princess of Wales. With the Establishment against her, though, she had more excuse than most. In later years, she was intelligent enough to see how silly it looked – that Taj Mahal shot! – and became a total trooper, putting her best foot forward, making sure they got her good side.

People who see themselves as vulnerable are often self-centred and insensitive. When men try it on, we see this in spades: Gazza and Beckham and Chris Evans, all blubbing at the drop of a ball.

Don't encourage men to 'show their feelings' more than they do, for the love of God! Men show their feelings every day; that's why we have road rage, rape and wife-murder. Now we've got crying and kicking to add to the roll-call. Bloody great. But some people do genuinely fit the definition of the word; those in danger, on the edge. Women sleeping on streets, girls in forced marriages, children terrorised by parents. Vulnerability brings out the beast, not the best, in those who have power. That is why it's so reprehensible to try it on for size as a stylistic tic. Grow up, girls.

10 OCTOBER 1998

You can say what you like about me, but I've never been a hypocrite. If a married friend tells me she's having an affair, I say, 'Brilliant! How long? And for what length of time have you been seeing him?' (Think about it.) If someone says they're pregnant, I enquire, 'And do you have a good abortionist?' If someone asks me to admire her immodest new dress, I say, 'The last time I saw a woman wearing a garment like that, she was walking through the bazaar in Cairo with a number on her back.' I can tolerate most low habits, but hypocrisy is one I am violently opposed to. It's such a cowardly vice.

I've heard some rancid old chestnuts in my time, but the limpest of them all is, 'Hypocrisy is the tribute that vice pays to virtue.' It's always men who say it and, like 99 per cent of the things they say, it's self-serving crud. More to the point would be, 'Hypocrisy is the raspberry that vice blows in the face of virtue.' Or, 'Don't do as I do, do as I say!'

Amid the liberal bleating in defence of Clinton, there was the implication that it is somehow reactionary and old-fashioned to call the President's sexual proclivities into question. To this, I would reply that it is extremely reactionary and old-fashioned to say that because some guy's a big cheese he shouldn't be prey to the same prying the rest of us have to put up with. The man in the street gets gossiped about in the street, so the world's policeman is obviously going to be up in the dock in front of the world. If he doesn't want to be a global village sideshow, then he shouldn't act like a global village idiot.

'In France, it's all so civilised,' the liberals moan. No, it's not; it's hypocritical. All that business in the Sixties was so that things wouldn't be like they are in France: the man with both a wife and girlfriend, and the women putting up with it. Neither France nor America – in the unlikely event that either would have a female president in the first place, so scared of women are they – would put up with a female leader who took on all comers. They'd revile her as a complete slag, and then dump her.

French women didn't get the vote until 1945; Paris is the sexual-harassment capital of the world; France has the lowest number of female MPs in Europe; and those that make it into government are tarred with the wink-wink, nudge-nudge brush that they're being rewarded for exciting *l'enthusiasme de Monsieur le Président*. In short, the French attitude to men, women and marriage is the last Western bastion of Victorian sexual values.

The gynophobia of the US is more wide-eyed, less jaded, but still in place. Go figure: as a proud career woman, Hillary was loathed; as a doormat, she is adored. Now go figure this: the sheer audacity of her 'better half' (*sic*), that love machine who ended every evening with his mistress masturbating over a lonely sink. What a stud! 'Am I making you hot, Sink, baby? Did the plumbing move for you, too? C'mon, Sink, baby, talk to me, make me hot!' While Clinton was busy spilling his seed down the sink, he was and is presiding over the dishonourable discharges, the ailing and the life-shattering of dozens of men and women from the US Armed Forces simply for the sin of sleeping with a colleague. He has also presided over a crusade against teenage 'immorality' and the removal of benefits for single mothers. It has even become possible actually to jail unmarried people for sleeping together, taken up by some small towns, to teach teenagers 'a lesson'. Imagine that happening in this country. Imagine.

No one held a gun to Clinton's head and made him do these Draconian sex things. No one made him make that sickening campaign speech in which he brought up family values and said that, unlike the Republicans, the Democrats weren't going to talk about family values – no, the Democrats under Bill were going to practise them! More than anything, it all proves that the man's arrogance and hypocrisy verge on the sociopathic.

'The people of this country do not mind fornication,' said Ramsay MacDonald, 'but they loathe adultery.' In the US and France, the opposite is true – which says a really good thing about us and our relative lack of hypocrisy. Hypocrisy was once the vice of the switched-off and reactionary, but in recent years there has been a move to repossess it for the liberal and the switched-on. The hypocritical look is the New Look, and no longer the stuff of serge-trousered under-secretaries of state: serious actors doing commercials that are seen only on Japanese TV; fashion designers slamming models for being temperamental and overpaid; Naomi Campbell moaning about being discriminated against because of the way she looks (black), while taking full advantage of looking (thin, 'exotic') the way the fashion industry fetishises; Martin Amis, author of a book about how the pursuit of money makes you lose your soul, abandoning his long-time agent for a huge advance; David Duchovny, sneering at *The X-Files* before taking the money and running; Madonna swearing she'll never let her daughter watch TV, not even MTV.

Notice that of the two Brits on the above roll of shame, one is resident in the US and the other is yearning to go there. Brits who go to America always say they went to escape Tall Poppy Syndrome, but they actually go to avoid Bullshit Detector Syndrome. And it is our mischievous desire to see the rich and powerful debagged for the hell of it that makes British society so much less craven, so much more irreverent than that of others across various ponds. The feminist comic's 'He's a man – he deserved it!' translates into our 'He's rich/powerful – he deserved it!' God help us if we ever start respecting the 'privacy' of those who seek power over us; then we really will be as bad a bunch of kowtowing suck-ups as the rest of them.

The people in power judge those who are not all the time; every time they slash their benefits ('Stand on your own two feet'), privatise their industries ('You can't be trusted') or send them off to war ('Be a man'). So they deserve all the judgement they get, be it in a kangaroo court or not. Prying and poking is the price the plebeians demand of the powerful, and long may it stay that way.

24 OCTOBER 1998

Although I can be quite amusing when surrounded by my nearest and dearest, I am generally a quiet person, in both senses of the word: I have a quiet voice and I say very little. When I was Queen of the Groucho Club, this was something of a problem. Just as Steve McQueen could not go into a bar for a quiet drink without some lush saying, 'Hey, McQueen, you think you're a tough guy – come outside and fight me', I could not sit down in the back room of the Groucho without some idiot swaggering up and demanding of me, 'Go on then, be controversial.' When I failed to rise to the occasion with a blizzard of *bons mots*, the inevitable jibe followed: 'You're not very funny, are you? You're not like your writing. Go on, say something!'

I rarely saw the need to respond to such rudeness, but would rather go and sit the other side of my husband and look at my assailant as if they were mad. This was because speech has always been my second language. To some extent, I was brought up to think that people who talked a lot were in some small way mad. I grew up in a quiet household among a people who provided a hat trick of reticence: the English West Country working class. To say we did not talk about our feelings is to put it mildly; if ever one member of the family seemed likely to lurch at another with protestations of affection, the targeted one would rear back and all but make the sign of the cross, as though a too-loud declaration of love was the first sign of a bloodsucker. Looking back, I think my people had something. I've seen loads of families, especially middle-class ones, who were very voluble about their affection for each other, but I would stand my parents' silent, stoic love against theirs any day.

There always seemed to me something very sad about compulsive talkers, people who could not stand to be silent lest they hear the self-loathing Babel inside their brains: tinnitus with a thesaurus. There is something about too much talking that speaks of deep loneliness. When I first came to London in the mid-Seventies, I was amazed to hear my first radio phone-in show, on LBC; all those people, in all those rooms, ringing up to air their views to complete strangers! I found myself bunking off nights on the town with boys from punk bands just so I could sit with my ear to the radio and marvel at this amazing example of modern anomie. 'You won't believe what they do up here,' I told my friend Karen in Bristol. 'There's this radio station, right, and all these complete strangers ring up and give their opinions about things! Often, they get really angry and shout.'

'You always were a liar,' she said, and hung up.

Now, of course, Bristol has its own phone-ins, as does the most outlandish district, and the days when gratuitous lip was a big-city vice are forgotten. But I have noticed that the ones in Bristol tend to be people arguing the toss about Cribbs Causeway, the big new shopping centre, as in Brighton they tend to be about the new mall, Churchill Square, and whether or not the street entertainers therein are a good thing or a damned pest. London talk-ins still specialise in lonely souls with loads to say and no one to listen. If they were younger and richer, they'd be edging shyly into Internet chat rooms; as it is, they turn to Talk Radio, inevitably their number-one number on BT's cruelly named Friends and Family tariff.

There's worse: there are people who are pursued by a solitariness so extreme that they have to get a reaction from all present in order to feel validated. Interestingly, though it is young working-class men whom we most associate with all types of noise pollution, I find that it is thirty-something upper-middle-class women who tend to talk the loudest about personal issues: Toff Totty with Tannoy.

When I was in hospital after having my last baby, I'll never forget the Hampstead type who ruined my ward's sleep by keeping up a running commentary, day and night, on the gruesome state of her vagina; the working-class girls either side of me simply sobbed quietly, which was far less intrusive. On a bus in Bristol the other day, I heard a posh woman describing her first meeting after 20 years with her absentee father, who was now 'riddled with cancer' and living in Australia to boot. You could tell she felt it was a toss-up as to which was worse.

But the woman I came across on the train from Brighton to London last month was the most amazing – I have honestly never seen a piece of fringe theatre like it. This woman, who had obviously read and taken to heart the accepted wisdom that the English do not talk to their children enough, and why oh why can't we be more like the French and the Italians, proceeded to be more like the French and the Italians for the next 50 minutes. And I have never passed a longer 50 minutes. Fixing her gaze on the rest of the carriage, making eye contact with us one by one before we turned our terrified eyes away, she explained to her daughter, who must have been about five, exactly how much Mummy and Daddy had wanted a baby just like Jody, exactly what they had done to get a baby just like Jody, exactly how Jody was born – you could all but smell the blood – and, basically, what had happened during Jody's every waking hour since.

The performance culminated in a demonstration of child massage that had the more censorious among us muttering things like 'Shouldn't be allowed!' as we pulled into Victoria Station. With this, the woman stood up and announced, 'We're getting off now, Jody, darling, because these people are so boring. So gloriously boring!' Then she was off, leaving us all staring at each other with total incomprehension. What had we been supposed to do? Join in with our own birth horror stories? Join in with the indecent massage? I'm sure most of us didn't blame ourselves for being overly dull, but hit, instead, on the pretty obvious truth: that this woman was, in some small way, mad and, as mad people do, said exactly what came into her head at the moment it came. In a culture such as ours, currently terrorised by middle-class mores and threatened with the extinction of those working-class values that did make us different from Italy and France, we must brace ourselves for more.

31 OCTOBER 1998

This month's Cosmopolitan magazine carries a poll of the alleged Top 50 Most Lovable Men in the world, voted for by its readers. Now, I don't read *Cosmopolitan* myself, because it speaks to a type of person who is as foreign to me as the people who read *Horse and Hound*: it speaks to the kind of woman who can't get a boyfriend, can't have an orgasm and really thinks that the circumference of your thigh matters a toss.

I came across the *Cosmopolitan* poll in last weekend's *Sunday Mirror*, which I was balancing across one vast thigh and flicking through while recovering from an almost aneurysm-inducing orgasm. 'Oh, look!' I exclaimed to my boyfriend. 'This is a hoot – it's a parody of those awful "sexiest men" lists, except they've got a list of the top 50 men who the idea of shagging is enough to make you want to sew yourself up!' He took the newspaper from me and shook his head. 'Then why's there no picture of Tony Parsons in it? Or David Baddiel? And what's Ewan doing here? And Leonardo? And your darling Richard Ashcroft?'

'Richard Ashcroft! Where?' I grabbed back the paper. 'But look,' I said, 'here's Chris Evans! And Richard Littlejohn, Nick Hornby, Harry Enfield, Tony Blair, John Peel. And Richard Branson at number 27!' I finished triumphantly.

'Yeah, but look – Robert Carlyle came first. It's just another regular top-50-favourite-men survey, my dove.'

I'm always accused of being a man-hater – to which my

answer is, invariably, 'Yes, I do watch the *Six o'Clock News*' – so just this once I'll treat you to my opinion on an area of modern life where men are way out in front: they are honest about what they like. Especially when it comes to the opposite sex.

Just look at any similar roll-call in any men's magazine, and you'll see the usual suspendered suspects slinking down the page: Denise van O, Melanie S, Mel B, Kate W and Cindy C. And quite right, too.

When the question 'Who do you fancy?' is posed, the answer should not come back, 'Whoever is talented/nice/clever/the Dalai Lama.' This is what's called crap logic, and this is just what women are always being accused of by men. They don't need more proof!

And yet there he is – the Dalai Lama, in with a bullet at number 26, a whole ten slots above Antonio Banderas. He's 63, he's celibate, he doesn't believe in votes for women, he looks like a prune that somebody played a silly game with ('Ho ho, let's draw a mouth and a nose on this prune and put some glasses on it so it looks like a face!') and hundreds of women say they adore him more than they do Denzel Washington!

The hell they do. Even though each reader's voting slip was only going to be read by a few members of the *Cosmo* staff, who don't even know them from Eve, they still had to lie about it! They felt they had to impress people whom they had never even met when answering a question about people they don't know! If that's not pathetic, then what is?

Men, on the other hand, would never be guilty of such gross hypocrisy. After all, men didn't put Mother Teresa at number 26 in the Women We Love charts while she was alive.

If men were answering such a poll, Richard Littlejohn (who was at 49 in the *Cosmo* poll – I mean, men didn't even put me at 49 when I was alive!), Nick Hornby, Tony Blair, Harry Enfield –

their equivalents would be Maeve Binchy, Harriet Harman, Pam Ayres. For Sting, read Cilla Black. For John Peel, the Queen Mother. Nelson Mandela? The late Indira Gandhi. See what I mean?

The woman who says that 'looks don't matter' may think she is a cut above the Essex girl screaming at a Chipperfield boy, but she is actually playing along with the oldest sexist game in the book: that women are as valuable as their looks, while men are intrinsically worthwhile. That women age, while men mature. That Michael Douglas snogging Gwyneth Paltrow in a film is normal, while Robson Green snogging Francesca Annis on TV is an 'issue', to be 'tackled', like incest or divorce. The 'Looks Don't Matter' sisters are the reason why Woody Allen (who I was amazed to see didn't make it into *Cosmopolitan*'s Top 50 – that's a first) feels free to go into his sixties romancing girls who are young enough to be his granddaughters – both on and off screen. From such strange normalisations does paedophilia draw strength and sustenance.

So, please, girls – just stop pretending to fancy the Universal Grandad. It's not clever and it's not cool. And rest assured: if you really did mean it, if you really do fancy His Holiness, then you are even more of a mess than I thought.

In the past, women were dependent on men, and in no position to demand physical as well as fiscal attractiveness from their mates. But when it came to fantasy figures, they judged in exactly the same way as men did; many was the dumb male beauty who made it in old Hollywood on the strength of his pecs-appeal alone, and was then dropped as soon as they dropped.

Any man of 68 hoping to have sex with a woman of 28 would have been laughed off the screen back in those days – he was W.C. Fields or Groucho Marx. Today, however, he is Sean

Connery, a stud, God's gift to Catherine Zeta Jones.

Now, women can choose men on a physical basis alone, if they want to; and, knowing this, their soft hearts creep in and croon, 'Looks don't matter! Honest!'

But you've got to be cruel to be kind. And telling Richard Branson that he is the 27th most lovable man in the world is not kind. Suppose he lost his money tomorrow? He'd be living in a fool's paradise. He might go around saying, 'I'm the 27th most lovable man in the world!' to cheer himself up. And then he might get put into an asylum, like men who claim to be Napoleon.

On second thoughts . . .

7 NOVEMBER 1998

One of the most embarrassing questions, right up there with 'Are you really going out with David Baddiel?', must be, 'Do you know who I am?' I must say that if I was a member of the catering calling and heard this one from a soused hack or actor, I'd be very inclined to answer, 'No. Do you? Another candidate for the Laughing Academy here, Bert!'

So it was nice to read that when Tom Cruise was refused the hire of a Blockbuster video because he did not have the required two forms of identification with him – even though his mugshot was stacked on shelves all around – he did not throw a temper tantrum. A source apparently said, 'Tom was not put out by the incident in any way – he understands the rules. One of the things he likes about being in England is the anonymity.'

Tell me about it; that's class, for sure, and it's the only way to be. It's an old line, but it tends to be true that those at the top and the bottom of the social scale have good manners, while the pushy scufflers in the middle, riddled with insecurity and terrified of being marked out as parvenus, pride themselves on Not Suffering Fools Gladly, i.e. being bloody rude. The antics of Michael Winner and now Jeremy Paxman – being rude to the help – mark them out as two specimens of that grisly modern type: The Man Who Thinks He's It.

There is nothing wrong with liking yourself; it's fancying yourself that frightens the horses and revolts the populace. Earlier this year, a newspaper gave its readers the chance to set moi some posers, and one of them was, 'Do you think that sometimes you have admired the view in the lake so hard that you have fallen in?' But I don't think I ever did; I loved the Eighties, but I cried out in alarm and shame when my friends used my name on the phone to get a table at a fashionable restaurant. (It always worked.) Left to myself, I used my married name; I found it far more dignified to go without a table than pull rank. It's nice to be treated like you're something special when you're young and insecure, I'm not arguing with that. There was one evening long ago, when I and three comrades turned up late at the Groucho Club. Peering into the back room, even I could see that every table was taken. 'It's no good; let's go,' I said to my friends.

'No, that's not a good idea,' said a voice in my ear; it was the totally cool owner of the club, Tony Mackintosh. In his hand, he held a table. 'Follow me.' We followed him as he carried his strange bounty to the centre of the room. He moved four tables aside, set the table down, pulled four chairs out of nowhere, winked at me and disappeared. There was quite a lot of silence.

'THAT,' my friend Tom whispered in my ear, 'was a Frank Sinatra Moment.' I purred. These days, on the other hand, I would run screaming to the blessed anonymity of Burger King. I do not want the attention. That was part of my old life, my

Eighties life. But when I say this, I am not slagging off the spirit of the Eighties, like so many movers and shakers who have shaken to a standstill and intend to spend the rest of their lives biting the hand that powdered their noses when they voluntarily stuck them in the trough. I am no conventional downsizer; it was I who wrote a book called *Ambition* in the last year of the Eighties and my twenties, and I'm certainly no advocate of young women opting for early marriage and mindless childbirth instead of a place in the rat race.

It's not a gender thing, it's an age thing. I believe that in the teens and twenties, the person who is not burning up with ambition and narcissism is either a saint or a simpleton. Ambition, like angst, is a necessary kickstart to the adolescent personality, essential to get us out of the playpen and into the real world. But like angst, if ambition hangs around too long, it goes a long way towards making a person boring and conventional – not to mention hideously unsexy. You have only to look at Branson, Carling, Madonna to see how ambition continued into later life corrodes the soul – and more importantly, the sense of humour. Viewing middle-aged ambition in action is as unappealing and embarrassing as seeing someone vigorously masturbating in a public place.

Superannuated ambition is even more disfiguring in a man than in a woman because men should be strong and silent and dignified, not pushing for attention and affirmation. How can you feel sexual desire for a man so desperate for attention that he'll get up at 5 a.m. just to speak for two minutes on the radio? And that's the bottom line – show me a man who's ambitious, and I'll show you a man who's bad in bed. It's a Napoleon complex thing, only Ambition Man tends to be short all over.

Women do not admire ambitious men as much as most people think. Of course, there is the occasional dweeb with low

92

self-esteem who thinks that 'Power is an aphrodisiac', but these are usually orgasmically dysfunctional broads who thus consider the fiscal more important than the physical. A recent dating bureau survey of Anglo-American professional women, though, concluded that the dream man of the average affluent Americanne is a carpenter, and they're hardly the richest or most ambitious breed.

Yet speaking as someone who for the first time in her life is dating someone without ambition, I can testify that it is a gorgeous experience, like putting your feet in a foot-spa after a long, hard day at the January sales. No more pushing and shoving, no more LOOK AT ME! Surely this is a man.

How different from the home lives of the London media I left behind; all those 'hot couples', those social dynamos and networking nonces who spend more time having their picture taken by the gossip columns than having each other. All those Jones girls and Hornby boys, the first addicted to aromatherapy baths, the second to playing with their toys in order to deal with the stress of Making It, finding no solace in each other but only a sad reflection of their own frazzled yearning for glory. It's a dog's life, really. So if at first you don't succeed – give it another half-hearted bash, and then give up. And get down to actually enjoying your one and only life.

14 NOVEMBER 1998

Wonderbra adverts, according to those behind them, are the Nineties equivalent of the SCUM manifesto: empowering to women, emasculating to men. I must admit, I've never really got this – if men are emasculated by women in their underwear, why do they pay through the nose to watch table-dancers? But the catchline accompanying Adriana Sklenarikova's poitrine rang a bell: I CAN'T COOK. WHO CARES? My waist measurement is about the same as Miss Sklenarikova's bust, but I don't care either, and I've certainly never met anyone who wouldn't go out with me because I don't know a bain-marie from a crêpe Suzette. (They both sound like table-dancers to me.)

Lots of women young enough to know better, though, seem to care terribly – or, rather, are being told they should care – about arming themselves with culinary skills in a way they would once have gone about the getting of sexual wisdom. In a new advert for Sealy beds – where previously an ageing Italian sex-bomb mercilessly vamped a dazzled young salesman – a blonde in light make-up, hair mussed, smile blissful, falls asleep in the afterglow . . . of reading the Marks & Spencer *Complete Italian Cook Book*, still clasped lovingly in her arms. This girl isn't post-coital; she's post-cookery, and gosh, darn, don't it feel good.

There's nothing wrong with liking a good nosh-up. I have been known to pick up a phone and have a hot meal on the table within 20 minutes, and I've never had any complaints from the boys (or girls) when it came to laying on a good spread. The weird stuff comes when food is made to stand for, or stand in for, other things, such as love and sex and self-respect. For instance, a lot of women now seem to cook for the reason they once used to screw; so men will talk to them afterwards. This is sad, in any language.

Then there's the torment element. Women are requested by society to keep thin if they want to be considered worthy of respect and attention, yet, increasingly, they are being told that the demon of the boardroom must also be the angel of the kitchen. Comfort eating must be avoided at all costs, only comfort cooking is allowed – for the consumption of other people, naturally. But the woman who cooks ceaselessly and never puts on weight seems to me like some sort of grotesquely self-denying freak – like one of those strange women who doesn't have sex so she can come, but 'for the closeness'. Yuk! This sort of broad's G-spot is somewhere towards the back right-hand side of her Aga, and if you try to find it you'll burn your fingers.

Then there are women who see cooking as a means of expressing themselves. I've got to say that this seems to me as sad as women who talk about expressing themselves through the way they dress. This is the logic of the addlepate; God gave us brains and tongues, and this is how fully functioning human beings express themselves – through thought and word. Slip below that, and you're on the verge of being a three-year-old, 'expressing' yourself through finger-painting.

As Fran Lebowitz once said of T-shirts with slogans on, 'If people don't want to talk to you, what in hell makes you think they want to hear from your T-shirt?' The same goes for your cooking.

The New Cooking could be seen as Marie Antoinettism – or just plain desperation. As recent celebrity break-ups remind us, the fantasy of home and hearth, perfect children and perfect wife waiting for daddy in a perfect kitchen, with something gorgeous simmering slowly on the stove, is a far more powerful and attractive dream for women than for men – who, as Hanif Kureishi recently put it, would gladly let their wives and children die in an icy sea for the sake of a really good shag. When lust leaves the family home, women often whip themselves into a cooking frenzy, and they can be extraordinarily dim about how little men actually care about the quality, as opposed to the quantity, of food. According to Eddie Fisher in his autobiography, when Debbie Reynolds realised that she was on the verge of losing him to the state-of-the-art Fifties femme fatale Liz

Taylor, her response was to cook him his favourite food – lima beans. He walked, fast.

So, while she's poring over the *River Café Cook Book*, seeking to put the spice back into their limp union, he's watching Italian Stripping Housewives in his 'den'; it's strange pussy, not foreign food, that would be a comfort to him on those long, dark evenings when he worries about his financial viability and that new whippersnapper sniffing at his heels. A little lady very visibly in the kitchen, far from making him feel like a Big Man, may well rub in the fact that things aren't like they used to be. He'd probably feel more secure with some tough career woman who can keep the boat floating if he drops his oars, rather than some Goddess of the Hearth who'll try to bail them both out with nothing more than a wooden spoon.

Many of the new cooks are from broken homes, and seek through ceaseless stirring to re-create the happy home they never had. Fine, but what is a personal salvation for them should not be made into a norm for the rest of us. Those of us who come from happy families – such as mine, where I never even saw my mother boil an egg – don't need dreary tableaux of domesticity; we know that love can be shown in more direct ways, such as throwing your arms around someone and kissing them until the pips squeak. Food is what you give people when you can't give them anything else.

It was Jerry Hall who, when her mother told her that to keep a man a woman should be a maid in the parlour, a cook in the kitchen and a whore in the bedroom, said, 'I told her I'd hire a cook and a maid and take care of the rest myself.' Seeing how much Mick has strayed, she might as well have hired a whore for the bedroom – but the point is still valid. When women can't stand the heat, they get into the kitchen. The stomach isn't the quickest way to a man's heart – his genitals are – but it is the quickest way to get a man to look on you as his mother. Pass that Perfect Pizza menu – I feel inspiration coming on!

21 NOVEMBER 1998

I don't know if the older *Guardian* reader knows who, or what, Massive Attack is, so, for their benefit, I'll explain that they are probably the greatest popular music combo ever to exist. Coming out of Bristol in the early Nineties, they have since recorded three albums and have changed the face of modern music.

Last week, at the MTV Music Awards, they went up to collect their prize for Best Video. Unfortunately – for her – the person presenting the award was the Duchess of York. Now, seeing as how pop stars have recently been falling over themselves to act as human spitoons, Wet Wipes, footstools and suppositories to the Prince of Wales, Sarah must have believed that Massive Attack would kiss her hand before attempting to crawl up her fundament. Imagine her surprise when they refused, literally thumbed their noses at her and told her to piss off. Asked to explain themselves, they answered with another question: what had the Duchess to do with popular music, the very existence of which is rooted in contempt for social hierarchy above all else?

You can blame the Duchess for being an insensitive, merit-free freeloader, but you can't really blame her for being surprised at their reaction. Over the past year, any well-connected nobody who can trace their bloodline back to beyond the Industrial Revolution has been sucked up to by pop musicians (and actors, and comedians, and every other 'outlaw' in the kingdom) in a way that would be sickening to behold were it not so funny. Someone who seems particularly keen on blue-blooded rednecks is the American rapper Puff Daddy, who not only asked Fergie to his birthday party, but also went to the trouble of flying those two national treasures, Tara Palmer-Tomkinson and Tamara Beckwith, out to Los Angeles to appear in one of his videos. Top candidate for this year's Most Performed Song must be 'Ghetto Superstar', by another rapper, Pras, of the Fugees, which is actually 'Islands in the Stream', an old MOR hit for Dolly Parton and Kenny Rogers. It seems likely that rap – never the most creative of mediums – is following an agenda that aims to record every crap white song ever played by Radio 2 before 2001: I am already awaiting the Wu Tang Clan's version of 'Sometimes When We Touch' by Dan Hill, or perhaps Snoop Doggy Dogg's treatment of Randy Edelman's 'Uptown Uptempo Woman'.

To get back to Massive Attack – two of whom are black, one white – there could not be a better example of the different turns that black culture has taken on either side of the Atlantic than to compare them with the moronic inferno that is rap culture. Massive Attack are very models of dignity and integrity, as their MTV outburst showed; American rap artists are, virtually to a man, bullies and braggarts, whose targets are inevitably those weaker than themselves – women, Koreans – and who have encouraged young black men to believe that education is worthless and ignorance cool. Dressed like Golders Green grandmothers, swollen by massive entourages, they are the soundtrack to Mike Tyson's career of beating up his fellow blacks for the delectation of rich white folk, and of beautiful black women tearing each other's hair out on *The Jerry Springer Show* for the amusement of white college students. With no notion of communal effort or responsibility, rap takes from the poor to give to the rich. It is the ultimate sound of the American Dream gone wrong, and it is eating its young.

Why are the most visible British blacks so cool and civilised, and their American equivalents such grotesques, from Oprah to Jackson to the Wu Tang, who boast of their friendship with Donald Trump and have a lovely little song in their repertoire about defecating on girls after sex? (A white music paper called this 'darkly humorous'.) Why is it always really awful when heavy-metal groups call women bitches and whores, but a bit of a scream when black artists spit these same curses? The difference is, as usual, love and socialism – that brace of beauties that tends to change everything. Black and white intermarriage in Britain is, proportionally, three times that of the US – here, I think of everything from the swooning reaction of our girls to the black GIs, and their refusal to be frightened away from them by the jealous white Yanks, to poor Marvin Gaye moving to Europe 'because the gals over there sure do mix!' In a country where black women marry white boys and black men marry white girls as a matter of course, the claustrophobic blame-throwing that exists in black American sexual politics – she's too strong: he's too weak – is neither here nor there.

Arthur Miller said that the greatest tragedy of the US was that it never had a real, viable mainstream socialist movement; for ethnic-minority Americans, the promise of the 'melting pot' was held out instead. But what they got was a sort of vicious mosaic, with everybody jostling for position and blaming other ethnic groups rather than white capitalism when there wasn't enough cream to go round. Rap is happy to badmouth other immigrant groups, or women, or homosexuals – but when it comes to really rich white folk, such as Donald Trump, it becomes a big, swooning fan who wants to be just like that. Over recent years, lots of soft, middle-class white boys have taken it into their heads to copy American rap stars, and there really can be few things sadder than a lily-handed boy called Tom or Toby talking about his 'bitch' (Emma or Zoe) in his 'hood' (Hampstead).

They, of course, can always opt back into their nice, white lives when the lustre wears off their medallions, but for the young American black men who play this game, it usually ends in tears – those of their mothers and sisters as they lower their best boy into the ground. To naïve white eyes, American blacks may have a certain desperado glamour that British blacks lack, but that is simply because they are desperate. Personally, I'd much rather be in panto with Frank Bruno and Ainsley Harriot than in the cold, hard ground with Tupac and Biggie.

28 NOVEMBER 1998

I get a letter from J. Walter Thompson, the advertising agency, asking me to hold a 'Masterclass' for its staff. The letter is charming and respectful, but it makes me want to weep: 'This entails inviting a Master, in his or her field, to talk and take questions for around 30 minutes . . . They are very relaxed and enjoyable occasions, which draw a packed audience. Past Masters have included Dave Stewart, Terence Conran, Richard Branson, Nicholas Coleridge and John Lloyd.' It's when I read those names that I want to cry. God, are those really the people I'm meant to be first among equals with? Say it's not true.

All those years ago, when I mooched around the tedious killing fields of the school netball pitch, sneaking a quick Sobranie and getting smacked on the back of the legs with a wet ball, what got me through it all? The belief that, one day, my name would be up there with all the great Neurotic Girl Outsiders: Zelda Fitzgerald and Radclyffe Hall and Sylvia Plath and Djuna Barnes! And I've ended up on some ad agency wishlist with the unbelievably dreary, mainstream likes of Branson, Conran and Nicholas effing Coleridge! Do people really think I'm that boring? I don't think I could stand it if that were so. I knew I was a lot of things, but boring was not one of them. It's always been Me versus The Bores. I'm not being a snob, but when I was Queen of the Groucho Club, there was always a point in the evening when I'd narrow my eyes, beckon one of my henchmen and instruct him to offer hard cash to a bore to vacate his chair at my table. Without fail, they were famous bores, by which I don't mean they were famous for being boring; quite the contrary: they were famous, and people had got into the habit of telling them they were the most scintillating sinners ever to crawl this Earth. But they were actually boring as hell, and fame had helped make them so. Famous people hang around with other famous people: 'I'm famous, you're famous, aren't we fascinating?' That's got to spell death to anyone's rapier-like wit. It's like when you see Madonna hanging out with Donald Trump; Nick Hornby summed it up as, 'You're famous now, so we can be friends', when he started getting post-*Fever Pitch* phone calls from household faces he'd never met.

Do people think of me as one of the herd of bores who crowd around the watering holes of London, talking column inches and byline size? I can assure them that I haven't walked that way for years, and am more likely to be found on Brighton Pier playing shove ha'penny or fighting over the last box of Oriental Prawn Parcels at M&S. I've gone out of my way not to have famous friends, and to cultivate those people I have met who have jobs for which getting drunk isn't compulsory. I remember being immensely impressed by an interview I read with the young Kim Wilde, in which she said, 'My best friend is a telephonist.' Ever since, I've pined for a telephonist BF. While not quite scaling those heights, I'm now friends with a beautician, a trolley dolly and a student of history, and it's going on five years since the time when I didn't have a single chum who wasn't part of the mediaocracy. I now find it incredibly comforting that my boyfriend works for the post office. It makes me feel like Mrs T. S. Eliot must have done, seeing him trot off to the bank every day. There is something euphorically tranquil-lising about putting one weary foot back into the lukewarm footbath of everyday life after so long in the self-adoring, self-boring, looking-glass world of the media.

To be frank, I've never had a drearier time than I've had with famous people, so I identified with the DJ Sasha, who recently told *Muzik* magazine of his night at Supernova Heights: 'The people I was with were really excited – I think they stayed all night. I got out. It just felt really seedy.' I don't think I'd much go for a night on the Tizer and Twiglets at Chez Gallagher, either; I'd be too worried that chatelaine Meg would be lurking with her trusty Polaroid, keeping a clear head while all around her got off theirs, just waiting for the right moment to commemorate our bosom buddyhood on film – right there on the front page, alongside Meg 'n' Kate (currently 'resting' in the Priory Clinic, feeling 'exploited by her friends', according to her father), Meg 'n' Anna, Meg 'n' Sadie.

The silent-screen actress Anna Mae Wong believed that every time her photo was taken, part of her soul was stolen, too; Meg seems to believe that her soul, and personality, and reputation are somehow added to whenever she stares into that half-inch of cut glass and hears that life-affirming click. The camera may not love Meg, but Meg sure loves the camera. In the world of celebrity friendship, 'How do I know what I think until I read what I say?' has become, 'How do I know who I like till I see how they photograph?' Mrs Gallagher's new gossip column in the *Sunday Times* is up there with Yoko's bum and Angie's free verse when it comes to embarrassing Rock Wife Droppings; with endless boasts about the length of their country house's drive-way (quarter of a mile, with room for a pony) and the number of paparazzi camped outside their town house, her scribblings resemble nothing so much as Joe Orton's cruel parody of society tattle, *Between Us Girls*. You would swear it was written by a woman-hater, not a woman. Yet isn't that the best possible way to sum up this, our pre-millennial condition: that what was once agreed to be the problem is now heralded as the solution? There is, sadly, no mystery as to why Meg wants to boast about her famous friends. They warn you about drink and drugs in the Big Playground, but they never warn you about the feeling you get from credibility by association – the most golden, glowing, duplicitous drug of all. What I do find inexplicable, however, is that Mrs G has chosen to be photographed twenty-four-seven, for, no matter how many thousands of pounds she spends at Gucci, she'll still look like a hod carrier who has just discovered Biba. That is, like a member of The Sweet. Which, I suppose, makes her just about as fashionable as a girl can get this late in the day, when it gets dark so early.

5 DECEMBER 1998

My Dad just died. Five years it took him, the tough old working-class hero, and never one word of complaint as the dark bloom of cancer moved through his body, inevitable as history, mysterious as a mermaid, sad as Cyprus. Just because once – for six months, 50 years ago, when he was a teenager – he worked with asbestos. I keep getting this picture of him in my mind, the tallest, fairest, straightest man I ever saw, getting up happily each morning and strolling off to work, feeling really grown-up, able to bring home the bacon for his large, extremely poor family for the first time. And, even then, the cancerous tumours that were to consume two-thirds of his body were taking root, making themselves at home. So that somebody who owned some factory could make even more money than they had already.

They tell you how many people communism killed, and how many fascism killed. But they don't tell you how many capitalism killed, and is killing, because a) they wouldn't know where to start, and b) it would never end.

Well, five years, and I never once mentioned it: no fly-on-the-wall documentary, no column, no book. That's not like me, not mentioning something. But I'm glad I didn't, because now I won't get royalty statements and make loads of money, and then go out and spend it on life's little luxuries, and come home and cry in the middle of a sea of shiny wrapping paper because I feel about as worthwhile as a gob of Satan's sputum. I know for sure that if I had made money out of the illness of someone I loved, especially myself, I would feel far worse than I do now; and I would feel worse partly because capitalising on the death of a family member seems about as wholesome as selling their body on the street, but also because I would feel that capitalism, as well as starting the joke, really had had the last laugh. We sell so much of ourselves already every time we go to market, us little piggies, so it has been something of a comfort that sex and death were among the very few things that we kept for ourselves, untainted by commerce, our secret gardens, things that shouldn't be bought or sold. That's why even the most broad-minded of us wouldn't really like our son or daughter to become a prostitute, no matter how much we approve of the idea of state brothels with wipe-clean surfaces and weekly health checks. We don't mind, so long as it's someone else's loved ones with their feet up in the stirrups, but, somehow, it's not quite what we want for our own dearly beloved. Yet, for some reason, some people see nothing wrong – just the opposite, in fact; it's a caring thing! – in profiting from their deaths. If I were writing for some shallower publication, I suppose I'd try and sell you the notion that death is the new sex.

It's funny; when I say I knew for five years that my father was going to die, of course I've always known. I've got to point out that we're not talking any ordinary death here, but the death of the person I've loved more than anyone, ever. That only happens to you once; compared with that, all the other deaths are just canapés. I've been waiting for this to happen all my life. This is, I suppose, why I began wearing nothing but black at 13, even when I was still the thinnest girl in the Western world, and why I began to develop the twin pillars of my existence – total hedonism and religious faith – at around the same time. If you're looking for a good life, I can thoroughly recommend the two taken together – you're going to die, so you should have a good time; but then, when you die, you'll have an even better one. All the surveys on happiness back me up on this one: happy people believe in God and have all the fun they can handle. The worst thing you can be, apparently, is a sober atheist, and there are so many of them around. The same people who tut-tutted at my wildness when I was young are equally disapproving of my mature serenity Only my friend Laura understands. Laura, who never doubted that her mother would go to heaven, which she imagined as an Edwardian garden party with gin and tonics as the sun went over the yard-arm. Laura says heaven for her will be a Venetian masked ball. For my Dad, it'll be some combination of communism and dogs.

But I have no doubt whatsoever that he's there.

I can understand why atheists get so upset over death; I wouldn't like to think of anyone I loved disappearing into a yawning void, either, though enough people seem to move to Surrey of their own free will. The reasons why believers weep buckets are more complex. The most obvious reason is for oneself; that you will simply miss a person terribly. There's just no getting around this one, and it's why human cloning is such a brilliant idea. Which one of us, no matter how opposed to cloning in theory, wouldn't throw those noble principles right down the toilet for a chance of looking up and seeing the person we loved most in all the world come walking through the door saying, 'Cheer up, it might never happen!' as we wept over their ashes?

Then there's the guilt thing. If the last words you spoke to one of your parents were, 'You're a vile old moron and I hope you burn in Hell', it's only understandable that you feel a teeny bit guilty when they join the majority. Myself, I find that, as soon as they start showing signs of wear and tear, it's best to say nothing to your parents but 'I love you, I do. I'd have been nothing without you, I wouldn't. You're the best parents ever, you are.'

After an adolescence spent at loggerheads, I realised in my twenties that it really wasn't their fault that they'd wanted me to be normal, and overnight everything was all right, as though I'd literally been born again. Even before my father's illness, and much to his alarm, I had taken to declaring my love for him so often that the poor man grew pale and left the room, taking the dog out for a long walk whenever I opened my yap. He had love coming out of his ears and, a naturally reticent man, he knew one thing for sure: it wasn't like this in Russia! He saw my sentimentality as totally uncalled for – the three of us all knew we loved each other – and he was probably right. But it certainly makes me feel better now.

1999

9 JANUARY 1999

First of all, I want to thank everyone for their letters. I don't often get the chance to do this, because it's hard to know what to say about letters that say 'Die commie/fascist whore' (especially when you know they're from your publisher), but the many notes I have received commiserating with me on the recent death of my father were extremely welcome and moving. And I feel much better now.

Well, that's over, then – my first Christmas as an orphan. I've still got a mother, of course, but she's as bereft without him as I am; two orphans together. At six o'clock on Christmas Eve, we cheered, albeit tearily: no more Christmas commercials on the TV, no more torment by jollity. From now on, just the sales, and he never liked the sales. 'Look at it!' he'd leer, gleefully. 'Capitalism! Straight off the starting block! God forbid more than a day wasted before big business starts cramming people full of rubbish they don't need again!'

He liked Christmas, though. His generosity and bossiness came into their own at Christmas. So much to give, so much to do! I'll never forget the way he cooked the Christmas dinner – you'd call it lunch – which we had at 12 o'clock: separate saucepans for everything, then a look at his watch and, 'Right, I'm up the top for a pint. Don't touch nothing. Back in half an hour.' I always wondered why grown-up women liked to advance the theory that cooking a simple meal invariably led to 19 nervous breakdowns; my dad said women were temperamentally unsuited to cooking, and that it should be left to men. My mother and I were happy to oblige, but that feather-bedding now seems like a sword of Damocles as my mother sits staring at a crooner advising her to 'Have Yourself a Merry Little Christmas' and I reel around the kitchen trying to remember whether sprouts are fried, poached or boiled.

He made everything look so easy. He could have done so much more, if he'd been born into a different class, and still made it look easy. I kept thinking of him as the Mandelson fiasco unfolded and my dad remarking a year ago that, much as he loved *Keeping Up Appearances*, it was a strange day indeed when the stewardship of Keir Hardie's party had been handed to Hyacinth Bucket for safekeeping. All those ponces that Mandelson mortgaged his soul to hang out with – the great and the good, they call them! But why? So far as I can see, the great and the good are in their graves, their bones turned to dust and their party become a businessmen's bunfight.

'Most people lead very humdrum lives,' Mandelson crassly gave as one of the reasons the Dome was needed. But it is he and his like who must lead unspeakably dreary lives that they depend for excitement on Domes and dream homes. For the rest of us, who engage in profoundly felt love and politics, life is a searing business. I've already stopped thinking of my dad as some sort of saint, and I like to remember the weird and quirky things about him. For instance, on Christmas morning, while opening our presents, he insisted that we watch the terminally ill children on TV opening theirs. So you know how lucky you are, madam, was the censorious subtext aimed at his somewhat indulged only child (moi?). But a rather morbid habit, nevertheless. As he lay dying, just before he was taken to the hospice, he shouted at me to 'Go and cancel that satellite TV crap, girl! Now!' I started to protest that my mother enjoyed UK Gold – 'Do it! Now!'

Why is it that we will do anything, anything, for our families, except spend more than three days at a time with them? Why do I roam this house, this three-up, two-down dream home – where I spent the best part of my time planning my escape – searching for the scent of my hero? In the scullery, I find the stations of the cross, the commode and the Zimmer frame he was too weak to use, and I place my hands where his must have been. I think of the years, from 12 to 17, when all I wanted was for him, for both of them, to disappear into the ether, for me to be orphaned and then sold into an illegal bigamous marriage with David Bowie and Bryan Ferry, who would take turns with me in a log cabin – well, I had just seen *Paint Your Wagon*. They're still here, and embarrass me in front of my young friends on *TOTP2* every week – 'You fancied THAT?!' – and he's gone. He never embarrassed me, but he thought he did, and I can only pray that I finally put him right.

In the lead-up to Christmas, the TV seemed to be taunting my mother and me with the sheer worthlessness of those left alive. We compare pet peeves: my mum says the kid on the Clover ad should be first to get it, but I raise her with Ruby Wax squawking as a small child in the supermarket, and we cackle over newspaper reports of her nervous trouble. Death has made us nasty, not nicer. We hiss at John Cleese yelling in the Sainsbury advert, and console ourselves that he sees a psychiatrist, too. And Chris Rea, ceaselessly driving home for Christmas: we wish he'd head straight into a pile-up, probably caused by black ice. Everyone else just seems like such a waste of space. Except dogs. He never met a dog he didn't like.

I stand by the sink, washing up, snivelling. My mum's on Prozac so she can't cry, so doing it loudly seems like showing off. Suddenly, I get this picture of my dad in my head; he's in Heaven, and he looks around him, and his slow, sly smile splits his face as he turns to God: 'You could do it this way. I'm not arguing with you, chief! But did you ever think . . .' Suddenly I stop blubbing and start to laugh.

I'm really going to try and make this the last column I write about my dad. I keep thinking of that *Private Eye* spoof of the Pakistan elections, in which Benazir Bhutto characterised the opposition as The Bastards Responsible For Daddy's Death Party. I have every intention of dedicating the rest of my private life to the pursuit of this party, but you may rest assured that by next week I will be back on track, chasing the bright, elusive butterfly of the zeitgeist. Cheers!

23 JANUARY 1999

There are two sorts of sacred cows, just like there's a Whopper and a filet mignon. The first sort of cow is one that we know is sacred, but we're – titter, snigger – covertly encouraged to attack it, both for pleasure and for profit. That would be the Queen and Cliff Richard. The second would be the Queen Mother and John Peel. Show me a filet mignon and I become a mad cow. John Peel has become 'our' – and, by that, I mean people who consider themselves enlightened and unburdened by tradition – Queen Mother. He needs taking out; if only in a caring way, for his own good. He is in danger of reaching hands-off, Help the Aged status: 60 years old, and he's still got all his own teeth, sorry, all his own Fall records! I've always loathed John Peel. It started in the Sixties when I was a child, still staggering under the first blow of benediction by black music. All day long on Radio 1 – most of all, on Tony Blackburn's show – you could hear great creamy earfuls of it: Motown by the mile, Philly by the furlong. But at night Radio 1 became a white desert. It became 'intelligent'. That is, it became male, hippie and smelly – it became John Peel.

I hated him in the Seventies, too, because he liked punk, long after punk – the whitest, malest, most asexual music ever – should have been left to die an unnatural death. I'd been a punk, and knew that the whole thing was, frankly, shit in safety pins. We came to bury the music industry; we ended up giving it one almighty shot in the arm. In the Eighties, someone gave me as a kitsch gift a Sixties pop annual. I'll never forget John Peel in it, talking about his father's absence during his infancy: 'He was off playing soldiers.' Reader, this man was fighting in the Second World War.

What did YOU do in the war, Daddy? Well, John Peel caught VD, and banged on about it. Until recently, Peel banged on a lot about sex. Like many an ugly Englishman, he went to America, where that nation's young women found a Limey accent so beguiling that they barely looked at the face it came out of: 'All they wanted me to do was abuse them, sexually, which, of course, I was only too happy to do,' Peel told the *Guardian* in 1975. 'Girls,' he said to the *Sunday Correspondent* in 1989, 'used to queue up outside . . . oral sex they were particularly keen on, I remember . . . one of my regular customers, as it were, turned out to be 13, though she looked older.'

This was the Sixties. Fleeing America after the authorities quite rightly objected to him having sex with young teenage girls, Peel was joined by his wife, Shirley, a Texan girl, who was 15 when he married her. Talking to the *Correspondent* about this young woman, now dead by her own hand, Peel seems strangely censorious: 'She fell in with some extremely dodgy people . . . she married three more times after me, and I was the only husband by whom she didn't have a child. All the children were in care. She did some terrible things, you know. She didn't deserve to die, though.'

Somebody give that man a medal! Scratch a hippie and find a sexist – well into the Seventies, Peel was drooling on about 'schoolgirls', in print and on air, where his Schoolgirl of the Year competition was quietly laid to rest during punk's tenure. I always thought the alleged Sexual Revolution of the Sixties was not a bid to advance women's rights, but rather to block them, to turn back the clock and push the brave new young working woman back to being barefoot and pregnant. Even the appearance approved for hippie women – long skirts, long hair – spoke of an earlier era, before girls raised their skirts and bobbed their hair and went out to earn a living.

Knowing of Peel's rather sticky track record on matters sexual, it seems both wildly inappropriate and somehow totally fitting that his latest venture is the radio critic's favourite Radio 4 programme, Saturday morning's *Home Truths*, which, as its name implies, is a deeply reactionary idea masquerading as a droll, down-to-earth sideswipe. *Home Truths* concerns itself with family matters, both bitter and sweet. These may be as unimportant as the reluctance of teenagers to tidy their rooms or as serious as the alleged False Memory Syndrome, but they are linked by one overriding belief: that after all politics, after all ideas, there is the Family. And that the Family, alone of all institutions, is as natural as breathing.

This is, of course, untrue; the Family is a construct like any other, one that has been propped up by a million years of hellfire warnings ('Marry or burn' – so-called 'St' Paul) and that, the moment the pulpit-bullying ceased, broke down with amazing swiftness.

Everyone's got a right to get old and fat – hell, it's practically my *raison d'être* – but I find it filthily objectionable for someone who has grown rich and respected for preaching the Sixties mantra 'If it feels good, do it!' suddenly to come over so cosy and domestic that it would have Oxo Katie reaching for an icepick.

Peel, being middle class, managed to survive the Sixties, and then thrive in the decades that followed. But for the young working class, the road of excess led to madness, alienation and incarceration; and for the girls who got hip to the Sixties slogans about sexual generosity, a joyless shag led to nothing but a council flat and the end of youth before they were entitled to vote. I don't blame Peel for changing his mind. But I do blame him for rubbing the nation's collective nose in the fact that the well-connected can walk on the wild side and return to the fold, whereas the working class need only stray once off the straight and narrow to be trapped in a cul-de-sac of sorrow.

A public schoolboy who calls his children after footballers, a lover of World Music who happily took the Order of the British Empire, a landowner who does commercials for toilet paper and PlayStations and yet calls himself a Bennite, a past 'abuser' of children who preaches Family Values *in excelsis*: it is not, as his fans like to say, a wonder that Radio 1 has not sacked him in 30 years. No, in all his patronising, phoney, hypocritical glory, he is Radio 1. Lord Reith would be proud.

13 FEBRUARY 1999

I've got another book out in a couple of weeks – *Married Alive*. It's my third book in the past two years, but my first novel since 1993's disastrously received espionage romp, *No Exit*. Since then, I've published my autobiography, which was certainly about me, and my biography of the Princess of Wales, which many reviewers said was about me and my loathing of the male sex.

The one good thing about the reaction to *No Exit* was that no one claimed that it was about me; quite the opposite. Everyone complained that I shouldn't have set it in Prague when, at the time, I had actually been no further than Jersey – and found that to be a bit too foreign for my liking, actually. But now the Peek-a-boo/I See You! chorus has started up again, with Jason Cowley in *The Times* calling *Married Alive* a 'confessional' novel, and Syrie Johnson in the *London Evening Standard* concluding that my husbands, Mr Parsons and Mr Landesman – peace be upon them – are well out of it. Miss Johnson is an interesting girl. She seems to disprove the theory that the test of a first-rate mind is the ability to hold two conflicting beliefs at once, though hold them she ceaselessly does. In her review of my new book, she says the heroine, Nicola, is me. But then she calls me a liar for making Nicola a thin, blonde, Nineties babe instead of a fat, dark Eighties *grande dame*, as I am! Well, Syrie, there's one reason I performed this audacious sleight of hand: because it's not me! Not me, living in a loft in Docklands! Not me, being a magazine illustrator! Not me, having her half-mad old grandmother to live with her! I'm sorry to sound shrill here, but I never thought that I, who effectively left school at 15, would be explaining the definition of a novel to someone who got a first at Cambridge. And yes, I would like that saucer of milk, thank you very much.

But Syrie will be happy to know that, thirsting as she does for even more information about Me, she can watch a 50-minute TV documentary on her favourite subject on the 23rd of this month. Yes, finally exhausted by repeated requests from the major channels to poke around in My Life Story – I turned down *Omnibus* on a whim because my son, when he was younger, used to call it *Ominous* – I have conceded defeat to BBC 2's *Close Up*. But that's the end, beautiful friend; I hope, with this documentary, to officially proclaim The End of Me. Because, over the space of 22 years in journalism, more than half my lifetime, I have, frankly, had a bellyful of Me, and I bet you have, too.

We are never less ourselves than when we are being Ourselves. Just as the silent-film star Anna Mae Wong believed that each photograph stole another part of her soul, so each column we write as a Personality steals another part of our personality. The more we show, the less we are. Up to the middle of the Nineties, I was a beacon for the strangest and sweetest of modern souls, like Robert Newman and Richey Edwards; when I met them, they would flutter and swoon and tell me that I was the wind beneath their wings. Bound as they were to the mast of modernity, only my siren song of Sovietism and soul music pulled them through the hard rocks of rationality. But I bet they wouldn't feel that way now, now I'm Bridget Jones's much-married sister.

When I became a Personality Columnist, we were pretty thin on the ground. Around 1984.

Not now! To open the Sunday papers is to be immediately transported to The World's Most Boring Dinner Party, to find yourself surrounded by well-groomed women with names that end in A and absolutely nothing to say while saying it very loudly. And the weird thing is, I used to know quite a few of these gals – and when you meet them, they're not half as boring as they are on paper. But it should be the other way around, shouldn't it? Like a comedian who can't, or won't, make funnies offstage, they should be saving the best bits of their minds for their work. So what has brought about the current state of columnists, where they save what insights they have for the dinner table and cast crumbs out to the paying punter?

And me sitting there right in the middle of them, asking, 'Shall I be mother?' Well, I've dined my last at the media trough of Me, and I'm going back to my rude roots. I made my first appearance in Peter York's book *Style Wars* as a 17-year-old who upset an older journalist when she overheard me saying, in the lobby of the Hammersmith Odeon, 'People aren't really very interesting, there's not much to be said for individuals.' Yet somewhere along the line I've become one of the dread breed myself, believing that I am interesting for myself rather than as my father's daughter or my class's warrior. But the point is that people become interesting only when they're not concentrating on themselves – rather when they're eaten up with wonder and curiosity about the world.

So whaddya think, then? No more of Me! Imagine it. No more screenplays about my dad's dog (*Prince*). No more novels imagining my then best friend as a far more fascinating woman than she could ever hope to be (*Ambition*). No more about my boyfriend, or my girlfriend, or the little white cloud that cried over my shoulder one day. No more of my dad – a man so modest he demanded no ashes and no headstone – being trotted out to testify to my humanity one more time. I can see his face, his sly, Stalinist smile: 'Leave it, girl!' Towards the end of his life, we were watching a TV programme about Russia under Stalin, and I murmured, as I had been taught since I was ten, that he was The Man For The Job: 'He was a madman, girl!' (Beat) 'You haven't been writing your rubbish about him, have you?'

No, you've seen the last of Little Me: all that's left, I hope, is my Talent – why I went into the racket in the first place – brought to bear on things that matter. I always dreamed of a world without Me: it's the oceanic bliss we Communists, alone, feel. And now, at last, it might come true. It'll be a wrench and a half, but I'll get there, day by day; with You, and without Me.

6 MARCH 1999

A couple of weeks ago, writing about the Vanessa scam, I pointed out that, while it had taken the best Oxbridge minds in TV several years to tumble to the fact that what purported to be life in the raw was actually am-dram, women from my working-class Bristol suburb who left school at 16 have always insisted that it was a fix-up, 'like the wrestling'. Their reason for not believing? 'Because people just don't behave like that.' For people, read 'women', and for behave, read 'have sex'. What my mother's friends had stumbled across came from observing their own lives, and those of their daughters and granddaughters – namely, that women – unless they are drunk, or mad, or abused, or prostitutes, or trying to prove something – are not generally sexually promiscuous. Neither are most men, but they probably would be, given the chance. Women are given the chance every day, and choose not to use it.

This fact has been obscured in recent years with much excitable chatter about 'ladettes' and 'female orgasm'. Whether either ever existed outside of the feverish minds of copywriters is a matter for debate, but I would refer said copywriters to the example of Zoe Ball. It took the genuinely affecting shock and delight she expressed on becoming engaged to pop star Norman Cook to throw into relief the filthy phoniness of her former persona as the resident non-stop-drinking, dancing, shagging party animal. In the face of her friend Sara Cox, betrothed of Leeroy from The Prodigy, there is the same unmistakable relief at not having to Put Out any more. Not having to be sexy has, paradoxically, made them both attractive, to women as well as men.

Miss Ball's statement that true love means you are able to pass wind in front of each other is simply a coarser version of Mrs Patrick Campbell's 'deep calm of the double bed after the hurly-burly of the chaise-longue'. In the Spice and Saints babies, and in the nesting of Denise van Outen with Jamiroquai, we see not a rejection of feminism, but an adoption by the most favoured and fashionable young women in this country of the working-class model (marry young, have kids, get on with career) over the middle-class ideal that has dominated the past couple of decades (slag around, get panicky, get married, take ages to conceive, become a mother, feel totally shagged out and retire prematurely). This tough-minded, clear-eyed, pragmatic attitude to sex and marriage, which can be seen in any classroom or call-centre, is at odds with the image of young and/or working-class women subscribed to by Vanessa Feltz and, it turns out, Germaine Greer – seething hormonal stews, their lives ruled by their vaginas, forever ready, willing and able to be dragged along the nation's high streets of a Saturday afternoon wearing nothing but a double-headed dildo by a group of lusty young men, and thence to be had in common in front of Primark.

In fact, there has probably never been a time in history when women knew so much about sex and wanted so little of it. The Sexual Revolution dreamed of by the turn-of-the century feminists – that women would make love when, and to whom, they pleased, without censure or coercion – is nearer to realisation than it has ever been. The Sexual Appropriation of the Sixties and Seventies, however, when women were persuaded to let men take all manner of joyless liberties with them, is receding. Women have voted with their vaginas, and the result is a generation of men rather surprised that they are getting less sex than a young man would have got 20 years ago, but bearing up gamely by resorting to porn, chatlines and the massive 80 per cent of all Internet hits that access pornography.

A new study, the biggest since the Kinsey Report, in the *Journal of the American Medical Association* found that 40 per cent of women have no interest in sex, compared with only 8 per cent of men. English women have sex twice as much as Americans, when they're having it, but 40 per cent of them also couldn't care less. Panicky sexologists have tried to explain this by pointing to health problems, lack of time, job pressures and money problems, but women are healthier, richer, more successful at work and have more labour-saving devices than ever. This is probably why they are having less sex: because they don't have to Put Out any more. We are not talking about women rejecting sex out of fear and shame, but out of enlightenment and confidence. And because of the very simple fact that sexual intercourse between a man and a woman will almost inevitably end in an orgasm for the man, but is unlikely to for the woman. This, more than tiredness or worry, is the point: for a lot of women, sex doesn't work – therefore, it is only sensible to stop it. A man puts 50 pence in the fruit machine and hits the jackpot every time: watching him for a while, a woman sooner or later starts asking herself why she should throw good money after bad, seeing as how she has put in a tenner and come up with row after row of lemons.

So sure are we, despite the reams of propaganda, that more women are faking it than making it, that the female orgasm has become a signifier not of wild, unbridled hedonism but of good manners and socialisation. When, in *When Harry Met Sally*, Meg Ryan does her number in the deli, it renders her even nicer, not nastier; on TV, the female orgasm is used to sell Organics shampoo. Can we imagine the male orgasm, in all its sticky authenticity, ever being used on prime-time TV to sell a product?

If most female orgasms are faked, there can be no offence in them. Apparently, men's pupils dilate when they see photographs of naked women – women's pupils dilate when they see pictures of naked babies. Houston, we have a problem.

In a rare moment of lucidity, Freud said that all a human being needed to be happy was love and work. How, then, could he ask, 'What do women want?' The very things that make a human being happy, of course. It is a triumph of the 20th-century woman that she has achieved both these things, against all odds. Is it any wonder that sex comes a poor third?

27 MARCH 1999

Seen *Smack the Pony*, then? Mmm, me too. Channel 4's new all-female comedy show was quite funny, I suppose, in a gentle, caring kind of way. Like 30 minutes of foreplay with no orgasm at the end of it: for those who like that sort of thing, as Miss Jean Brodie said, that is the sort of thing they like. I tend to think that women actually aren't as funny as men, but that's because a) they're not as ridiculous as men, and b) they aren't as cruel as men (present company excepted, of course). That's why they inevitably turn out 'gentle humour' or 'a sideways look at' – both of which are polite ways of saying 'not funny'.

But they shouldn't really care about this, as it's a sign that they're doing something right, not wrong. Commercial humour has always reminded me of commercial sex. Why can't you get it from your friends, or do it yourself? How can you possibly do it with someone you don't know? Did you really mean it when you laughed so hard you sneezed, or were you just faking it? The to and fro of heckling mimics the rhythm of dirty talk between lovers, building to a pitch and then reconciled before a mutual round of applause.

But laughter, like sex, takes on a sour tinge when it is bought and sold in the marketplace; hence the rancour of the buyer and the sulkiness of the seller. And let's look at the character of comedians. It's more than 'The Tragic Clown' or 'The Tears of a Clown' cliché, which actually makes them sound quite sweet and vulnerable; no, from Chaplin to Bruce to Woody Allen, comics are known to be utterly nasty pieces of work, hard as nails and particularly vicious to anyone they perceived as further down the food chain. Ask anybody who ever worked at the Groucho Club who the really arrogant, finger-clicking, money-waving, drug-demanding clients were, and they won't say the hacks or the ad men, but the comics. Contrary to what the publicity would have you believe, the only use for the milk of human kindness most comics could possibly have would be to break a bottle of it over some lackey's head and call it Knockabout Humour.

Laughter is more and more portrayed as the best medicine, but when laughter becomes commercial it can actually be bad medicine – the sound of ideals dying, or the sound of nasty little characters keeping certain clapped-out ideas alive. In recent years, the better-than-bottling-it-up school has argued that the most vicious racist and sexist jokes are, in some way, 'healthy', as they actually render the fact that women have periods or that ethnic minorities sometimes eat different foods harmless to beleaguered, bemused white men. But why anyone over the age of five is bothered by these facts in the first place is the real joke; and propagation of the idea that they are in some way 'deviant' only strengthens, not weakens, prejudice.

David Baddiel's ceaseless crusade to rehabilitate pornography as a valid recreational choice for the discerning modern man – opposed to what it was seen as ten years ago: a pathetic prop for men who were too crap in bed to engage with real women – is the sticky end of the wedge. But there has always been the sad air of sexual failure around the comedian, up there in the spotlight and talking rude, hoping that Mum will come home and give him a slap. Many people who mistake themselves for sadists are in fact masochists, who only know how to get the bruising they want by taunting others. It shouldn't really bother women that they aren't really up to joining this saddest and most dysfunctional of sects, really.

Of course, you don't have to be a comedian in order for your joyless misogyny to qualify as biting satire – any old art will do. John Lennon was a perfect example of a man who – like Chris Evans, his greatest fan – went straight from speccy nerd to playground bully without ever considering the option of becoming a sweet-natured, sentient human being. New newspaper adverts for Amnesty International feature photographs of John Lennon at the height of his hippie phase, with a centre parting and moustache; they say dogs get to look like their owners, and of no twosome was this truer than John and Yoko. Remember, it was at this peak of animal attraction that they chose to exhibit themselves naked – back and front on the gatefold sleeve of their long-playing record *Two Virgins*, leading EMI chairman Sir Joe Lockwood to muse sweetly, if somewhat missing the point, that 'If one of them has to strip off, couldn't it be Paul? He's so much prettier.' Beauty may be only skin deep, but Lennon's ugliness went all the way through. It was he who shot back 'Queer Jew!' in the Sixties when then-manager Brian Epstein asked, 'What shall I call my autobiography?' It was Lennon who later led the chorus, 'Baby, You're a Rich Fag Jew', on the track, 'Baby You're a Rich Man'. It was also Lennon who happily sang along with the words to 'Taxman', a right-wing whine against the horror of having to pay income tax, and who headed the Fab Four's negotiations to buy an island from the Greek fascist junta. In later life, it was Lennon who, soon after imagining 'no possessions' in his famous song, bought his wife a whole apartment beneath their own in the extortionate Dakota building and then filled it entirely with fur coats, just so they could be kept at the right temperature.

In short, Lennon was a scummy little man, forever ready to take his non-specific rage out on someone, provided, of course, that that person was weaker; waiter/waitress accepted, Oriental preferred. 'Through his life, his statements, his protests and his songs, he left a legacy to the world,' the Amnesty International advert snivels. 'A legacy of peace, understanding and compassion.' But in his actions, as opposed to his statements and his songs, Lennon exhibited largely selfishness and spite in his time on earth. Am I alone in thinking that Lennon is about as worthy of representing Amnesty International as Arthur Koestler would be posthumously fronting public announcements from a rape crisis helpline?

3 APRIL 1999

Well, hand me down that white feather, baby, and call me 'Conshie' – I've finally found a British military engagement I'm violently opposed to. When it came to the conflicts against Iraq (invading peaceful little Kuwait) or Argentina (invading peaceful little penguins), I practically had to be restrained from handing out white feathers to all apparently healthy men over 16 whom I saw walking down the street. This time, I feel like I'm behind enemy lines. Why? Well, I suppose I never dreamed I'd see my country going to war on the same side as the Luftwaffe. Simple, really.

What is wrong with Tony Blair? Is he in love with Bill Clinton? Is there literally no mess he would not willingly follow him into? I can't help but think that if Blair was sitting in the bath and Clinton asked him if he could just try this thing out – with this electric fire, dropping it into the bath and seeing, uh, what happened – Blair would beam and say, 'Be my guest!' If Clinton wanted to try out a nuclear bomb in Blair's back garden while Cherie and the kids were having a barbecue, Blair would say (adopting horrible 'Howdy, pardner!' American accent), 'Sure thing, Billy Bob! And after, if you need to cool down, get the little lady to give you a beaker of her special punch – it's wicked!'

It most certainly is. It gives me no pleasure to say this about anyone, least of all the leader of my country – which I love; and only slightly less than I used to, now that it's got French flu, German measles and Dutch Elm Disease – but if the US was fighting the Vietnam War now, and Clinton was President, and Blair still had this insane desire ceaselessly to step down in the dominance hierarchy (something to do with playing a girl in school plays), I can easily see him going on TV to explain why My Lai was necessary. Or, 'In order to save this village, it was necessary to destroy it' – I can imagine that one from Nato any minute now.

Yugoslavia; we're bombing Yugoslavia. Gorgeous, integrated, independent Yugoslavia, where the rich kids at school always used to go on holiday while the rest of us sizzled on the Costa del Sol. And which the West always congratulated on Standing Up To Stalin and staying out of the Warsaw Pact. It was a country that fought off the Nazis, held off the Soviets and bent the knee to no one: it was the Cuba of the Balkans – a holiday in the sun that didn't leave a bitter taste in the mouth because it was a puppet of neither the USA nor the USSR.

Maybe that's what we can't stand: a country that shows us you can do it alone, without sucking off a superpower for survival. The Blair government has been horribly silent about Cuba, in this 40th anniversary of its revolution, living under siege from Uncle Sam, yet conquering both illiteracy and meningitis. The Cubans, and now the Serbs, make us realise what a pathetic suck-artist our potentially great country has become, so, naturally, we don't like it. It might give other countries ideas. That US general, Wesley Clark, telling us on TV how America The Beautiful planned to 'devastate and degrade' Serbia – he had a lot of medals, didn't he? I wonder where he got them. Vietnam, perhaps? I wonder what he did to get them, and what permutation of women and children were involved. Come on, it wouldn't be the first time – it's practically the American Way, to avoid the able-bodied fighters and go straight for the crèche with the napalm. That's what sticks in the craw about America – it's got so much blood on its hands, it's a wonder it can still hold a gun steady. What are the Serbs supposed to be doing to the Kosovars? Are they putting electrodes on their genitals? Dropping them out of helicopters? Torturing children in front of their parents? Like all those Latin American regimes the US has been installing and maintaining since the Year Dot. Ah, but that was US's backyard; that was different. They have a right to feel secure. Funny, isn't it, how the US gets to have a whole continent as its backyard, but Serbia's not even allowed to have a province as its? I'm certainly not saying that Milosevic is Mr Wonderful – though the Nato attack has certainly made him a good deal more attractive to the proud Serb people, who will now see him as interchangeable with Serb pride itself – but there are a good many countries with unhappy minorities. When we were mistreating Catholics in Northern Ireland, would the Catholic Nato countries have had the right to bomb us? Somehow, I can't see us accepting that. We have two million Muslims in this country, and many of them, particularly during the Rushdie affair, consider that they've been so badly treated that they formed their own Muslim Parliament.

But we're not about to let them have Bradford. If every miserable minority is allowed to have its own country, we'd soon end up like the film *Passport to Pimlico*; a curious desire, when we in the UK are being told that we must give up our national identity and cleave to a federal Europe.

Who died and made the Germans king? That's what I want to know. Who decided that Croatia has more right to national sovereignty than Great Britain? As Tony Benn pointed out, Croatia never existed until the Germans invented it for their own ends during the Second World War – and then, of course, they were the first to 'recognise' it when it wanted to break away from Yugoslavia. Of course they recognised it – they invented it! Croatia's not a country; it's a bloody division of the German armed forces – scratch a Croat, find a Kraut.

And because of Germany's stirring, every street in what was the peaceful, prosperous country of Yugoslavia is now designing its own flag. Great work, guys! Whatever is happening in Yugoslavia now, whoever is killing whom – the West did this. The glorious West, which has so little faith in its own lousy system that any little country that thrives under anything remotely like Communism has to be destroyed. To the West, anything was preferable to a socialism that worked – even Balkanisation and genocide. Well, they've got what they wanted.

Blair keeps telling us that it's legit, because it's just like the

Second World War. He's right. It is. Except this time, by reducing Serbia to rubble, side by side with our buddies, the Luftwaffe, we're the Fascists.

17 APRIL 1999

A friend of mine was taken to a party by a grizzled old golden boy last year, and all the usual suspects were there: men who'd been young when feminism was called Women's Lib and who said, 'I love liberated women: they're so easy to get into bed!' until well into the late Seventies. Peter York summed them up best as 'the grey-haired, blue-jeaned boys'; and it was they who made the world safe for Jeremy Clarkson. It doesn't get any worse than that.

So, there's Christopher and Mart and Salman. Apparently, Salman, when he's in his cups, recites Bob Dylan lyrics. And the grey-haired, blue-jeaned boys look at him with pride, as if he were a dog walking on its hind legs. It wasn't long before he was prancing about with Bonio. Now, he's written a novel about rock music and Bono has written a song about the book. This, then, was why Teds tore seats out of cinemas when they first heard 'Rock Around the Clock': to make rock safe for sissy-boys.

Why is the sight of posh people 'digging' modern popular music so vile? Is it because beat music comes from blues and country, the inarticulate speech of the heart of black and white poor, and to see it taken up by public-schoolboys is akin to having your culture seized and manhandled by an invading oppressor? Or is it just that the educated, wealthy and/or old are bloody embarrassing when they try to 'get on down'? 'Why don't you write about music any more?' people ask me. 'You wrote about it so well.' I have to remind them that a) I don't write about it because I am 39, and b) I wrote about it so well because I was 19 when I left the *NME*'s employ. I'll grant you that 39 is, by the standards of newspaper pop writers, a veritable spring chicken, but I happen to believe that pop/rock/dance music is the province of the young. This is not a view to which most newspapers subscribe – when Emma Forrest began working for *The Sunday Times* at 16, she was told she was 'too young' to write about pop music. There is a dark cloud over popular music: it is the shadow of a million middle-aged, middle-class men who can't, or won't, let go of their youth and are thus contributing to a culture that is becoming increasingly bland, homogenised and one-size-fits-all.

From Clarkson to Rushdie to Blair, we are all meant to settle down to the same soundtrack: one nation under an arthritic groove. We all love rock and roll now, and the fandom of all is welcome. (Except, of course, that of working-class teenage girls, who just scream. Though why screaming is a less valid reaction to pop than filing CDs alphabetically, or reciting Dylan, has yet to be explained to me.) Maybe I'm immature and over-sensitive, but this state of affairs makes me want to scream and break things and listen to the Goldberg Variations.

This month, a succession of bands played concerts to celebrate the 60th birthday of John Peel, the Schoolgirl's Friend. I'd stop that, for a start. Then I'd make it illegal for anyone over 30 to start or join a pop group, or to buy records by anyone not played on Radio 2. If the grey-haired, blue-jeaned boys really really wanted to get the new Orbital record, they could hang around outside a Virgin Megastore and beg passing teenagers to go in and get it for them. These may seem Draconian moves, but desperate times call for desperate measures – and Rushdie's new novel, *The Ground Beneath Her Feet*, is an embarrassment too far. Readers of a delicate disposition should stop here, for Rushdie describes his fictional band, VTO, as 'more Righteous than the Righteous Brothers, Everlier than the Everlys, Supremer than the Supremes'. For God's sake, man, go and listen to your Glenn Gould records and leave youth to the young.

Men seem much less willing to surrender their youth these days than women, which is a new twist: youth, and its accompanying beauty, used always to be valued in women far more than in men, so it should mean more to them to lose it. But walk down the street, and for every piece of female mutton dressed as lamb you'll see ten pieces of male scrag-end dressed as sirloin steak. Perhaps women have an easier time coping with the fact that youth is finite because their plumbing sends a message when it's time to come in, your time/eggs is/are up. With men, everything just sort of slides, gradually – there's no internal hectoring from Mother Nature to bring them to their senses.

I really think that men don't believe they age. Hanif Kureishi, 44 (that's his age and hip measurement), newly ensconced with a 23-year-old, wrote in his last novella of his ex-partner's 'fat, red face'. Bob Geldof (50? 55?) calls Patti Smith 'Grandma'. David Bailey, who seems obsessed with 'fat lesbians' criticising his smutty snaps, bristles when interviewers bring up his aged girth, and says that his looks are 'not relevant' to any discussion of women's beauty or lack of it. In one interview, Bailey revealed that he rarely sees his sister because 'she's old'. She's two years younger than him.

But at least most fat lesbians know what they look like. They do not (apart from me, that is) prance around in miniskirts and cleavage before noon. None of the above men could possibly understand just how horrible they themselves look, else they'd never say the things they do about women. When men turn 40, the health service must give each of them a free distorting mirror, which makes them look forever tall, upright and slender: they look in those mirrors, and porky, greying Hanif, Bob and David see Leonardo, Matt D and Ben A staring back at them. It's the only plausible explanation. But you can't fool all of the people all of the time, and even Salman must watch as his 20-year-old son turns his back on rock 'n' roll – put off, no doubt, by too many evenings watching Dad do his Mick Jagger impersonation. Instead, he goes 'clubbing all the fucking time – too much for my liking'.

I'll bet. For dance music has given popular music back to the young, the working class, the female; all of those shut out of the debates about Bob Dylan and Keats, and none of them giving a damn. Those who can, dance; those who can't, recite reams of rock lyrics in their cups. Youth will always find a way of stepping on the blue suede shoes of the oldsters and letting them know whose party it really is.

24 APRIL 1999

Apparently, the rude actor, Mr Valerie Kilmer, spent an entire Arizona-to-California flight recently doing 'body crunches' in the aisle in front of the first-class toilets. I wish I'd been there, because I'd have kicked him really hard at the base of the spine – for cheating on Joanne Whalley and making *The Island of Doctor Moreau*, among other crimes – and then he'd have had his body 'crunched' once and for all. A while ago, another actor, Ray Liotta, freaked out on a plane, screaming for hard liquor; then there was the time Minnie Driver went raving mad because *Good Will Hunting* was showing on her flight and her name wasn't listed on the entertainment-guide credits.

If I can think of one thing that could possibly make the

experience of air travel worse, it would be having to put up with hyperventilating thesps to boot. Flying is a horrible thing – not the turbulence or the bumpy landings; that's just like being on a really big, scary theme-park ride – no, it's not the thought of dying that makes air travel such a vile experience, but rather the reality of living.

It's amazing that only 30 years ago flying was considered sexy. Sexy! What else did we think was sexy in the Sixties, you've got to wonder. Chilblains? Nose hair? Mick Jagger? What did these people do when they couldn't afford to catch a plane anywhere but wanted to replicate that sexy feeling? Get someone to lock them in a cupboard for eight hours and spoon vomit down their throats halfway through? Anyone who ever found flying in the least bit erotic would definitely be the type of man with desires so dark that only a handsomely paid prostitute could endure them. I've just come back from Las Vegas on Continental Airlines, and it wasn't the worst flight, by any means – decent scoff, video games on the back of every seat and stewardesses who didn't look as if they wanted to throw you out and watch you drop. But it did make me think of terrible flights I'd endured in the past: Monarch, as I recall, was pretty depressing, not least because at that time its stewardesses were dressed as Romanian torturers; but the pig of them all must have been American Airlines, which charged five dollars for the privilege of using one's own earphones to listen to the film, and that served food so shocking that it made a tough friend of mine cry, literally.

Remember when all those types used to get up and demand, at gunpoint, that the aeroplane fly to Cuba? They weren't really revolutionaries; they'd just tasted American aeroplane food for the first time and instantly cottoned on to the fact that any system that can oversee and condone such an atrocity is inherently evil. In an aeroplane, on a long-haul flight, you have to sleep in front of strangers. We don't use the phrase 'sleep with' for 'have sex with' accidentally – it's one of the most intimate things you can do with someone. Shoved up against a total stranger, the shy among us will know true mortification as we start awake with our head on some old geezer's shoulder and our drool all down his tie.

But there is a way around the terror of losing one's personal space, and therefore one's dignity: fly first or business class. The only problem is that, if you do this, you have to sit with the scum of the Earth – and I say this as one who last year refused a British Airways upgrade on a flight back from the Bahamas. Humiliating as it is to have to file past the creeps at the front of the plane getting foot massages from the Dallas Cowgirls as you make your way to Sardine City at the back, it is even more humiliating to be one of those creeps – I know from experience. This being Britain, and so properly suspicious of those who give themselves airs, no one bound for economy looks at the first- and business-class fliers with anything like envy or respect; instead, they look at them with sheer, molten contempt. They think you're a jumped-up ponce, and you are.

The staff think so, too. One of my best friends is a trolley-dolly who has worked for a wide range of English airlines, and the stories I've heard about what they do to the food and drink of the first- and business-class passengers would make your gorge rise. I'll just enlighten you as to why those gratis glasses of champagne keep their fizz so well, considering they were poured before you ever approached the plane – earwax. Just a little bit. *Salute!* The people who work on aeroplanes for red-mist shifts and lousy pay can, with their ruined complexions and chaotic menstrual cycles (and that's just the boys), comprehend fully what a pup we were sold when we bought into the myth that flying is in any way, shape or form sexy. You can tell that they're still dealing daily with the fall-out from a dozen Seventies British sex romps, which insisted that 'air hostesses' were panting for it second only to nurses, even though the reality is that every form of transport apart from aeroplanes – cars, trains, ships, even buses – is rife with sexual promise.

Everyone remembers being a bored teenager and making a long bus ride under parental supervision bearable by arranging one's fellow passengers in ascending order of who you'd have if there was a nuclear war and only those on the bus were left living. But it would take a character with an extremely strong stomach to attempt this in a plane, where dehydration and lighting conspire to make everyone look as though they have just come round from a particularly hefty dose of general anaesthetic. It's my belief that the Mile-High Club was never about sex; it was actually nothing but an excuse to have that forbidden fag in the toilet afterwards. Yet, nevertheless, this summer will see most of us paying through the nose for the privilege of experiencing hell at 30,000 feet. Like marriage and mortgage, flying represents the triumph of hope over experience. So long as we understand that the feeling of dread, depression and disorientation we call 'jet lag' is nothing of the kind, but rather the realisation that, no matter how far we fly, we can never escape ourselves.

1 MAY 1999

David Beckham has had his infant son's name tattooed on his back, to match the Brooklyn embroidered on his football boots. It is to be hoped that a glamorous US sports star will be similarly moved to have the name of an English suburb branded on his person and peripherals – 'Surbiton' has a nice ring to it. Joking aside, it is cheering to see how eagerly Beckham – much mocked by thirty-something media critics, myself included, for his lack of book-reading – has taken to fatherhood. He has taken to it as gracefully as a dolphin to water, as previously he took to monogamy and uxoriousness; George Michael, on seeing Beckham and Posh at close quarters, said that she is, literally, the centre of his world.

A recent interview with Victoria mentioned how Beckham, who was doing a photo-shoot next door, repeatedly came into the room to show her the Polaroids: 'Wear the other shirt . . . you look nicer when you smile . . .' she kept advising him. Apparently, he lapped it up. What a slap in the face for the piggy scientists who insist that, to be happy, an alpha male must be out spreading his sperm around every minute of the day. Well, Beckham is happy – with all his wealth, skill, fame and looks – and he's settled down at 24.

Doctors released some highly unsettling statistics last month, indicating that around 20 per cent of all pregnant women will be attacked by the father of their unborn child at some point during the pregnancy – one of those little facts that makes you realise how much families need fathers. This is only a personal opinion, based on what I have seen and heard of working- and middle-class men, but, despite the received wisdom about education and its positive effects on the human spirit, I'd hazard that educated men feature strongly among these most cowardly of assailants.

It has obviously never occurred to Beckham that the pram in the hall is the enemy of promise; no, it takes an intellectual to come up with a worldview as craven and woman-blaming as that. The recent revelations of male writers' behaviour towards women – from Ted Hughes telling a female friend, as he prepared to marry his third wife, that Assia Wevill, at the time overweight and aged after the birth of their daughter, had to dye her hair to hide the grey, to Hanif Kureishi's charming line, 'There are some fucks for whom a man would leave his family drowning in a freezing sea' – prove that women are right to fantasise sexually about carpenters.

Just as the most vilely woman-hating rap music sells principally not to inner-city black men but to suburban white ones, a man who is unable to hold his own in a closing-time fight may find that a woman is the only person he is physically able to beat. In my experience, there is far more of a taboo against hitting women in working-class homes than in professional ones. (Here, some bright spark will point out that for every wife-worshipping Beckham there is a wife-beating Gascoigne, but Gazza is so dense as to be almost a sort of intellectual, in much the same way as the extreme right and left meet at some point.) I cannot imagine a working-class rapist who kept assaulting the wives of his friends being given the level of toleration, and even protection, that, say, Arthur Koestler was by his peers, where the general feeling seemed to be that attacking women made him rather more, not less, of a formidable talent.

A non-intellectual man doesn't give a damn if his wife can run rings around him. On the contrary, she becomes a status symbol: look at Denis Thatcher, forever happily bumbling after Margaret. (Compare them with the couples of the 'thinking' Labour Party, where high-achieving wives and girlfriends seem to be doing their best to resemble Nancy Reagan after a lobotomy.) If I wasn't so happily settled, and was looking for a decent marriage prospect, I would much prefer a sweet-natured artisan to a jumped-up ponce with a library ticket, a filthy temper and a nagging suspicion that knowing how to spell Nietzsche makes him less of a man.

*

I would like to thank the many readers who have written supporting my claim that perhaps, just perhaps, every last one of the Serb people – the nurse, the car mechanic and the snotty-nosed schoolchild – is not directly descended from the sperm of Satan, and so do not necessarily deserve to have napalm dropped on their nursery schools, as, I am sure, Jamie Shea, the People's Propagandist, will announce was absolutely necessary any day now. For once, I won't be replying personally, having spent the past six weeks suffering from two minor but energy-sapping illnesses in a row, but I'd like to thank everyone who wrote in support, especially the many veterans, both military and civilian, of the Second World War, and Edith, a German lady, born in 1934, whose own experiences at the dark heart of Europe have given her a wisdom and perspective denied to the rather more callow and excitable type of New Warmonger Lite.

Reading my postbag, I could not help reflecting that, whereas my supporters largely have some experience of war and came from the more proletarian areas of Britain, my opponents seemed to have an unhealthy representation in middle age (thirties and forties, middle-class, Home Counties). By their own admission, a lot of them were, like Blair and Clinton, life-long anti-war types who have now discovered a warlike streak as the blood grows old and thin.

I do not doubt the good intentions of my cross correspondents, but, as we all know, the road to hell is paved with such. And, leaving aside such issues as whether Milosevic is a monster or the KLA truly wunnerful people – albeit ones whose empire is built on drugs and prostitution, like most friends of the West – I speak more in sorrow than in anger when I ask them whether they honestly believe that the Nato strikes will leave fewer Kosovars dead and less of Kosovo destroyed than if they had not been inflicted. When this conflict is over, I swear that not one nanosecond of gloating will come from this direction. I only hope that you, dear, cross readers, will be able to say the same about regret.

8 MAY 1999

If there's one thing I love, it's lidos. More than parks, more than pubs, more than President Clinton's penis, they seem to me to be the greatest expression of a very public hedonism, attractive and accessible to all, regardless of age, sex or social status. If you go to the theatre or to football, you can get a better seat by having more money or by knowing the right people.

But at a lido, wherever you lay your towel, that's your home.

Indoor swimming baths make people feel cramped and sweaty and supervised; swimming takes us back to our soupy, primeval state, and when done inside it merely rubs in just how far we have come from our early grace into an alienated and lumbering maturity – little wonder that pool rage has been reported at some indoor baths in London. But under the sun of an English summer day, all six of them, the lido makes you feel baptised, blissed out, born again. Will Self once memorably said that orgies are so depressing because there is always a naked fat man eating ham alone on the stairs, but there are no such wallflowers at the lido. There, everyone finds their place in the sun.

This being so, of course it makes perfect sense that lidos are in the process of being wiped out. With the same local-council logic that sells books out of libraries while subsidising the Internet – what lonely outsider wants to read novels, after all, when he could be learning how to make nail bombs instead? – a shocking number of lidos have been ruined or closed down over the past 30 years.

In the course of my life, I have had the luck to live near three beautiful lidos. The first, the rather unfortunately and certainly inaccurately named Fishponds Lido in Bristol, was less a lido than a man-made Waterworld made up of endless miles of loosely linked pools of various sizes surrounded by foliage. They closed it down 20 years ago. Then there was a more conventional lido in Weston-super-Mare, a square of cold, turquoise water the size of a football pitch, with a slide on each side and a scary, scooped-out bit beneath the towering edifice of the diving boards that went down some 15 feet. It's still open, but it's called the Tropicana now. They've concreted it over, so that it's a quarter of its original size, the water's kept at bath-tub temperature and a wave machine comes on every half-hour. It would be easier, frankly, to swim in a spittoon.

Then there is Saltdean Lido, just outside Brighton, the most beautiful building in Britain. Saltdean has had its problems in the past, but recently became our first public art-deco building to be reconstructed, and will be open for business soon. And it hasn't been ruined much: the original pool was 140 feet by 66 feet, going from 4 feet deep to 10 feet, and was designed to hold 500 people. They've cut about a third off the length, and turned that part into a paddling pool, even though there was a paddling pool already. They've filled that one in.

But we are lucky to have Saltdean Lido at all; many seaside towns have a sad, rectangular crater on the seafront, like an open grave where pleasure has been buried. It wasn't Tony Blair who started closing our lidos down, but there does seem to be something about them that is the complete antithesis of bland and priggish Labour Lite.

For lidos are both opulent and socialistic, encouraging individuals by the hundred to find true happiness by merging into one big faceless, sun-worshipping mob. Unlike the new regime of 'fun pools', where you have to queue constantly to experience exactly the same thrill as the person in front of you, the classic lido is a blank space on which any fantasy may be projected. Above all, they are an open invitation to do nothing. Perhaps the most damning indictment of this government is that it is impossible to imagine any of them in a lido – unless it's Robin Cook, ogling women in bikinis.

Talking of adulterous politicians, whenever some sad, strange little man of Westminster gets caught with his trousers down, and citizens quite rightly start pointing and laughing, there's always some berk in the papers who can be relied upon to start banging on about la France and how 'civilised' they are over there about old l'amour. 'Why, it's practically mandatory for men to have mistresses in France,' they chuckle reassuringly.

Well, someone has obviously failed to inform French women of this, because France Telecom was recently forced, at great cost, to discontinue issuing itemised bills after thousands of affairs were revealed to enraged wives who clearly weren't privy to the fact that, for a Frenchman, adultery is as natural as collaborating with invaders and blowing up Greenpeace vessels.

The fact is that Frenchwomen have always had to put up with a wagonload of crap because, as befits this pathologically prosaic nation, the marriage contract is literally that: no matter how badly a woman is treated, she will find it hard to obtain a divorce unless her husband agrees to it. This supposedly sophisticated agreement actually shrouds a good deal of pain and deceit, and is responsible for a stratospheric rate of illegitimacy in a country that, like Catholic Ireland, nevertheless stigmatises illegitimate children severely.

The 'civilised' nature of the traditional French marriage has always been a by-product not of enlightenment but of repression; France, don't forget, is a country with fewer female

Members of Parliament than most other Western European nations – they didn't even get the vote until 1945 – and also has one of the highest levels of male-on-female violent crime.

The hypocrisy and sham of French marriage, in fact, pretty well sums up France itself: a country where appearance is all, and where the truth is seen as an ill-mannered interloper with no sense whatsoever of *comme il faut*. The French traditionally dismiss us as a nation of shopkeepers, but can anybody think of another country so pathetically bereft of things to boast about that the right to cheat on one's wife is the only national characteristic ever evoked by the envious men of other nations?

15 MAY 1999

Tragic though Jill Dando's death was, the words 'death' and 'journalist' are hardly strangers. She seemed to be a good woman with a curiously old-fashioned dignity, and elements of valour and chivalry that might have blossomed into bravery with the right job. I can't help feeling that, in the long run, the company of David Blundy and Veronica Guerin may suit her more than that of Cliff Richard and Gloria Hunniford. But another columnist and broadcaster of extreme working-class blood royale recently returned from the Priory Clinic – £300 a day, average stay two weeks – with the word from the Mount that he'd been locked into a cycle of hedonism (i.e. having a good time) because there'd been no books in the family home when he was growing up. And a young female hack, married to a TV personality but certainly no Tara P-T, has gone there, too, battling stress and a death in the family. A death in the family, no books in the family . . . can the day be far away, you have to wonder, when someone books into the Priory because their horoscope was mediocre, or because they mislaid a bangle? Add to this the antics of Geri 'Heartbreak' Halliwell and Sinead 'Suffering' O'Connor, and you appreciate the old-fashioned common sense of the glorious Cerys Matthews when she says of fame and fortune, 'I haven't found anything particularly harrowing or moanworthy about it . . . it's just pure pleasure.' Pure pleasure. When was the last time you heard anyone say that about success? We did a lot of it in the Eighties, and were condemned as champagne-snorting, Thatcherite scum-surfers. They had a point. But the national mood that has replaced our triumphalism is even more narcissistic; it's just Narcissism Noir. The callous high spirits of the Eighties have not been usurped by any move towards a more political society, rather to one that spends its spare time crying into its navel and expecting to be accepted as a 'serious person' because of it.

Of course, I'm not talking here about refugees or children raped by their fathers, but if your life is fairly decent and you're still not happy, nine times out of ten it just means that you've got into some very sloppy cerebral habits, encouraged by a century of voodoo babble about 'letting it all out' and 'dealing with it'. The criminally irresponsible psychotherapy racket persists in encouraging people to dwell on problems that might be best swept under the carpet. Copious counselling is now being offered to the students of Columbine High, but perhaps if teenagers were not so encouraged to take their every little grievance so seriously, those morons might not have felt so justified in going to war against their 'persecutors' in the first place. The Goths are merely the latest line in the culture of complaint that Freud started all those years ago.

The irony is that, before psychobabble, Geri at one end of the English class system and Tara at the other would both have had a stiff gin, taken the dog for a walk and resolved to cross that bridge when they came to it. Now the resources of the working and upper classes are being drained by the deadening, destructive reach of the middle class and its repulsive habit of self-analysis. Thankfully, there is light at the end of the tunnel. New research indicates that bottling things up is healthier than letting it all out. The child psychologist Professor Richard Harrington, writing in the journal of the Royal Society of Medicine, says that children who undergo counselling after the death of a parent take longer to recover than those who do not. A Dr Bushman at the University of Iowa claims that those who scream and shout when angry are less fit and die younger than those who keep a stiff upper lip; when people express anger, apparently, they are effectively 'practising' being upset, and thus lock themselves into a vicious cycle. A study at Vanderbilt University shows that psychotherapists admit that 6 per cent of their patients' 'lasting deterioration' is due to therapy itself. The only people to benefit from counselling are the counsellors themselves, most of whom are lazy, stupid and unemployable in any area that demands any sort of rigour.

My father died a horrible and lingering death last year, and the only three books we had in our house were a biography of Khrushchev, a history of the trades union movement and *Married Love*, all, for some reason, kept on a high shelf in the kitchen. Yet I would no more dream of going to the Priory than fellating Simon Fanshawe. I owe tens of thousands to the taxman and my last three books bombed. Yet I am happy as the day is long. How? Why? Because I want to be. At the end of the day, happiness is a habit, like any other, and one that must be learned as soon as possible, if anything at all is to be snatched from our brief and floating lives.

22 MAY 1999

'Look at me!' Geri Halliwell demanded – and a nation murmured, 'I'd rather not . . .' It would be a hard soul, indeed, who, having seen the recent tearful televisual study, did not laugh rudely at her trouncing by Boyzone in the singles chart last week, muttering in the manner of cruel supermarket mothers, 'There! Now you've got something to cry about!'

Geri's problem, perhaps, is that there is just so much for us to look at these days. Can it be long before our eyes start to take up more space on our faces than they do now? Will the day come when we are, literally, all eyes? We have been told so often that the camera never lies, that we can always believe the evidence of our own eyes and so on, that seeing a thing happening, even if we know it's not real, has become more relevant than the same thing done but unseen. This is why an actor will get several million pounds a picture for pretending to be a doctor – or a policeman, or a fireman, or, in the case of women, a prostitute or a stripper – while the poor sucker who actually does the job will remain resolutely overworked and underpaid.

On 11 August, thousands of lost souls will flock to Cornwall to see the moon block out the sun for a few minutes. I am not being sexist, racist or classist when I imagine what the majority of these people will be like: white, middle-class men of a certain age, to a greater or lesser degree resembling Mike Leigh's unfortunate Keith from *Nuts in May*, dragging along dispirited and docile Candice-Maries for the treat of a lifetime. Indeed, there is a very good television play to be written about an eclipse bore who has invested so much time and energy in planning the perfect sighting that all around him his family is falling apart – wife having affair, kids necking Es like Smarties, dog lousy with fleas. He's effectively blinded by the eclipse without even looking into it.

You just know some joker's going to do that, too – gaze directly into the thing, just like they're warning us not to. Don't look at it directly, don't look at it through sunglasses, don't look at in a mirror, don't look at it through binoculars, cameras or telescopes; view the eclipse only through a special Mylar or polymer viewer bought from a reputable source. Either that, or poke a hole one millimetre wide in a piece of cardboard, stand with your back to the sun and project its light through the hole on to a white surface two metres away.

I don't know about you, but for me one of the best things about growing up is not feeling beholden to waste a good part of my one and only life on *Blue Peter* projects any more. By the time you've gone through all this palaver, why not simply go the whole hog and watch the eclipse through a cathode-ray tube – television? But no: someone, some man, and more than one of them, is going to look at the eclipse with the naked eye and do himself irreparable damage. But at least he'll have seen it – and in a way the Blair-Joneses next door didn't, either. They may have the money to see the eclipse from the Orient Express (£635, with a glass of champagne) or even Concorde (£1,550), but did they look right at it? No, the wusses! People are obsessed with looking at things. Whether it's the sad sacks who have been camping on America's sidewalks for weeks, waiting to see The Phantom Menace (which does, as one wag pointed out, sound like a particularly creaky episode of *Scooby Doo*), or their more cultured brethren waiting all night in the rain to see the Monet exhibition, we place a pathetic faith in the transforming power of gaping, slack-jawed, at something. And surely the human face never looks dumber, less intelligent or sensitive than when it is looking, be that face at a fashion show, a strip show or a football match. Tourism, of course, has elevated gaping to a global concern. 'See the pyramids along the Nile' went the old American song of the Fifties, before going on to list, in a very banal manner, all the delights the world had to offer. Americans abroad have always been keen on seeing, rather than experiencing, a lot, leading to the unmistakable if-it's-Tuesday-it-must-be-Belgium syndrome that is now also beloved of the Japanese. 'He who has seen one cathedral 50 times knows something; he who has seen 50 cathedrals once knows nothing,' said Sinclair Lewis in *Dodsworth*, his great warning against tourism, but it would be a strange traveller today who would turn down 50 cathedrals glimpsed in favour of one known well. The wonders of the world have been reduced to a collect-the-set swap-meet, and it is not unusual to be on holiday in one of the most beautiful places in the world only to have the Americans next to you banging on, in horrible whiney voices, about the country they 'wanna' visit next. Having 'seen' the gorgeous vista before them, they have 'done' it, and see no reason to hang around any longer than is necessary.

One of the really cool things about being in love is how it makes the rest of the word disappear, like it did when the two lovers meet in *West Side Story*; just fading away to a non-specific blur.

All that gazing into a pair of sparkling eyes is so irritating to others not similarly afflicted, because it proves that the lovers have effectively opted out of the society of the spectacle: they are, for each other, literally the only thing worth looking at. So much of what we fill our time with is a sad attempt to replicate that fascination. In short, those who can, do; those who can't, look.

Dear, dear, dear ... so Melanie Gulzar Brown, breastfeeding heroine of the National Childbirth Trust, is now living in a separate wing of her mansion from her husband Jimmy after a mere eight months of marriage. No doubt their baby, the triumphantly breastfed but depressingly named Phoenix Chi, will now be the subject of an unseemly legal tussle. And that'll be just the start of her problems, with a name like that. Frankly, if someone called me Phoenix Chi, it'd take a bit more than a nipple in my gob every four hours to make me forgive them. According to 'friends', Melanie is short-tempered and volatile, while Jimmy is bored with their stay-at-home lifestyle. Oh dear: the curse of breastfeeding strikes again.

Mmmm ... a lovely clean row of bottles all lined up in the fridge, an unbroken night's sleep from a baby getting eight ounces of milk at each feed, a cheery mother-in-law to wave you on your way for a romantic dinner à deux: such, alas, was an impossible dream for poor Mel and Jim, for all their millions. Still, never mind – while spending her fortune on lawyers' fees, Mel can at least bask in the knowledge that she is the inspiration behind the NCT's current plea to 'Spice Mums Everywhere!' to give their babies 'what they really really want!' My recent measured and calm essay in the *Guardian* – in which I dared voice the thought that, perhaps, children should be weaned off the breast by the time they can open beer cans with their teeth – brought me a torrent of mail; at least half of it, I was interested to see, from men.

Breastfeeding is, like war, cars and abortion, one of those subjects about which men are so obviously the experts that I sometimes think it doesn't behove us girls to get involved at all;

just let them make the laws/lay down the law, and we'll do as we're told.

Far from seeking to change the minds of these natural law-givers, I'd just like to agree that if I, too, was a man, faced with the prospect of being outperformed intellectually by females from the age of eight, I, too, can think of nothing nicer than a process that miraculously removes thousands of highly educated women between the ages of 20 and 40 from the workforce each year, and leaves my pathetic performance in my chosen career looking far less dispensable. I'd especially welcome having a wife who was confined to the home, and who was a tearful slave to her hormones and whose suspicions about my fidelity could be laughed away with coy references to such. I'd love to have such a watertight excuse – breastfeeding women being extremely unin-terested in sex – to plunge into an affair with a hard-faced career girl to whom breasts had never been anything but purely decorative.

And when my wife pointed out that I was spending 15 minutes a day with my children – 50 per cent down from 1990, according to a two-year study by Edinburgh University – I'd point out that I was doing it all for her and the kiddies, wasn't I? And I'd walk away whistling to work with a clear conscience, leaving the wife leaking from eyes and breasts simultaneously, dreaming of a dirty lunchtime with hard-faced Hannah. Who at this moment is watching the blue line appear on the pregnancy test and looking distinctly dewy-eyed.

The letters from women were also extraordinary. About half of them seemed to say that anti-breastfeeding opinions should not be given space – which seems odd considering that they think their case so flagrantly and obviously just. Why the panic? A minority I found distinctly creepy – much was made of the 'lovely, sensual pleasure' of breastfeeding; I must say that, like the solid citizen who took Julia Somerville's boyfriend's nudie snaps of her daughter to the police, I was all for contacting the boys in blue here. All I can say, more in sorrow than in anger, is what a strange picture of the British adult is emerging here: the women using innocent babes for sensual gratification, and the men beating their tiny daughters on the bare bottom in public places for the heinous crime of showing fear. And people wondered why Charles Manson called his sex-crazed, self-righteous, psychotic gang 'The Family'. I could have told you that Mel B's marriage would soon be in trouble the minute she took on her husband's name – the rather ugly 'Gulzar' – for professional purposes. Professional women who have worked hard to make their family name famous and then abandon or add to it when they marry may as well get a tattoo on their wedding finger saying 'I'm a wuss! Please disrespect me!' Joanne Whalley who became Whalley-Kilmer (making a silly name sillier); Pamela Anderson who became Pamela Anderson Lee, then Pamela Lee, then Pamela Anderson once more after divorcing and jailing the brute; Robin Wright Penn, who recently got upset when her slob of a husband answered, 'Two hookers and a bag of cocaine!' to the question 'What is your idea of heaven?' on a chat show where they were both guests: don't these silly women know the first thing about men? Have they never heard of treating 'em mean and keeping 'em keen? And don't they know that, especially to the sort of neurotic, egotistic wreck of a man who succeeds in showbusiness, to give up one's name is tantamount to giving up every last vestige of honour, identity and self-respect? It's the grown-up version of doing that thing that 12-year-old girls do – going around writing your 'married' name on pencil cases the minute you fancy somebody – i.e. Julie Stalin. Like a lot of things, it's fine when you're 12.

I am afraid that some women still cling to the idea that a man marries a woman he 'respects', whereas often the opposite is true: he marries the woman he respects least. The more famous the man, the more this stands. Frank Sinatra once toasted his new bride in front of thousands of paying punters one night in Las Vegas, and was genuinely perplexed that she had been upset at his words: 'I finally met a broad I can cheat on without her finding out! I love ya, honey!' If I was a man, and a famous woman changed the name she had slogged so hard for just to please me, I would have such contempt for her creepiness that I would make a point of cheating on her with all the bridesmaids and the best man before I went on honeymoon.

26 JUNE 1999

I don't think the residents of Russell Square in central London are permanently on tenterhooks for the first swallow of summer like the rest of us. They get a lot of that all year, apparently. When the sun goes down in old Bloomsbury, so do the scores of gay men who haunt the park in search of fast love. Yes, nightingales may sing in Berkeley Square, but swallows can be heard in Russell.

And now Camden Council and the Bedford Estate plan to erect (oops, Mrs!) gates and close the park after dark. The naughty night-crawlers are understandably cross about this. This is Bloomsbury, after all, and one can imagine the ghosts of Lytton Strachey and his erudite bum-chums smiling down benignly. I don't know about you, but I find it rather sweet (I've got property just down the road, so it's not as if I'm a nimby). The poor buggers don't start up until around 11 p.m., and it's always pitch dark by then, even in summer.

According to one report last week, the boys move out of the

floodlights and into the bushes to do their business, and not one shriek or moan is to be heard. They seem to cause remarkably little public nuisance. I'll bet you any money that this initiative has more than a little to do with the fact that the Russell Hotel, so beloved of US tourists, overlooks the square. God forbid that we should let the natives upset Massah when he comes over to inspect Airstrip One.

The safety of foreign students and backpackers, who might use the park as a short cut at night, is being spoken of as an issue – but when did you last hear of a gay man raping someone in a park? It'd be like stealing food at an all-you-can-eat buffet. On the other hand, we are always hearing of women being raped and murdered when they take short cuts through parks – and having penises flashed at them in public parks ('flashers': even the name is light-hearted, like a type of firework) is something little girls have to learn to deal with before they even know what That Ugly Red Thing is – but I don't recall ever hearing urgent calls for the closure of those after dark. A man's revulsion is more of a cause for concern than a woman's death, as per usual. God forbid that a straight man should know how it feels to be treated as a piece of meat!

How dare Camden Council interfere in the discreet canoodling of gay men at a time when all children should be in bed. Those same children can walk into any sweet shop in Camden during the day and see, along the top shelf and among the respectable men's magazines in the middle, naked women for sale. It's a shame that the sensibilities of women who live in the area aren't treated as tenderly as those of itinerant backpackers: a seven-month-pregnant friend was regularly accosted by kerb-crawlers, and her eight-year-old daughter was often propositioned by men on her way home from school. If there's one thing that might teach such men to behave themselves, it'd be having a couple of cocks waved at them when they least expected it.

I would far rather children formed their idea of sex from glimpsing the shadow-play of Russell Square – free, for fun, a meeting of equals, involving no coercion or bribery – than take on board the current heterosexual mode, in which one side has the power and money to take any number of joyless liberties with the other side: pornography, prostitution, lap dancing. The allegedly caring Nineties have seen a creeping belief in the ultimate capitalist creed that anything a man can afford to pay for is by definition okay – far worse than in the supposedly brutal Eighties, when it would have been considered way beyond the pale for liberal pop stars to patronise strip clubs or for naked women to be bound and gagged in the pages of *GQ*. Women, especially famous women, seemed to have a great deal more respect for themselves in the Eighties, and saw getting their tits out not as 'empowerment', but as the sign of a stupid slag not fit for anything else. I remember a lot of bitter, jealous, scaredy-cat male hacks mocking we 'Thatcherite bitches' for our 'power-dressing' at the time. Well, now they've got their way, and power-undressing has replaced it. Except that no matter how hard she smirks, a naked woman in any commercial context looks like a victim, a bride stripped bare by the grabbing hands of the market.

Who was it who first had the bright idea of selling pornography in sweet shops as opposed to barbers' shops or wherever saddos went to get their grubby little meathooks on them before? A newsagent, a councillor, an MP? I'd really like to know so I could knee him in the nuts because I think it's such a sick and stupid thing to do. If any man has trouble imagining how random pornography makes women feel, imagine nipping into the corner shop for a packet of fags and being confronted by a line of magazines showing young men bending over and presenting their bums to you, while inside those covers they show off a wide variety of huge, plush erections. It has nothing to do with not liking sex, and everything to do with an *Alice in Wonderland* feeling of disorientation, of everything being in the wrong place.

Some independent newsagents have pulled porn from their shelves. To walk into such a shop is a delighted thrill of recognition of the world spinning backwards and correcting a fatal error. Porn would be less offensive, contrarily, if men were up there being objectified and commodified alongside the women. But, for some reason, female genitalia is considered cheap and male genitalia mysterious and sacred – which brings us back to the proposed gating of Russell Square. Those men just aren't respecting themselves – not like lap dancers. *The Sunday Times* reported last week that many doctors are still 'curing' male homosexuality – with, wouldn't you know it, pornography. Like the doctors who decided to give Viagra to a convicted rapist with no girlfriend, it makes you wonder what the medical profession consider a 'normal' man. Peter Sutcliffe? The fact is that what goes on in Russell Square is not the result of homosexuality (can you imagine 25 lesbians rutting in bushes? Go on, I know you've tried) but of male sexuality, with the female element of restraint removed. Forget the colonel's lady and Judy O'Grady: it's the *Loaded* lad and the Bloomsbury bender who are brothers under the foreskin.

3 JULY 1999

I was reading a newspaper the other day, when an item caught my eye so sharply that I could have sued the organ concerned for physical injury compensation. It was one of those moments when you feel so shocked and baffled that your secondary reaction is to explain away the situation by telling yourself that it's you who's the strange one. But I wasn't mad. Nor could it be explained away as a screamer plucked from one of those full-page personality interviews: no, this item – 'Actress Bridget Fonda hasn't given up on marriage despite two failed love affairs,' it began, and went on for another 30 or so words, along-side a pleasant, but not traffic-stopping, head-and-shoulders shot – was in a column called The World Tonight, and was sandwiched between an item on the state of the India-Pakistan conflict and one on the plight of whales at the hands (paws?) of homicidal polar bears in the Canadian Arctic.

What's all that about, then? Of course, we've known for a long time that newspapers are getting more magazine-y and opinion-led, all the better to give themselves the edge on news broadcasting, but the Fonda item has to be the benchmark of how unrecognisable newspapers of today are, compared with their post-war forebears. To put it simply, it seems as though the women's page has eaten the world. It is not inconceivable, if things carry on like this, that in 20 years' time we will buy newspapers purely for entertainment, and turn to glossy maga-zines such as *Now!* and *Marie Claire* – both of which are extraordinarily good on the plight of women suffering under the yoke of 'tradition' in the developing world – when the desire for real news, real reporting, becomes too great.

I haven't physically worked in a newspaper office since I was 19, and then it was only the poncey old *New Musical Express*, so I readily admit that I have always nurtured a highly romanticised idea of what such places are really like: hives of testosterone-rich activity as men in trilbys with press passes shoved in their hat-bands make life-and-death decisions between bouts of saving the world – a cross between Clark Kent in *Superman* and Arthur Christiansen in *The Day the Earth Caught Fire*. But the Fonda item has finally convinced me that I was wrong, and that newspapermen are, in fact, no different from you or me.

When I first went to work at the *NME*, having quickly proved myself useless at both reviewing and interviewing, I was given the task of looking through armfuls of foreign magazines in which, once every few hours, I'd find an interesting or freakish snippet, which I would then rewrite for the Thrills! pages. Now, apparently, this is the journalistic norm. I envision newspaper offices not as thick broths of testosterone, but like the sleepover scene in *Grease*. I imagine hacks sitting around with face masks on, bare feet on desks, toes separated by wodges of sponge to stop nail polish from smudging, only looking up from copies of *MovieLine* when the editor runs out of his room screaming that he has a lunch date with Liz Hurley in half an hour but has just broken a nail.

In fact, considering the ubiquity of Miss Hurley in those newspapers that last got excited during the Suez crisis – in the *Telegraph*, in particular, she pops up everywhere, like a hyper-sexy Zelig – it ill behoves the broadsheets to pour scorn on the alleged plans to invite her on to *Question Time*. Are they suggesting that television is a more serious and respectworthy arm of the media than print journalism? How very self-loathing of them.

One of the best pretexts for getting a big photo of Liz on the front pages of the broadsheets is any sort of 'scientific' survey of what men and women find attractive in the opposite sex. A new book on beauty and its biological imperative must have made the papers think Christmas had come early and, sure enough, there were the old pictures of Marilyn Monroe to illustrate how important the waist-to-hip ratio is. You have to wonder how long the human race has to stop doing a thing for scientists to catch on that something has changed – soon, they'll notice we've started walking upright – and it is a fact that the most enduring symbols of female beauty over the past decade (Madonna, Diana and Kate Moss) have all had a low waist-to-hip ratio. The hourglass figure is notorious in its absence at the most fashionable gatherings and, when it does exist, makes its owner less universally admired than the butt of jokes about stupidity and artificiality. Across America, you can hear the slurp of silicone balloons being removed from women who found owning an hourglass figure added nothing at all to their quality of life.

Similarly, the idea that alpha males are driven by their desire to impregnate as many females as possible should have gone out of favour at roughly the same time as property and inheritance laws first saw the light of day. Every week some rich and/or famous man is splashed all over the papers denying he is the father of this or that child; many, like Michaels Winner and Parkinson, boast of their infertility. The most sexually profligate men are not alpha males (Bill Gates, orgy-master?) but no-hopers on sink estates with no other way to prove their manhood.

You might have noticed that one of my ex-husbands, Tony Parsons, is touting a novel around based on circumstances not entirely unlike my bolting from the marital home in 1984, leaving him to bring up our son single-handedly. The novel has pressed a few buttons, as former 'hard types' such as Jeremy Paxman and James Brown testify that This Novel Made Them Cry.

Crying does not necessarily indicate intelligence and sensitivity in a man; look at Paul Gascoigne.

As Nora Ephron pointed out, 'Beware of the man who cries; he cries only for himself.' To quote Mr Parsons during the early years of our marriage – before he became Barbara Cartland and developed a taste for blue eyeshadow and droning on about the Family being the basis of everything decent in society – he said, after seeing a clip of *Kramer vs Kramer* on TV and whistling in contempt, 'Look at that! A man does what millions of women have to do, as well as going to work, every day of the year, and because he's a man, he expects the effing George Cross for it!' Thank you and goodnight.

10 JULY 1999

So the world didn't end, then. Don't you hate it when that happens? But that's worlds for you – don't get involved with them. I was all ready, for once. I had removed myself from my beloved boyfriend and my beloved Brighton, and gone back to Bristol, where I assembled a sort of Cultural Atrocity Exhibition of all the things that it would be wonderful never to have to see again: the films of Michael Winner, the plays of Steven Berkoff, the novels of A. A. Gill, the music of Mick Hucknall, the embarrassing and self-serving journalistic ramblings of long-dumped husbands, plus a packet of Cheese Strings. Looking around, I felt quite serene. Soon, all this would be dust.

I've never understood the things people say they'd want to be doing as the world ended; nice things, such as having sex or eating one's favourite scoff. How horribly poignant to have that snatched away from you! Still, there's no accounting for taste. I'll never forget how we all howled when Martin Amis finally realised – 30 years after the Aldermaston marches (always first with the trends, our Mart) – that there were these big scary things called nuclear weapons, and wrote an essay trying to imagine what he'd have to do if the warning went off. The first thing he wrote, with a presumably straight face, was that he'd have to get physically from where he was to where his wife and children were – and then kill them! This was the bit that made us fall about, I'm afraid, though it wasn't really a laughing matter: Amis, in Incredible Hulk mode, strangling Mrs Amis and the little Amises with his bare hands. 'You and whose army, Martin?' went up the cry at the Groucho Club – I bet he'll have to get Julian Barnes and Speccy McEwan to help, though the best thing would, of course, be if Christopher Hitchens was in the country at the time. Now there's a man who could give you a damned good throttling: mmm, you'd know you'd been throttled, and you'd stay throttled. But Martin, getting all Othello on your ass? Come on.

So even while I was waiting for the end of the world last Sunday, I was giggling like a fiend remembering this. But then, I'm not very good at solemn occasions: I got told off for laughing at both my weddings (both times, I'm ashamed to say, it was the line about forsaking all others that did it). Then, because I'm a bitch, I started thinking in an extremely malicious way about the people I despised, and how miserable they'd be feeling as the world ended. That self-pitying buffoon C, who'd been contemplating his novel for the past 20 years and took a whole morning to write a thank-you card – well, he was going to die unpublished. And that irritating cow H, who did get her novel published and made a mint from it – but, heh heh, she's been banging on about her biological clock since she was 30, and no way is she going to get the chance to spawn now! It really cheered me up, remembering that I'd had children and a number-one bestseller, to think of all the tossers – all of them barren in both departments – who'd sniped at me, now going to meet their maker. In fact, it cheered me up so much that I decided to call it quits in the Armageddon department and instead switched on the TV to watch a programme about amusing animals.

As I've got older, I like to think I've become more tolerant – I can certainly put up with stupid, boring people better than I used to – but show me a miserable person, someone by definition both stupid and boring, who believes that they are both clever and interesting, and I have to be restrained from doing a Marty on them. My favourite recurring fantasy at the mo involves me, Woody Allen, a locked room and an extremely large cheese grater.

I'm afraid that when I meet an able-bodied misery these days, I instantly transform into The Man With The X-Ray Spex and case them coldly, imagining all the lives their hearts, blood and kidney could transform. I have become The Harvester Of Eyes whom Blue Oyster Cult sang about. That old Great War song, 'We Really Hate to Lose You But We Think You Ought to Go', goes through my mind. And though I know *Logan's Run* is a rotten film, its underlying premise of glorifying suicide, so long as it's voluntary, actually has a lot going for it. You could take away a lot of the stigma of suicide by setting up a sort of reverse Samaritans for a start: Go on, do it! Think of all the lives you'll save! No longer the coward's way out, suicide would come to be seen as a club fit for heroes. Truly, the gift that keeps on giving.

17 JULY 1999

Summer is here. I know that because I know all the songs in the Top 20 again. People of my age, unless they're sad, ageing swingers, usually go through spring, autumn and winter staring in dull dismay at *Top of the Pops*, the ghost of their parents' contempt ringing in their ears even as it drops from their own lips: 'Call that music!' But you know it's summer when you can tell your Shanks and Bigfoot from your Phats and Small, and explain in fewer than 40 words just why Basement Jaxx's 'Red Alert' is the ultimate analysis of the situation in Kosovo.

When I was a teenager, I watched *TOTP* as though my life depended on it, just as I'd listen to the Radio 1 chart every Tuesday lunchtime in the school cloakrooms. We all did, grimly rooting for our favourites with an edge of hysteria. For working-class teenage girls in the early Seventies, listening to the new chart was the nearest we'd ever get to the feeling our grandparents had when they listened to Chamberlain's speech declaring war on Germany. Things could get pretty grim in that bunker: when monstrosities such as 'Grandad', by Clive Dunn, or 'Ernie', by Benny Hill, put down roots and refused to move from the top slot for months on end, I sometimes feared mass suicide à la Jamestown.

Even though the chart is not what it was in terms of sheer unit-shifting, it still packs a tremendous emotional punch for performers and punters alike – it makes us feel like children again. I'm sure Geri Halliwell must have had a moment of mindless Violet Elizabeth Bott-type rage when her single only got to number two, before collapsing with what the papers called 'exhaustion' but was probably sheer temper. To this day, hearing a beloved song on the radio is as near as godless teens get to a spiritual experience: 'Unfinished Sympathy', say, still brings tears to my eyes. I'm sure that record sales continue to plummet because the growth of pop radio has brought home to people the transcendent purity of hearing a favourite song at random. Next to such everyday epiphany, the prosaic process of going to a shop, handing over a fistful of change and piping, 'Can I have "Saltwater" by Chicane, please?' seems unbearably Pooterish, as does the idea of 'listening' to music (as men tend to) rather than using it as a handy prompt for human narratives (as women tend to).

I know all the songs in summer because it's only then that I spend all day with Surf 108 on in the background as I work beside my swimming pool. Well, work between swimming, ray-catching and trying to work out which of the three heroines of *Valley of the Dolls* I most identify with – Anne, the shy, smalltown survivor; Jennifer, the ravaged sex goddess; or Neely, Miss Box Office Poison of 1965? (It's got to be Neely.) It's not such a bad life if you don't weaken or talk to the gutter press, whose advances I've been resisting since they branded me The World's Worst Mother, Including Rosemary West And All Those Women With That Weird Syndrome That Makes Them Feed Needles To Their Children In Order To Get Medical Attention. So I hide out, and I work on the opening pages of my new novel – the one about The World's Worst Mother who has somehow ended up with the world's best life, working on a new novel about being The World's Worst Mother in winter.

While cloudy skies encourage brooding and introspection, the sun gives everything 'too much fucking perspective', as Nigel Tufnel once said of Elvis's grave. You can understand why races from cold countries who fetch up in hot places – California and Australia, say – are portrayed as amoral air-heads, always whipping off their tops and saying 'Whadever!' before jumping into a Jacuzzi with a dozen like-minded young marrieds. There is something about the sun that sneers 'Seen it all!' and encourages one to behave like a leathery, lecherous multiple divorcée – not much of a leap of imagination in my case, I know, but anyway. Doing The World's Worst Mother in winter would be much more of a cause for concern than it is now, when choosing between factor five and factor three sunscreen is far more of a pressing dilemma.

Until this week, sunbathing was Bad and breastfeeding Good, so imagine my surprise to read that, once again, it's all change in the crazy world of pop science. It gives me no satisfaction to know that all those ferocious lactators, who wrote me evil letters in their own breast milk, claiming that I would go to hell for opposing breastfeeding, are now panicking because, it turns out, they've been feeding Junior huge whacks of pesticides, lead, arsenic, mercury and sex-changing chemicals along with Nature's Best. No wonder you see kids who could open beer cans with their teeth still hanging on the nipple: they're addicts.

The WorldWide Fund for Nature last week published a study identifying more than 350 pollutants in breast milk, with two-month-old babies regularly receiving 42 times the safe human level of dioxin, the chemical involved in the Belgian food scare. We bad mothers, sitting by swimming pools writing self-adoring novels, on the other hand, are apparently soaking up enough vitamin D to protect ourselves from putative heart attacks, while at the same time giving our mental health a massive boost. I never doubted it.

There has not been a society on Earth that has not felt the need to control and process women. Religious and intellectual rationales for doing so have collapsed, at least in the West. And here, health education has stepped in: no longer 'It's bad!' but 'It's bad for you!' is the message women now receive about everything remotely enjoyable. It's still scolding – but it's scolding in a caring way, as Dame Edna might say.

How enlivening, then, to hear that selfish, narcissistic sunbathing has benefits, and self-sacrificing, exhausting breast-feeding drawbacks. Insofar as I have any philosophy of life left, it might best be summed up in an old black American phrase: 'Don't trust Whitey', Whitey being, in this instance, male-devised moral strictures of any kind. There comes a point, as Valerie Solanas said, when any decent, fun-loving, self-respecting woman just has to say NO to everything expected of her, on principle, and set about creating her own moral universe. That's what I'll be doing by my pool this summer. I'll be sure to let you have the first peek when it's finished.

24 JULY 1999

The other morning, I went out to my pool and found swimming in it what I took to be a beautiful fluffy grey duck. It had an intelligent face – for some reason, it reminded me of Kirsty Young – and looked at me out of the corner of its eye. 'Hello,' I said conversationally. 'Are you lost?' It walked off quickly, as though I'd propositioned it at a bus stop. It didn't fly, so, thinking it might be injured, I called the PDSA.

'Describe it,' said the lady. 'Is it as big as a swan?'

'Easily!'

'What colour is it?'

'It's grey and fluffy. I think it might be foreign.'

'Is there a lot of seagull activity over your house?'

'Yes. I think they're jealous of it. They might want to kill it, because they're ugly, and it's sweet.'

'Look at it again. Is it really as big as a swan?'

I went back. It was sunning itself beside the pool. When it saw me coming, it jumped in and began swimming in circles, as though it had been up to something illegal. It was much smaller than I'd thought. 'It's not as big as a swan,' I admitted. 'That's because it's a seagull. It's a juvenile. It has got itself separated from its group, and that's why you've got so many seagulls flying over your house. They'll shriek at it until it flies. It should be gone tomorrow.'

When I went out the next morning, Kirsty was gone. Bastard seagull, pretending to be a duck like that! For a moment, I felt murderous, like a disgusting, old-fashioned man who buys a girl dinner and then blows his top because she won't sleep with him. Bitterly, I called my pool boy to come out and wipe away any stray traces of the perfidious bitch. That night, I saw a similar thing on *The Sopranos*, in which the don's depression is brought on by the desertion of a family of ducks who've been living in his pool.

I've always had a thing about having a wild animal living in my garden, and really thought that Kirsty might be The One. I told my posh fox-hunting friend this, and she laughed, triumphantly. 'Aha! If you had a fox in your garden, he'd have killed her.' 'Well, yes, but I wouldn't really have minded, because then I'd have had a fox in my garden.' Only last week, I read a piece by a man who puts a chair by his garden wall so that a vixen and her cubs can play in his garden and then leave when they've had enough. The man lost livestock to the foxes, but he didn't care: he had a fox in his garden!

This made me think that it's not we anti-hunters who anthropomorphise foxes, thinking that they're cuddly little oofums (as we're always accused of doing); it's the pro-hunters. 'Foxes kill chickens! They deserve to die!' That's only a short philosophical jump from those mad medievalists who put pigs on trial for stepping on mice, thereby 'murdering' them. Anti-hunters expect foxes to kill other animals; they're only animals, for God's sake, and don't know any better. They're naturally equipped with claws, fangs and speed, so that they can chase another animal and kill it easily. We're not, and that's why, if we want to chase and kill an animal, we have to ride horses and employ hounds.

This may be what particularly repels people about hunting (don't forget that around 80 per cent of country-dwellers are in favour of a ban, the very people who, say hunters, suffer most from sly Mr Fox's antics): it's the bullying, mob-handed aspect that appals – it's not just humans who chase foxes, but humans, horses and dogs. If something takes that much effort, chances are that it's not a 'natural' way of controlling vermin at all. The idiot pleb apologists for hunting who say it's not a class thing only make their case more grotesque when they point out that 'ordinary people' follow hunts on bicycles and in cars. Right: that's people, horses, dogs, cars and bikes . . . chasing one fox. No wonder the British love of fair play finds this hard to reconcile. Despite the sentimental eyewash talked about our island way of life, there is something about hunting that seems completely un-British. It belongs to the dark mainland cruelty of Europe, all those Germans torturing beautiful stags or Spaniards chucking little donkeys off church roofs.

We are the species that produced Beethoven, Shakespeare and Christy Turlington, made in the image of God. It seems blasphemous, then, that we should want to turn ourselves into beasts, foaming at the mouth with bloodlust. And it has nothing to do with freedom: people don't even have the most basic freedoms to do what they like with their own bodies, so why should the right to play God with another life be paramount? Just as society bans drugs because it wants to save people from themselves – and I bet old Camilla, apparently devastated by her son's little habit, believes that drugs should not be legalised – we are going to ban hunting for the same reason. Hunting coarsens the human soul. It sets up a thoroughly unwholesome link between excitement and blood, which leads to a casual accept- ance of cruelty as a part of everyday life. You have only to look at upper-class attitudes to children, women and war to understand that life is cheap to them – it becomes cheap during those first years in the saddle. It would be good for them to take a long, cool look at what they do. Someone like Camilla Parker Bowles, say, who has been raised with every chance to obtain learning and culture, instead has a life that, according to even her friends, consists of nothing more than waiting for the weekend to come so she can go out and kill something. Seen with compassion, this is a human tragedy of Dostoyevskyan proportion. What goes on in that mind of hers?

In the end, my objection to fox-hunting stems not from the fact that I feel animals are as good as us, but because I believe we are a higher species who should not lower ourselves to behave like animals. If we want to behave like animals, we should trade in our voting rights, say, for this privilege. Are you a human being or are you a beast? You decide, and you take the consequences.

On the other hand, a compromise solution occurs to me. Foxes are vermin, but so are the upper classes, as the great Aneurin Bevan once pointed out, Why not form a People's Pest-Controlling Militia, and on horse and by bike and by car go after the lot of them every weekend until they are all dead? Then, perhaps, we can get on with the business of being human.

14 AUGUST 1999

Every time I see a picture of Catherine Zeta Jones these days, all I can think is, 'What kept her?' Of all the women who were born or built to be film stars – more even than, say, Uma Thurman, Jennifer Lopez or Cameron Diaz – it seems ludicrous that anyone ever assumed that Zeta Jones could be anything else. Her eyes always seem to be looking at you from a pillow, and she appears to carry her own Klieg lights secreted on her person, for wherever she appears there seems to be a sudden burst of radiance, almost a Pentecostal flame. For once, that erratic actor Michael Douglas has got his expression just right: sheer numb, dumb gratitude.

What seems most perplexing is not that Miss Jones is now the only female star apart from Julia Roberts who can open a film, but that she ever wasted so much time cooling her heels over here on Airstrip One, making films playing the love interest of Wurzel Gummidge's son and doing dull things with sticky-backed plastic and a *Blue Peter* presenter. But just when you thought we'd be making merry with the Tizer and bunting at her success, it's all gone quiet. When you think about the pathetic way in which we tried to talk up such obvious non-starters as Julia Ormond and Helena Bonham-Carter, it's rather sad that the only recognition we can now give Zeta Jones is that she's really hooked herself a live one. Way to go, gold-digger! Naturally, I feel a little perturbed that she has put the kibosh on my theory about actresses with three names never really making it – Mary Elizabeth Mastrantonio, Mary Louise Parker, Sarah Jessica Parker, Mary Beth Hurt – but, that apart, I am really pleased for her because she has bust out; she has found her old life not worth living and gone and got herself another one. If men do this, we're meant to regard them as sexy old dynamos, but if a woman does it there is still a great deal of no-better-than-she-should-be-ing. Women are supposed to stay where they're put.

Indeed, Zeta Jones was so far down the showbusiness food chain that even Michael Winner felt free to be bitchy about her. Seeing how he sucks up to anyone famous, even O. J. Simpson, this is really quite a first. 'She's just a former dancer,' he is quoted as saying in my precious copy of *Who's Really Who*. 'They're almost always rather nice, jolly people who go through life having a ball. But you never seem to hear much about them when they get older.' Either Zeta Jones never read this, or she's much more forgiving than I am, because last week she was all over *OK!* magazine being all over, among others, Michael Winner.

Most likely she just thinks he's a stupid old man. Although, in civilian life, old geezers are finding themselves redundant and disrespected, I'm afraid that showbiz seems to be the last refuge of the wrinkly. There used to be that special Oscar they'd give John Wayne or Hank Fonda just for Not Being Dead Yet, but these days such greybeard worship seems to be endemic, I'm afraid. Just look at all the fuss about Des Lynam! What's all that about, then? And Jack Nicholson! If I hear one more woman say how sexy he is, I'll puke – when did it start being sexy to hire prostitutes and beat them up when they ask for money? Nicholson is a walking, breathing affront to women, and if he was young and fit, somebody would have blackballed him years ago. There seems to be some unwritten rule that old blokes can get away with things that would have young men pilloried as psychopaths fit only for locking up. 'Poor old General Pinochet – he's on his last legs, bless him!' Good: the quicker he pops his clogs in clink, the less money the wretched British taxpayer will have to waste on him. I bet all those people he had tortured to death would have loved the chance to die of old age in jail – compared with what they went through, Pinochet's having an all-expenses-paid Saga holiday.

People of a certain sensibility would be the first to ridicule and reject the sickening displays of brown-nosing recently laid at the bunion-blighted feet of the Queen Mother, yet these same people, the Hip Squares, practically wet themselves and genuflect every time they mention John Peel or, God help us, Jeffrey Bernard. Longevity, pure and simple, has a great deal to do with it – such people hit critical mass only when they hit 60. Before that, only a handful of dismal misfits had ever heard of them. Add on William Burroughs, Ken Kesey and Steven Berkoff while you're at it, and what a sad-sack selection of septuagenarians we've put up there in the counter-culture canon! Makes you kind of envious of squares proper, what with Compo and Rompo and the rest of them.

And what does this rogues' gallery have in common, apart from providing a good argument for forcible euthanasia? Yes, fight fans, you've guessed it: an attitude to women that is in equal parts Howard Hughes's attitude towards money and Hitler's attitude towards the Jews – as a wise (Jewish) man once said of the old pop group The Knack. You will look for old women in the Hip Square canon in vain; they were long ago killed by their spaced-out husbands or dumped for younger models.

For my sins, I met Jeffrey Bernard a few times, and I do not for the life of me understand his continuing canonisation. I can only suppose he appeals to people who are foul-tempered, burnt-out and who will never produce anything of worth themselves, because at last they have someone they can feel superior to. Intellectual women, like what I am, always have to exercise caution when praising glamour icons; you can make yourself look terribly over-heated and lecherous and lonely, like when poor Professor Paglia starts banging on about Catherine Deneuve and Cindy Crawford, and comes out of it looking like little more than the thinking dyke's Benny Hill.

But, as tales from Theatreland go, I find the Catherine Zeta Jones Story – girl from nowhere dancing in West End show at 15, on the scrapheap at 25, then conquers world – far more poignant and affecting than the old, old story, now playing at the Old Vic until Kingdom Come, of how a man was born with every advantage life had to offer and frittered it all away.

21 AUGUST 1999

Last Saturday night, I went to a party thrown by the two most beautiful lesbians in Brighton in a house in the most beautiful square in Brighton. As you can imagine, it was a right hoot, full of lovely creatures of all persuasions, but there was only one pair of eyes I wanted to gaze into.

'Can I go in and see him now?' I kept badgering the hostesses every half-hour from 10.30 p.m. to 4.30 a.m. 'Please, just for a minute.' 'He's asleep!' they cried each time. 'Leave it, will you? It's starting to get weird!' You'll have guessed by now that the object of my request was a cat: Mr Slippers by name – a male kitten, dark grey in hue, of around six months. Finally, I was allowed to see him, and I felt that the 15 minutes spent in his presence had made everything worthwhile.

There were some charming people at the party, and I had some brilliant conversations – though, um, I can't remember them now – but I can honestly say that Mr Slippers (who is also known, for some reason, as Satan) ran rings round all of them. A few days later, a friend rang to say that a close mutual mate had been savagely beaten up and robbed when he left the party, and I'm afraid my first response was, 'Oh, my God! And he never even met Mr Slippers.' There was a quick intake of breath, and then she put the phone down on me.

I've always been mad about animals; my first memory of the cinema is of the house-lights being turned up before the end of *Born Free* and myself being led to the manager's office, there to be plied with sweet confections that might make me stop howling at the top of my lungs at the plight of Elsa the lion cub, soon to be forced back into the callous bush from the comfort of her Adamson home. As time has gone on, though, I've definitely got weirder about them. When I say 'animals', I don't mean the poor brutes bred for food and I don't mean the wild animals you see on TV whose lives seem a bit too much like ours for comfort – all that sex and death and people nosing at you, trying to take pictures. No, what I mean, of course, is pets – dogs and cats, but cats in particular.

During the first year we were together, my boyfriend was shocked one day when I confided in him that I sometimes had a fantasy of getting on a bus and seeing where it went and leaving my life behind, taking on a new identity just for the hell of it. 'Only, of course, I couldn't do it,' I added quickly – he looked touched and started to smile – 'because of Patsy.' Patsy was a goldfish who belonged to my air steward friend, Marcus, but who lodged with me.

'Anyone else?' asked my boyfriend.

'Um, no.' He then gave me what I believe is called an 'old-fashioned look'. It wasn't for weeks that I worked out what I should have said.

Last month, after four years of bliss, it happened again. We were in Torquay, which – and I know this is an unusual taste in one of my sensibility; far stranger, say, than a penchant for absinthe or frottage – I find to be just about the most glorious place on earth, and I was going on about how I was just going to disappear from Brighton one day and disappear to Torquay and take up hotel management and find a new identity. And then my boyfriend, very slowly and lovingly, as if talking to a beloved backward person, said, 'But you wouldn't, would you, because of . . .?' I thought for a minute . . . 'The cats!' I exclaimed, pleased with myself. The cats, Fluffy and Sox (sad, but true), are twin tabbies who have owned me for more than a year now.

I got That Look again. Three days after we got home, I realised what I should have said. Perhaps I, like many other people, am over-attached to my pets, but these weird attitudes don't just come out of the blue, you know. Human history is a veritable vale of tears, and one day you just hear about one too many developing countries where they can't afford food but can somehow afford nuclear bombs, and your string snaps. This is why young people are so massively disillusioned with politics, but will happily throw themselves under a lorry to save the life of a veal calf.

'People who love animals hate people.' There's always some misery-bucket lurking around muttering this, usually in conjunction with the amazingly original observation that 'Hitler was a vegetarian and an anti-vivisectionist, you know!' So? Hitler was also an Austrian, a house-painter and a man, and if we said that just because he was a mentalist then everyone in those groups is, we'd be accused of being bigots and alarmists.

The statement implies, of course, that people who don't like animals spend half their time mopping up on the killing fields of Rwanda and the other half disposing of their income to the poor and needy, whereas it simply means that they're just too tight to spring for a can of Kattomeat: 'What's in it for me, then?' It really is time to nail once and for all the rumour that every time one feeds a duck in Sussex a fellow human being dies of hunger in Ethiopia. The one has absolutely nothing to do with the other. If someone really has no time for pets, what it reveals about them to me is not an all-embracing love of humanity, but rather an absolute lack of a sense of humour – and that's just about as unsexy as it gets. For it is the very preposterousness of cats and dogs that is so enriching and enlivening.

In a world where, increasingly, human beings are bred to live out their lives like beetles on a dung-heap, scurrying around attending to their own piece of ordure with no glimpse of a greater plan, the very existence of pets is proof that some things actually prove their excellence by not being a profit-making concern. To be born with a leg at each corner, and a tail – a tail! – and to exist solely to be stroked and loved: well, it makes a lot more sense to me than putting a bomb under somebody because you want to see a different piece of material fluttering from the flagpost on high days and holidays. Frankly, animal-lovers have no further need to put their case – lovers of humanity, on the other hand, have really got their work cut out.

28 AUGUST 1999

I still remember the day I first read the amazing quote by that society broad who turns down a suitor with the words, 'No, darling, I only sleep with the First Eleven'. I remember running to my friend, Viking Ann, to ask her with a tremulous voice, 'I only slept with the First Eleven, too, didn't I?'

Viking Ann roared, 'Course you did, darlin! The first eleven that asked you! This was, perhaps, the one time in my life that I have been forced to admit that women can be as evil as men.

Most of the time, there's no competition. No matter how rabid a masculinist he is, I do not believe that any father of small children has not said to them at some point, 'If you get lost, go and tell a LADY!' No parent, not even David Thomas, says, 'Go and tell a MAN!' It remains a statistical fact that a girl child is safer, sexually speaking, sleeping under the roof of two strange lesbians (though not too strange) than she is sleeping in the same house as her blood father.

Women may not be nicer than men, which was always used in the past as an excuse for men to behave like beasts and women to put up with it, but there can be no doubt that they behave better. Despite all the tired gags about PMT, they do not seem half so ruled by their emotions as men, for what is a murderer but someone who has completely lost control of himself? Men are far less capable of objectivity than women: when a judge, say, lets off a rapist with a pat on the head, you just know that, nine times out of ten, he's looked at the victim, fancied her and thought, Cor, I'd rape her myself if I thought I could get away with it!

You know it's silly season when the newspapers start banging on about how much more violent women are getting: invariably, the headline will be the reekingly cheesy Deadlier Than The Male (question mark optional). This searingly original query also raises its head whenever a cold-blooded female killer is sighted, though, of course, the fact that we can recite the unholy canon of Myra Hindley, Mary Bell, Beverley Allitt and Rosemary West simply demonstrates how rare such women are. If we tried to recall the list of cold-blooded male killers who've been brought to justice over the past 40 years, we'd still be here at Christmas. Christmas 2005.

Last week, the *Daily Mail* ran a piece about how the female prison population has doubled in five years; that is, 17 per cent of prisoners are now women, in for shoplifting, fraud and dropping fag ends out of moving car windows, while men, the veritable little Peace Pledgers, remain steady at 83 per cent with rape, murder and child molestation. Attaboys! Why can't a woman be more like a man?

We have become so used to men being rapists, murderers and child molesters that we, least of all the *Daily Mail*, never question why they feel the need to do these things. But I'm old enough to remember the Seventies, before the *Daily Mail* became the champion of our dusky brothers via the Stephen Lawrence case, when the headlines came thick and fast as to how black youth was driving a violent crime wave that would one day engulf the country. We can only surmise that the accuseds' families read them, too. Questions are constantly posed by the right wing about race and criminality, but no one ever sees fit to ask why 83 per cent of all prisoners are male, and what can be done to stop men raping, murdering and molesting.

I'd like to point out here that I am not speaking with my feminist hat on, but rather my Responsible Citizen *chapeau*. It is a fact that young men are more likely to be victims of violent crime at the hands of a stranger (women are lucky: they get killed by their nearest and dearest) than any other group. On behalf of us all, women and decent men, it would behove right-wing pundits to tackle the sticky problem of why a minority of men are so responsible for wreaking such havoc on society.

I think I have the answer. I've known lots of gay men and lots of genuinely straight men, and most of them were absolute angels. However, I have also had the misfortune to come across a large number of men who pretended to be straight, worked overtime at it, in fact, but who, in their heart of hearts, were profoundly gay. This made them misery buckets when sober, dangerous when drunk and a thoroughly unhealthy influence on society in general. I'm not going to name names, but we all recognise those men who have what can be politely called a tormented masculinity built on sexual confusion. (Hemingway was one.) The novelist who takes karate lessons. The actor who says that being in borstal was the best time of his life. The rastafarian who won't let his girlfriend into the kitchen when she's on the rag. The wife-beating footballer who never seems happier than when he's got his tongue down the throat of his equally repulsive mate (that word is such a giveaway). Any man under the age of 50 who loves football or boxing, though not, paradoxically, all footballers or boxers. Men who talk about ard men or geezers, or who read books by violent criminals, or who liked *Lock, Stock and Two Smoking Barrels*. Benders, benders, benders.

It is the desire and fear of a large minority of men when it comes to bending that, I believe, cause so much upheaval and misery in our society. Earlier this month we were warned by the boys in blue that the blessing of live football on TV several times a week would damage the level of policing generally as more resources were poured into keeping the peace around various hotspots. Can you imagine women's hockey causing such bother to any civilised society, or that society putting up with it? Just so a bunch of pencil-dicked dickheads can have an excuse to get pissed and grope each other.

If women think they may have lesbo tendencies, they get merry on Babycham and fall giggling into bed with their second-best friend; we're brought up with so much soft-core, girl-on-girl eroticism that it doesn't seem a big deal. Men, though, have still got this ludicrous, operatic solemnity about their manhood, and not being made a woman of.

So they bottle it up, and it makes them ugly.

Eventually, they are violent one too many times and get sent to jail. Where, hey presto! its acceptable to bend, blow and bugger to kingdom come. It's very clever, what these geezers do, when you think about it; like a dog eating grass to make itself sick. They end up with exactly what they want. It's the rest of us who have to suffer.

4 SEPTEMBER 1999

As the English summer draws to a close, the good General Pinochet down there in darkest Surrey (wasn't there something inevitable about him ending up in the Home County that has always seemed the most likely to go fascist, probably on the premise that it would make the 8.14 from East Sheen run on time?) need not shiver yet; unless in fear. Because this enchanted, chilly island is hanging on to its place in the sun by, uniquely, making sure that the three top pop singles all move to that Latin beat: Lou Bega with 'Mambo No. 5', 'Much Mambo' by Shaft, and 'Mi Chico Latino' by Geri Halliwell, with Jennifer Lopez and Ricky Martin hanging on in the albums chart. Not since the heady days of 'Her name is Rio, and she dances on the sand' and Madonna crooning, apparently, 'Last night I dreamed of lumbago', has it been so politic to get yourself into a rumba skirt, flash those eyes and yelp hopefully any combination of 'Viva!' 'Ariba!' 'La Vida!' and 'Loco!'

I'm usually a really cheerful person – insanely so, I feel, coping with bereavement, bad book sales and being a size 18 with a *joie de vivre* born of a genuine belief that it's all a momentary blip and, hey, look at that sunset – but cod-Latin music, whether by the Munich-born Italian-Ugandan Lou Bega, or by Miss G. Halliwell of Watford, is the one thing I can think of that makes me feel really depressed. Because, whenever I hear it, I think immediately of the Chilean folk singer Victor Jara, who had his hands cut off in the Santiago football stadium soon after the Pinochet coup, and who was told by his torturer, 'Go on, then! Play the guitar!' before being killed.

Funny thing is, I've still never heard Jara sing, and I really hate folk music. But since that moment I've been obsessed by Latin

America, and its ceaseless agony and bravery, which far surpass anything that Eastern Europe had to go through, yet which never seemed to matter when it came to the Cold War and all that cant about human rights. I don't know where these things come from: one moment, I was a sexy, blond teenager with a headful of clothes and disco music standing by a bus stop in south Bristol opening my *New Musical Express* and frowning to find a double-page spread on the Chilean fascist coup and the killing of some hippie; the next, I was reading it and the world seemed to spin wildly around me, and everything to be beyond control.

I confided in my friend Bambi that, because of a coup in a faraway country of which I knew nothing, the ground seemed to have melted away from under my feet. Even though she didn't get it, she got the joke, and put her hand up without fail just before double games: 'Miss Simcock, Julie B can't do netball. She's worried about Chile/Paraguay/Uruguay.' You bet I was popular!

In the early Eighties, when I found out that the British government was giving money, through Reagan, to the Nicaraguan Contras – rapists of bridesmaids, to a man – I got totally distraught again, and spent many an evening weeping in my armchair in a bungalow in Billericay, where my then husband insisted we live (if that is the word). 'Pull yourself together, will ya?' was the testy riposte more often than not, doubtless because my crying got in the way of Tone's enjoyment of his Chas'n'Dave records. Well, I tried to cheer up and get with those Latin rhythms.

Soon, old Kid Creole was on the scene, and Ze records was getting into its stride – celebrating the joyous Latin American way of life, while over in America's backyard the fields ran red with the blood of peasants, trades unionists and anyone who didn't think that the profits of the United Fruit Company were the most important thing in the world. But despite the bum-sucking support which Ze got from *The Face* (despite its achingly hip reputation, the magazine was always terrifically naff in its enthusiasms, from sailor suits and lederhosen to Irish republicanism), it was a bit of a turkey that clucked all the way to the remainder racks.

I bet Kid Creole's kicking himself, if not his Coconuts, for peaking too soon – he is now treading the boards in *Oh! What a Night!*, an Eighties greatest hits review that nevertheless manages to sound like a Will Hay second feature and was dubbed by the *Surrey Comet* (note the Surrey motif) 'The musical of the year'.

Perhaps Pinochet might fancy it as an evening out to take his mind off his troubles. Failing that, they could always wheel him out to an Irish theme pub. Over the past few years, I have viewed the rise of these pubs with the same father-forgive-them horror with which I once contemplated the selling of the Latin beat. They'd never have been tolerated in the Seventies and Eighties, when the mainland felt that it was genuinely involved in the civil war, but during this decade – which, predictably, has been less about caring and sharing and more about doing any dirty thing for a quiet life – they have become a signal from the English population that we are prepared to sell the Loyalists down the river for a pint of Guinness, a Pogues song and a touch of the blarney.

If the English had not embraced the Irish theme pub so wholeheartedly, I find it entirely probable that Mo Mowlam would not have rolled over and played doggo for the IRA so enthusiastically.

I'm still the only person I've known who has always distrusted Irish Republicans for left-wing reasons – their persistence in targeting civilians, especially women and children, was always more the action of a right-wing goon squad than the genuine freedom-fighter; while their adherence to misogynistic, anti-life Catholicism always made me reflect that, yes, what the world really needs is one more country opposed to abortion, contraception and divorce.

So, the recent news that they would just as soon bully and butcher working-class Catholics came as no great surprise. I do hope that we can get our heads around the idea that there is more to Ireland than pop stars, trendy beer and 'the creach', or whatever it's called.

I realise that the Irish Problem is a bit of a bore, and not half as much fun as a cheap weekend in Dublin. But it might behove us to realise that a real fight between good and evil is taking place in Northern Ireland, just as it is in Latin America. Then, if we still choose to turn up the mambo and get blind on half-price Guinness, rather than see justice done, fair enough. Let's ask the General while we're at it! What price good and evil, when happy hour lasts for ever?

25 SEPTEMBER 1999

What about that Kenneth Branagh, then? What a shameless hussy! I write two weeks ago that I used to fancy him, and he dumps Helena Bonham-Carter as smart as you like after five years of Luvviedom. That'll teach you to 'drink loads of Diet Coke and belch and use the F-word', Hels – you were just too common for a well-brought-up boy like our Ken, after all. He wanted a lady, like what I am. But sorry, Ken, I'm taken – you could have had me in 1994.

It's been a bloody good month, gloatwise, for me. I seem to get a very deep, almost sexual satisfaction when someone I've always loathed – and who by common consensus is the best thing since pore-strips – is finally revealed as a rotter. The farmers first. Half a billion pounds of our money, they're getting! Like they need it; my friend's going out with a farmer from West Sussex, and he's got a CD player, television and Sensurround sound in one of his tractors. She calls it the Shaggin' Wagon.

Why do politicians suck up to the farmers? When they stuck those 50 pigs' heads on poles along that motorway recently, they were showing their true colours at last. Just think of all the children who must have seen that gory bit of grotesquerie. WE KILL THINGS, US! – that should be the motto of the National Farmers' Union. They make their living killing things and damn me if the moment they don't get a bit of leisure at the weekend, they're off killing things for fun. When they can't sell their polluted product – and here, suddenly, they're all socialists who deserve a state subsidy, unlike when they're doing well and all voting Tory – they kill the poor swine anyway, just for kicks. All that crap about how the countryside wouldn't exist without them – sod off, then! We'll keep that half a billion pounds and give it to task forces of idle youths. They can keep the hedgerows tidy for far less than that.

Funny, I never heard anyone on *The Archers* sympathising with the destruction of the mining communities when the pits were being closed down. I can't stand to listen to *The Archers* any more, with Brian and Jenny moaning on about how they can't afford a new Merc and she's still tootling about in last year's BMW. Only a group as savagely right-wing as farmers could complain about *The Archers* being too 'radical'; in fact, it's a reactionary disgrace. The new money (Lynda Snell) and the working-class Grundys are shown as complete buffoons; only the feudal tyrants of the various Archer branches are shown as sensible, competent human beings. And all that fuss when

Elizabeth had her abortion! You'd have thought she'd killed a baby or something!

And what about old P. G. Wodehouse? All my life I feel I've been a freak because I find his twee little books about as funny as having vomit come out of my nose and always knew he was a wrong 'un, doing that Lord Hee-Hee thing for the Nazis. 'Silly ass', my foot! He was actually in the pay of Joseph Goebbels: £3,500 a month in today's money, plus limitless expenses and travel, and a plush billet at a swank Paris hotel, for 'assisting in decomposition work, involving the destruction of the morale of Allied personnel'. What ho, Jeeves! indeed.

Talking of traitorous finks, I once burst into tears in an English class when I was about 12 because I couldn't explain to my sympathetic teacher exactly why *Animal Farm* was such an execrable book. I thought it had right-wing public-schoolboy written all over it, for a start. No, everyone kept insisting to me down the years, it's a masterpiece and Orwell was a great English socialist. And it turned out he was working for the CIA all through the Fifties, fingering fellow writers as Communist sympathisers – especially, charmingly, if they were Jews, a race he wasn't very fond of. Lovely chap.

Ted Hughes. Another pet hate of mine. His poetry is like being slapped around the face with a wet mackerel, and I don't mean that in a sexy way. I was always with the grave defacers on this one – Sylvia Plath; Hughes was her slave name. In her new book, Emma Tennant describes him as squandering the Plath estate on Dom Perignon to lubricate his lunchtime assignations, bad-mouthing his long-suffering third wife and suggesting that Tennant attends a School For Witches (talk about taking coals to Newcastle). What a creep – and what cretins those women were who were attracted to him. They're the thinking man's equivalent of those sickos who write to jailed serial killers offering to marry them. Yeuchhh!

Finally, it's been a bad month for popes. Popes, eh? Don't get involved with 'em. They've always been a bad lot. In this age of FaithZone@The Dome, there is a meat-headed feeling that we must 'respect' all faiths equally. Well, I don't mind respecting the Quakers and Methodists and withholding judgment on the Jews, Hindus, Sikhs and Buddhists, but I'm damned if anyone is going to demand that I respect any religion that believes that contraception is a sin (Catholicism) or that the word of one woman in a court of law is worth half the word of a man (Islam). Frankly, I would just as soon respect fascism.

As John Cornwell's new book, *Hitler's Pope*, reveals, Pius XII was a deeply wicked man, complicit in the deaths of thousands of Italian Jews. Yet the present Pope, John Paul, is dead set on canonising him! Those Catholics; if they're not canonising Nazis, they're raping children.

The extent of child abuse by Catholic priests and monks in Ireland will probably never be known, but the current investigations into the terrible crimes of the Christian Brotherhood children's homes – about half a million children are thought to have been raped in them over the past 50 years – goes quite a long way to convincing one that the Catholics heard the phrase 'Suffer little children' slightly the wrong way.

Say what you like about the Church of England; they may be boring, but I don't know many vicars who take six little orphan boys to the seaside as a treat, and every one of them has to be hospitalised for anal bleeding when they get back (as recently happened in Eire). It's pretty damn obvious why the Catholic Church is against abortion; too many of them, and there'll be no more unwanted, vulnerable children left to rape. God forbid.

2 OCTOBER 1999

I've got no time for autumn. I take those months – September, October, November – and I divide them into two. The first half I think of as a nasty bit of summer and the second half I think of as a balmy bit of winter. I like extremes: boiling by my swimming pool with a gal pal, or wrapped up by the fire with my boy. Spring is frustrating because it's like constant foreplay and autumn is crap because it's like post-coital tristesse, and frankly I don't go in for either.

Do it or get off the pot, autumn! Autumn's always dawdling; always – appropriately enough – kicking its way through the leaves on corners. I imagine it having that wheedling, whiney voice that New York fashion people have: 'Do I haaave to? I'd rather nooot.'

Who could possibly enjoy such dog days? I know: liking autumn is for people working overtime at being adult. The colour of the leaves, my foot! Apart from the fact that you're extremely likely to trip A over T in them – no wonder they call it fall – what is so attractive about autumn leaves? Seven shades of dysentery, if you look closely. And rightly so: autumn is about rot. There's no nice way to talk about things rotting. As Joan Collins, in her mighty book *My Secrets*, put it, 'Rancid nuts, meat, vegetables, dairy produce, or any food that's past its sell-by date, are liable to make you ill.' If you add men to that list, this is as near to a philosophy of life as I have, I'd say.

Autumn's for people who don't flinch when they see the words 'wistful' and/or 'rueful' in novels. Myself, I'd throw them down, whimpering. I don't think I've ever acted wistful and/or rueful in my life, and if I ever see anyone doing so I'm going to kick them really hard where it shows.

I'm totally not a mood person. Recently, Bill Deedes persuaded me to have luncheon with him at an Italian restaurant on the Strand, to talk about his close friend and my major crush, the Princess of Wales, and wrote afterwards that I had a streak of melancholy. Well, I'll tell you for nothing why that was – it was because the Ladies' stunk to high heaven. Holding my nose and touching up my lipstick in the mirror, I muttered to myself, 'I bet he never brought Diana here.' I wouldn't have minded, but the Savoy was just across the street.

When I think of the 'rueful' and 'wistful', I think of Edna O'Brien. What would we do for kicks without the old girl, I invariably ask myself when I read the reviews of her latest novel. Is there any other writer, apart from me, who consistently makes such a show of themselves for the benefit of the gaiety of nations? Now, she's definitely an autumnist – rueful, wistful, shoulders drooping with regret and ennui (yet rallying bravely with each whiff of spring), carrying her emotional baggage under her eyes. I bet her lovers (autumnists always have lovers, never boyfriends or shags – not rueful enough) tell her that her hair is the 'colour of autumn leaves' (i.e. rotting). That must be why she keeps it that preposterous colour.

But even Miss O'Brien's hair is not half as florid as her prose. In her new book, fields 'translate into nuptials, into blood', a lake is a 'great whooshing belly', while 'fathoms deep the frail and rusted shards, the relics of the battles of long ago' do their worst. And it really doesn't get much worse than this. To me, people can be divided into two types: those who have read *Cold Comfort Farm* and those who have not. And those who have not should have their voting rights removed forthwith; and, if they are scribblers, all writing implements taken from them, too. This is not cruel treatment. On the contrary, it is compassionate, like removing the belt and shoelaces of a potential suicide.

Autumn brings out the worst in all artists. Like sirens on the rocks of public ridicule, cheap metaphors beckon by the bushel-load – rotting, renewal, taking stock, husbanding resources, gathering in: a regular little Harvest Festival of homilies. Under autumn's fusty, musty, thoroughly unwholesome influence, even a team such as Anderson and Weill will come up with a monstrosity like 'September Song', the sentiments of which pretty much amount to 'Get your kit off, I'll be croaking soon!' Justin Hayward had it about right with his smash Eighties hit, 'Forever Autumn', in which the season is shown as one colossal hangover, about as much fun as licking out last night's ashtray.

When I was little, I belonged to the Puffin Club, and one month we were all asked to write about our favourite month. Naturally, we all wrote about December, because we got presents then.

Imagine our distress when, in the next newsletter, the Puffin Club announced sniffily, for the first and only time, that it was severely disappointed in its young members and that though there would be winners, only two winning entries would be printed, and those with a bad grace. The more priggish and eager-to-please of us got the message then that liking Christmas best was babyish and greedy, and that if we wanted to be taken seriously by grown-ups we'd have to go for something less obvious. Less fun, in fact.

Well, that left summer out, because summer was such a blast, all candy floss and funfairs and being sick on the way home from the seaside. Spring doesn't really occur to children as being a season – it only takes on real resonance when you've had your heart broken a few times, being almost as full of cheap metaphors as autumn. Which left autumn itself: a season with a face that surely only Mother Nature could love, the eternal party pooper, forever raining on one's parade. In a culture that seems to think there is something noble and moral about deferred gratification, autumn is the natural season of choice.

Not mine, though, for I am a confirmed live-now, pay-later summerist, who cannot help but believe that youth, health, wealth and beauty are meant to be fuel, to be burned in pursuit of pleasure, and not fruit to be pickled in anticipation of some future famine. (Hang on a minute and I'll get my sequins out and give you a quick rendition of 'My Way'.)

So I'll crank up Bob Marley singing 'Sun Is Shining', despite the evidence of my own eyes, and leave it to the autumnists to 'take stock' over a nice cup of thrifty broth, have a good old brood over Christmas and then, in spring, 'turn over a new leaf'. No doubt they'll learn from their mistakes, and I never will – but then again, they're rotten bores who count their change in restaurants and complain about the service, and I'm not, so I definitely know who I think got the better deal.

9 OCTOBER 1999

When do you think you can finally be called old, without fear of contraception? Surely there are enough physical signposts along the way. (I always think of them being cruelly defaced and deceptive, like the ones the wonderful Welsh Nationalists left behind in the Seventies.) Sure, a spreading girth and salt-and-pepper hair won't make you Homecoming Queen of Kookai's communal changing rooms, but weight can be lost and hair can be dyed and suddenly you're not the sticky end of the lollipop any more.

No, you know you're really old when your mouth starts

looking like a cat's anus. For those of you who haven't had the pleasure recently of having a puss shove its butt in your face (I'm told it's a gesture of affection and respect, but I'll take a box of chocs any day), look at recent photos of Iggy Pop. See it? The body's still buff, but those lips: it's like there's a tiny man standing on his tongue sewing his mouth closed from the inside. It's sort of ruched, and sort of frilled, and altogether horrible. Mick Jagger and Jeffrey Archer have it, too – and so does Edna O'Brien, judging by that lovely big picture of her in the paper last week.

An equally visible, though even more irritating, sign of becoming old is a tendency to cry more on happy occasions than on sad ones. Last week, I went to an awards luncheon honouring what I believe are called Everyday Heroes. (I'd never been to anything like this before.) With me was my longest-serving friend, Mrs Karen Wilson, who has known me since I was three and has spent a great deal of the subsequent 37 years regarding me as 'a hard-faced bitch spawned in Hades and just not deserving parents like yours because, frankly, you're a total cow, Julie, and you'll never get a boyfriend!' (Mrs W at 13.)

Imagine her delight, then, when I became a heap of quivering mascara before the second gong had left the MC's hands. I wasn't even drunk, and I cried through it all. Predictably, it was the bursts of pertinent music accompanying the heroes' trium-phant progress to the stage that started me off. I began okay, with just a lump forming at the back of my throat – which I told myself was a bit of badly digested chicken chasseur – as four giggling teenage girls who'd rescued the old lady who'd fallen down the stairs went up to got their award to the strains of 'Help!' – a sentiment I was soon silently echoing by the time a little girl who had been physically unable to smile until six months ago trotted back to her table to 'The Most Beautiful Girl in the World'.

I grabbed my napkin and blew my nose in it, hard.

'What in God's name are you doing with that serviette!' hissed Mrs Wilson, appalled. 'It's not a serviette, it's a napkin!' I hissed back, equally so. Then I stopped, poleaxed with horror. The master of ceremonies was now treating us to the story of a 77-year-old man who had fought off a drug-crazed burglar, and I just knew what soundtrack they'd use to accompany his long and painful walk to the podium. Yes, it was! 'I Will Survive'. Oh, no! I started blubbing really loudly. Thankfully, the applause drowned my racket.

We moved quickly through a supergran (three lorry-loads of goods for Bulgarian orphans – 'Wind Beneath My Wings'), a good Samaritan teenager (picked up man with broken neck in street, didn't mind when paramedics cut the roof out of his uninsured new car – 'Driving in My Car'), a meningitis-surviving tot ('Every Little Thing She Does Is Magic') and, I'm afraid to say, I made a complete spectacle of myself to that awful song from *Friends* when we honoured a gentleman who'd given a kidney to his dying daughter – 'I'll be there for yoo-oo!' will never sound the same again. By the time the beautiful teenager in the wheelchair was leaving the stage to 'Isn't She Lovely', Mrs Wilson was threatening to take me outside until I calmed down.

Then something really bad happened. We were told the awful story of a Pakistani family whose shop was set upon by 25 sacks of scum in human form, ending up in a terrible beating for the husband, the wife and their two sons. After initially deciding to close their shop and move away, the family had decided to stay put. As Mohammed and Zubalda supported each other to the stage – they must have been at least 60 – the familiar sounds of Chumbawumba's Tubthumping rose up: 'I get KNOCKED

DOWN!/But I get UP AGAIN!/You're never gonna keep me down!' Even this bit seemed inappropriate and crass, looking at the heartbreakingly gracious and dignified couple making their way through the tables of big, loud white people.

Then I remembered the next bit, and I prayed that the organisers had thought to edit the song in an appropriate manner. But no. As the Faqirs got on to the podium, the applause dropped and that bit boomed out loud and clear – 'PISSING the night away/PISSING the night away' – before moving on to the gimmick, 'He drinks a whiskey drink/He drinks a cider drink/He drinks a vodka drink/He drinks a lager drink.' I ask you, could anything have been less suitable? Not only were the Faqirs extremely likely to be religious, and so opposed to alcohol, but it seems extremely likely, going on past evidence, that the 25 heroes who attacked them had probably been at the whiskey, cider, vodka and lager drinks themselves.

I found this thought immensely upsetting, and started laughing in a manner I can only describe as hysterical. The whole thing made me think about the sheer inappropriateness of music at certain times, yet how it has become ubiquitous; how every famine, plane crash and war comes served up with a song, as though the sheer fact of human tragedy wasn't enough and we need extra pathos to squeeze our shagged-out hearts. I remember how horribly crass I found the use of The Cars' 'Drive' – a tu'penny ha'penny song about the breakdown of some dreary little relationship – over footage of crying, starving children during the Live Aid crusade. I'm sure that if the concentration camps were liberated today we'd see the footage on TV with Celine Dion singing 'My Heart Will Go On' over it.

Just as the Nazis could cry over Schubert sonatas at the drop of a hat and then go back to torturing children without missing a beat, the emotions which music arouse in us can obscure, rather than illuminate, the cause of human suffering. Please, BBC: when we see the inevitable *Panorama* about the Paddington train crash, spare us the Manics doing 'If You Tolerate This, Your Children Will Be Next'. Sometimes, incredibly, the sound of silence is the only appropriate response.

23 OCTOBER 1999

There's a great bit in Nora Ephron's book *Heartburn* where the heroine's editor reveals to her that he is devastated due to his wife running off with another woman. When the heroine looks confused, the editor says, 'What? Did you think she was too attractive to be a lesbian?'

'No,' admits the heroine, predicting the Lipstick Lesbian craze by a good decade, 'I didn't think she was attractive enough to be a lesbian.'

I don't know when it happened, but the same thing has happened with feminism. Thirty years ago, if you saw a hatchet-faced harpy hissing at a beautiful blonde, chances are the first would be the feminist and the second the anti-feminist, relying on her physical charms to get what she wanted out of men. These days (and I say this with no desire to wound, being something of a hatchet-faced harpy myself), the first is likely to be the anti-feminist hissing at the beautiful career girl to get back to the kitchen. Reading the newspapers – especially *The Sunday Times* and the *Daily Mail*, which are fast becoming the respective broadsheet and tabloid parish magazines of that sad cul-de-sac of Middle England that is kept awake at nights by the idea that some woman, somewhere, is having fun – it is striking and surreal to see educated women, those beneficiaries of the long, hard struggle for women's rights, explaining why women have too much freedom, and why the Spice Girls and Denise van Outen should be burned at the stake for setting a bad example to impressionable young gels.

Apart from anything else, women who write anti-feminist pieces are hypocrites, and that's never a nice thing to be. If these women really want their crackpot views about girls robbing boys of their education and women stealing men's jobs to be taken seriously, they should stop writing and get cooking. There are thousands of unemployed male journalists out there, many of them with families to support, who could be filling that space instead. For some reason, women captains of industry are bad and unnatural, but women journalists aren't. Funny, that.

When I see an anti-feminist, she is invariably suffering from one of two plights: the younger sort can't get a boyfriend, no matter how hard she tries, and believes that putting other women down will make her attractive to men; the older sort is usually married, has long ceased to enjoy sex, and naturally feels that the easygoing, snout-in-the-trough attitude to sex displayed by younger women will make hubby likely to stray from home and hearth. The crankiest of this sort is obsessed with women she sees as home-wrecking career girls, forever hiding behind the water-cooler with their skirts around their waists, beckoning the poor salaryman as he attempts to scuttle home to his wife and two veg.

There is a horrible, priggish strain of you're-not-going-out-dressed-like-thatism among older once feminists when they look at younger women. You can all but hear them sucking their teeth over the garden fence and saying, 'Well, and she's no better than she should be!' as they watch Denise sashay down Media Street in her pussy-pelmet.

These women talk about how glad they are to be no longer slaves of the sexual marketplace. The fact is, they are stark, staring mad at young women because young women, like young men, will always be more physically beautiful than old ones. I've never been able to understand such spiteful envy myself. Though my youth and beauty have long since fled, I find that I am sometimes moved to tears by the sight of beautiful, brilliant, young women – especially when they show them getting their exam results on TV; that kills me. When I see pictures of Zoe Ball, Samantha Janus or Kate Moss, to name but a few, I want to stand up and punch the air and make that moronic woo-woo noise that Americans make when watching sport. THAT'S OUR TEAM, THAT IS! Look at those golden girls GO! My generosity to young women in journalism is legendary, and just because I've had sex with a few of them, the principle's still the thing. There are few things as widely enjoyed in some circles as catfights, and when these old boots start up criticising young women, they are staging such a low entertainment with the sole aim of sucking up to men. It's very undignified – and I know how big they are on dignity.

What fear must have been struck into these women's wizened old hearts when a recent survey revealed that, for the first time, young men are more concerned that a prospective wife should have good career prospects than a perfect figure or an ability to cook! I wasn't a bit surprised; the fact is that, for the first time, men and women have truly become mates in something other than the biological sense, and are having a bloody good time together when they're left to get on with it. Far from being terrified of girls like van Outen, young men are actually madly attracted by that combination of sexiness and matiness, good humour and assertiveness.

Heavens above, they don't even seem to mind that she breaks

wind frequently and finds it amusing! Whatever next? Shameless hussies eating in public? But how will they ever fasten their corsets? I know it's never fun to glimpse a fantastic-looking party through a window and know you're not invited, but try to get over it, ladies!

It is, I believe, largely sexual frustration that leads women into becoming anti-feminists, forever spitefully lashing out at the likes of the Spices and van Outens, girls who dare to Have It All – that is, a career and a love life and children. 'It all!' It's strange that what is considered a greedy mania for women is considered basic human rights for men. Imagine saying a man wanted 'it all' because he refused to rule out either work or marriage, and you'll see exactly what a silly, ill-sorted idea this is. It used to be said of feminists that all they needed was 'a good seeing to'; life being rich and strange, we have now reached the point where, incredibly, it is the anti-feminists who need a good seeing to in order to calm their resentful envy of young, sexy, ambitious women. Maybe even a little light lesbo action might put a smile on their miserable faces.

On second thoughts, no. I'll do a lot to further the feminist cause, but I won't do that.

13 NOVEMBER 1999

My friend comes back from New York to visit, and the first thing she says as she comes through the door is, 'Have you heard that really rude record?'

I try to narrow it down: 'What, rude-sexy? About sex?'

'No, just rude! It's the rudest song you've ever heard!'

It took us ten minutes to find it on MTV: 'Larger Than Life', by The Backstreet Boys. The chorus goes, 'All you people can't you see, can't you see/How your love's affecting our reality/When it goes wrong/You can make it right/And that makes you larger than life!'

Hear that, girls? You're not just a many-mawed monster, good only as a market for shoddy merchandise – because you love The Backstreet Boys, you're a star, too! Hmm . . . I think I prefer the straightforward contempt of Guns N' Roses, who were wont to urinate on their devoted fans from hotel balconies.

On another level, at the recent launch of Tina Brown's *Talk* magazine (I wonder how many advertising executives were paid how many millions of dollars to come up with a name that sounds like a magazine your mum would read?), Demi Moore was reported to have gestured at the nearby celebrity-watching crowds and remarked to Tina, 'Can you imagine how we look to those people?' What Moore looks like is, probably, a woman who hasn't had a hit film since Drew Barrymore was a druggie; whose massive investment of time, money and energy in her physical appearance has resulted in a body that, the more of it she reveals, the more tightly the paying punters seem to hold on to their cash, and that proved insufficient glue to keep her boastfully 'hot' marriage together. And there she was talking to a woman who looks like Lulu. I couldn't swear to it, but I bet the expression on those pilgrims' faces wasn't so much sheer, molten awe as mild curiosity, like the faces of people looking into the monkey house at the zoo. Look, they're almost human.

Celebrities have very little idea how indifferent most people are to them. As Planet Hollywoods and Fashion Cafés take a nose-dive; as docu-soaps, animal shows and decorating and gardening programmes trounce big-budget TV star vehicles; as *The Blair Witch Project* (with not a star in sight) becomes the most profitable film ever; as pop groups who, a few years ago, believed that a good section of the young generation would gladly lay down their lives for them now face losing their record labels (Duran Duran's John Taylor was even reduced to advertising for a girlfriend in the *Spectator*); and as video games continue to eat into the profits of the music industry, there seems only one conclusion: if you want to get ahead, make sure you're smaller than life. Hey, babe, take a walk on the mild side. Even men's sexual fantasies, apparently, are mostly about women at work or the girl next door. The members of the Fame Club will hang on to their illusions for as long as they can, of course: what, exactly, would an individual with as few inner resources or as little life of the mind as Demi Moore (who, according to one recent report, was visibly intimidated by Liz Hurley's intellect at one Hollywood dinner party) do or be if she weren't famous? The Fame Club acts as sanctuary and soft cell to all the needy souls who find that life as a little person inflicts far too much psychic damage on them – it's a place where they can meet to lick each other's wounds and whisper in each other's ears of their specialness. The Fame Club throws up the strangest alliances: Demi and Tina, Puff Daddy and Ivana Trump, Fergie and Billy Connolly – even Rupert Murdoch is happy to appear on *The Simpsons* as a power-crazed maniac because, hell, it's *The Simpsons*! Let some faceless hack call him that, on the other hand, and he'd be on their case.

Once in a while, however, a star is born who shows no understanding of the Fame Club's rules and lays about them with all the glee of the little boy pointing out that the emperor really does have no clothes. They remind us that you don't strictly have to be a bum-sucking toerag to make it. Jennifer Lopez is delightfully dismissive of the co-stars who have tried to bed her and the dishwasher blondes who walked off with the roles that were rightfully hers because they once sat on Steven Spielberg's knee when they were a babe. Sophie Marceau recently made a splendid show of herself: Michelle Pfeiffer? 'So boring.' *Titanic*? 'Boring and completely stupid.' Robert De Niro? 'A funny little man I didn't even recognise.' The late President Mitterrand, who once sought to impress her over dinner? 'Really weird and touchy.'

For whatever reason, stars have become smaller. When we look at photographs of Bogart and Bacall, Gardner and Sinatra, Monroe and DiMaggio, they give meaning to that raddled old whore of a word, 'charisma'. But when we see pictures of Brad'n'Jen, Tom'n'Nicole and Gwyneth'n'Whoever, we know that we could find ten couples in the local disco who appear more sexy and compelling. I have always felt that the true test of whether a celebrity couple has it is whether we can imagine them having bigger, better and weirder sex than us. I can just about believe that Ava Gardner had more fun in bed than me, but Tom'n'Nicole? Come on – Pinky and Perky hit the wilder shores of love with greater regularity.

Stars are not the people who are best at what they do; they are merely the people who want it most. Madonna, the biggest star in the world, demonstrates this more than any other: a million girls are better-looking, better dancers, better actresses, better singers, but did any of them want it more? Closer to home, Geri Halliwell and Chris Evans prove that needing it is a better bet than beauty or talent every time when it comes to making it; perfectly suited in mediocrity, as in colouring, they have all the steaming chemistry of the little couple living in the weather-house.

The stalking of stars is a terrible thing, but it's surprising that it happens as little as it does. To achieve fame, a person must work obsessively at pushing themselves into the consciousness of millions of complete strangers; this is very odd in itself, and easily as odd as the act of stalking.

'Look at me! Love me!' demands the star. Can they really be so surprised when the odd unbalanced civilian takes them at their word? When the star is stalked, he or she has achieved the logical outcome of their ambition: to one sad soul, at least, they really are the most important thing in the world – truly, larger than life.

20 NOVEMBER 1999

Just recently, I've started having the scariest dreams. Not wake-up-screaming scary, but scary in their banality. Last week, I dreamed that I was thirsty and wanted an icy Fanta from the fridge, but that it was too cold to go and get one. And do you know what? When I woke up, I did go and get it, even though it was cold. The next day, I dreamed that my boyfriend gave me a lift to Marks & Spencer on his way to work – and yes, within two hours, I was rooting around in the Luxury Fish cabinet. Either I've achieved the gift of prophecy, or I'm just incredibly boring. However, this week, there was great excitement when I dreamed that a) the journalist Miranda Sawyer had won a small part in a television hospital drama, and b) that I'd broken my favourite Frosti-Mug. So far, neither has transpired.

Is this what I've got to look forward to: a lifetime of dreams about watching paint dry? It has been suggested to me that this is happening for exactly the same reason I don't have sexual fantasies any more. When you've packed an awful lot in, so to speak, in a relatively short time, and you've spent your life pretty much following your desires wherever they may take you, there isn't an awful lot of slack for the mind to play with.

'Dreams': the very word conjures up sumptuous vistas of the barely believable, fantastic transports of delight. Is this what I get for having a happy private life at last – dreams that make *Watercolour Challenge* look exciting? It wasn't always this way. In my teens, twenties and early thirties, I had the most amazing dream life, which would more often than not wake me up in a blushing muck-sweat, glancing across the bed at various husbands, to see if I'd been rumbled. My first husband actually caught me out committing adultery with my second when, having fallen asleep on the marital sofa one night under the loving gaze of Husband One – 'Exhausted herself baking cookies, poor sweet!' – I began to talk loudly and extremely graphically about what I would do to my lover next time I saw him. How we laughed!

During my second marriage – my husband having been a bit of a lad, though by then totally uxorious – I was tormented by the most amazingly rude dreams of his putative adultery, often with the most unlikely people (Princess Margaret once, I remember), which would leave me in such a fury next day that I would often not speak him for the next 24 hours, reducing the poor follow to the depths of despair.

Then, in the early Nineties, when I'd gone off both of them, I started to have the most outrageous dreams about famous people – it was during this period, of *Modern Review* Rat Pack repute, that I probably got a bit carried away by my own publicity, shall we say, and was so intent on admiring the reflection in the pool that I tumbled all the way in, self-adoringly treading water in the shallow end of my own psyche. In the space of two weeks I had the following dreams:

A week after Elizabeth Hurley became the first actress to advance her career by putting on her clothes – That Dress – and was popularly believed to be about the most desirable thing on the planet after her boyfriend, I had the most amazingly realistic dream that the pair of them were fighting over my sexual favours outside the front door of my flat. I dived under the bed, all the better to protect my honour, but such was their frenzy that I could clearly hear their voices from my lowly sanctuary.

'Leave it, Liz! She's straight, I tell you!'

'Oh, sod off, H! I saw her first! In the Ladies', at the Groucho!' Sound of savage shin-kicking. 'Now get out of the way!'

In my dream, I moaned to my husband, 'Make them go! Get the police!' Then I woke up.

A week later, I was travelling across Siberia with Madonna sitting opposite me in the first-class carriage of the Trans-Siberian Express. Wrapped in soft furs, she looked beautiful and alluring, much better than her photographs. She was staring at me. But when I leaned forward to speak to her, I saw that she was crying, very quietly and softly, perfect tears dropping like tiny diamonds from Max Factor'd lashes.

I sat back in my seat, confused. At that moment, though, the train stopped and Oprah Winfrey got on. She stepped up into our carriage, cast a look at Madonna and sat down beside me. As the train started moving, I whispered under cover of the noise, 'Oprah, why's Madonna crying?'

Oprah looked at me with that famous steady gaze, and then at the now openly blubbing Madge. Then she spoke: 'Girl, she used to be the most famous woman in the world. Now you are.' Leaning across the carriage, she tapped Madge smartly on the knee. 'I said, get used to it, bitch!'

Those were the days. Now I'm reduced to listening to other people's celebrity dreams with the open-mouthed, green-eyed envy that sumptuously appointed globe-trotting inspires in the impoverished and deskbound. Recently, my boyfriend dreamed that Tom Hanks had kidnapped us, my friend Emma and Ken Livingstone, and that he'd tied us all to hospital trolleys and was masturbating over us prior to torturing us to death. 'And you all thought I was such a nice guy, huh?' he kept saying as he whetted the chainsaw. I know it must have been damned unpleasant – my boy can't even watch *Big* any more (previously one of his favourite films) – but I felt nothing but covetousness. The bittersweet phrase, 'I can dream, can't I?' takes on a hollow ring when you can't.

11 DECEMBER 1999

Heard the one about the sexist, racist, middle-aged French model agent? You're right, it's a trick question. Because perhaps the strangest thing about the Gerald Marie affair – unspeakable boss of Elite Models, exposed by *MacIntyre Undercover* as a lecher and a cad – is not that Elite attempted to reinstate him so quickly last week (two days after his agency accepted his resignation for his 'shocking, unacceptable and highly inappropriate' behaviour) but that he was ever suspended in the first place. (Only the last-minute intervention of Elite's American chairman, grand old John Casablancas, scuppered French Elite's sneaky plan.)

As with the reviled It Girls and Fat Cats, and now poor Posh Spice, Marie has done nothing at all unusual or bad by the standards of his tribe. Young, upper-class women lead useless lives, shopping and lunching taking the place of the loving and working that Freud said it takes to make a fully rounded human being; businessmen make vilely unfair profits from the sweat of the workers; young female entertainers purge themselves of every pinch of excess flesh, all the better to evade the ceaseless nagging and sneering of the *Daily Mail*. This is considered, most of the time, the perfectly desirable, naturally ordered way of things in *Daily Mail* Land. But once in a while, as a kind of human sacrifice to appease the gods of the Twitching Net

Curtains, one of their number must be thrown to the wolves so that this most excellent state of affairs may continue.

Modelling is totally about sex. To let anyone who is not a heterosexual woman, a gay man or a eunuch have any position of power in it is as irresponsible as letting a child molester work in a crèche. To be faced daily by scores of physically perfect women at the peak of their fertility asking you to inspect their breasts, hips and bottoms – well, really. How can you expect any straight man not to feel like a cross between a kid in a candy shop, a miser in a counting-house and a sultan in a harem?

The thoroughly 'respectable' fashion and cosmetics industries frequently use models under the age of consent as the apex of female beauty. I remember a particularly repulsive American advertisement for perfume which, under a photograph of a ten-year-old girl, read: You're A Wholesome Woman From The Very Beginning. In an industry that considers glossy hair, extreme slenderness and unlined skin the most important things a woman can offer the world, of course teenage girls will be the most desirable females. And desirable means physically, as well as fiscally, desirable. Marie's crime appears to have been that he is the only honest model broker in a world of cant and correctness. Personally, I was less offended by his comments than by the recent participation by supermodels in the Fashion Targets Breast Cancer appeal. Frankly, if I was a woman facing a single or double mastectomy, the last thing I would want to look at would be photographs of beautiful women with perfect breasts in tight T-shirts telling me how sympathetic they were to my breast cancer.

Modelling is about selling the bodies of women to the highest bidder. Model agents are, Marie pointed out, highly elevated pimps. Even his 'racist' remarks are not easily condemned if you think for more than half a minute about them. In expressing a preference for the looks of white women over black women, he was doing nothing more than what the fashion and beauty business does as a matter of course; he was discriminating. Why it is okay to discriminate in the matter of tall over short, thin over fat, beautiful over plain, but not black over white, no one has yet properly explained to me. It is all very well for Naomi Campbell to throw a strop over how she only earns £5 million a year as opposed to the £10 million she'd be getting if she was white (Iman earned £2 million in her 'worst' year of modelling) – but how can we talk of 'fairness' when a woman born arbitrarily beautiful can earn in an hour staring into a small circle of ground glass what a nurse can earn in a year? Incredibly, that's no exaggeration.

When it comes to beauty, you can't pass laws about what people should like – 'The heart wants what it wants,' as Woody Allen pointed out, the only smart thing he ever said. I wouldn't sleep with a blond or ginger man, or a bald man, or a fat man, or a man over 29 – sue me!

The fashion and beauty businesses have nothing to do with real life and real women; a cross between a huge international brothel and Never-Never Land, they are utterly fantastic, and should be treated as such. To demand that they act 'responsibly' by using a certain quota of black models, fat, old models or disabled models is to credit them with far more respect and influence than they deserve.

With splendid insouciance and bad taste, the cosmetics giant L'Oréal Paris has just seen fit to mark the millennium with a new range of make-up 'which combines universal appeal', as *OK!* magazine puts it. 'L'Oréal has captured the essence of feminine beauty from all corners of the globe . . . four looks which allow each woman to achieve an individual look to fit her own personal style.' This accompanied by the make-up collections

Indian Saffron, Western Blush, Asian Fever (dangerously close to 'Yellow Peril' I'd have thought) and, wait for it, African Ochre. The choice of models is extraordinary – or rather would be, if modelling, fashion or beauty made sense. The light-skinned, half-black model Vanessa Williams is India, the French Laetitia Casta is the white West, while Milla Jovovich turns up as Asia.

Even stranger, at a time when the beauty industry is under fire as never before for ignoring black models, Jovovich turns up again as the main attraction, African Ochre, daubed all over in blue, red and black paint. This is, apparently, 'A homage to the beauty of the women of this continent, including colours inspired by the unique landscape of Africa'. A razor-thin teenage Ukrainian girl, so white that she must glow in the dark, painted blue to represent the beauty of black women? It's mad – but no madder than a young woman throwing over her education in order to go into a profession where she will have to display her body to millions of disgusting men and be finished by 30. In a mad world, surely only a mad reaction makes sense? R. D. Laing himself, I cannot help but feel, would be proud of poor Gerald Marie.

2000

22 JANUARY 2000

My mother died last week. Shut up at the back, there. I know that you're whispering, 'Oh no – she only just stopped banging on about her father dying, and now we're going to be treated to her mum's untimely demise in 50 episodes, too!'

Well, no, you won't be, because it was the shortest, sweetest heart attack in history. This isn't going to be one of my 'poor me' pieces, but rather an essay on the elegance and appropriateness of the English way of death, which I think gets rather a bad press these days – not least from George Monbiot in this very newspaper last week. In my mother's case, her death is also a testament to the devotion of the English working classes to their pet animals. When my father died 14 months ago, one of the last things he said to my mother was to be sure to look after the dog, a cheerful mongrel called Benny. Some months ago, the dog became ill with tumours, which was what my dad had died of. On 8 January, Benny joined the majority. On the 10th, my mum followed him.

There seems to be something so inevitable, so cosy, about this that an untoward show of grief would seem selfish and silly. It hurts to be stuck here like a lemon without them but, hey, you have to try and take the long view.

'Are you in shock?' some of my friends have asked me, but I don't reckon I am. I've had a good snivel, alone or with my boyfriend – and you do feel a bit better afterwards, like a radiator that has been bled. However, my very warm, very kind, very working-class extended family made it clear to me within an hour of my mother's death that blubbing *en général* wasn't the thing to do at all.

'You're going to have to be a bit braver than this, Julie!' snapped my Auntie Dolly, a saint of a woman, when I tried it on when we were driving home from the hospital.

'Y-y-yes,' I stuttered like a brave little soldier. Then I blurted, 'Auntie Doll, do you believe in an afterlife?'

'No!' came the answer from the front seat. 'Once you're dead, you're dead!'

I went mulishly silent at this. There is too an afterlife! I thought to myself. I believe very much in life after death, very much in the conventional mode of soft mists and eternal content, and can easily imagine my mum, dad and dog romping through some celestial meadow together, like in some Timotei advert. I suspect that I may have spent too much time at Sunday school as a child, but too late to change that now. It keeps me happy – and, anyway, I'm not the one rushing out in search of grief counselling.

The thing is that not giving in to grief does actually make you feel happier. You know that the dead person wouldn't want you to be sad and – supposing I'm right and there is an afterlife – it's going to be raining on their parade a bit, to say the least, if they're up there having the time of their (after) lives and they can see you, whom they loved, carrying on like Niagara down here, isn't it?

I'd started out whining, 'I can't do anything! I don't know what to do!' and yet, after just a little bit of a scolding, I had the funeral booked, the organ, cornea and skin transplants signed for and going ahead, and the death notice in the paper, all within 24 hours.

What I'm saying is, if I can do it, anyone can – and they don't half make you feel better, all those formalities and tidying-up jobs.

But, according to George Monbiot, I'm not doing myself any favours. In his opinion, it would bode a lot better for my future mental health if I were to 'kiss and embrace corpses, wailing and keening, paying tribute to the undeniably dead', as the ever-estimable 'other cultures' do.

His argument reminded me of a Victoria Wood joke that was intended to show up the passionlessness of the British: 'In India when a man dies,' she said, 'his widow throws herself on the funeral pyre. Over here, she says, "Fifty ham baps, Beryl – you slice, I'll butter."'

But in reality, of course, those widows are thrown on to their dead husbands' funeral pyres – they don't jump. I know which alternative I prefer, and also which shows the most respect for life.

Later in the same article, Mr Monbiot approves warmly of the Dani people of West Papua, for whom the dead, he explains, are everywhere. Apparently, when the living sit around at home of an evening, they leave spaces for all of the dead members of the family, and even give them as much tobacco and as much food as they give to the living.

I'm sorry, but I just do not believe this. For instance, where do they draw the line? Surely, as time goes on, there is simply not enough room for all the dead Dani ancestors to crowd into those modest-sized huts of their living relatives – it's not for nothing that they are called 'the majority', after all. Also, I'm sure that food and tobacco aren't so plentiful in West Papua that the Dani can afford to waste it nightly on a bunch of fussy eaters – i.e., the Dead. What's more, I really don't see why I should respect this tradition any more than I would a childless Western couple who nevertheless leave out a mince pie and a glass of Baileys Irish Cream for Santa Claus every 24 December.

Far from suggesting an ease with death, such gluts of weeping, wailing and generally having the ab-dabs – whether in Mexico, Mombasa or Morecambe – surely signal its exact opposite: a childish refusal to accept death as part of life, but rather to view it as something that is perpetually shocking and upsetting. The British way of death, on the other hand, says simply that life goes on. You slice, I'll butter.

This is not life-denying; instead, it is the most life-affirming notion that the human heart can hold: that we all – living and dead alike – go on together, and that nothing can really divide us. A socialism of souls, if you like.

There may well be some pretty unfortunate consequences of English 'repressing' – though judging from the general state of mental health in let-it-all-out America, this seems increasingly debatable – but our hands-on, heads-down, get-on-with-it attitude to death is not, I think, one of them.

29 JANUARY 2000

I seldom go to the cinema – largely for the same reasons that I rarely, if ever, lick out toilet bowls or watch paint dry – unless it is to accompany my 13-year-old son to one of those three-and-a-half-hour subtitled films about the Dalai Lama, which he feels are such a vital part of his spiritual and artistic development.

However, once a year comes a film so deliciously preposterous-sounding and so roundly and universally ridiculed that I am forced – in the interests of hilarity and sociology – to abandon my rule and treat myself. By and large, this divine error will be to see what they call a 'British film', usually one that has been adapted from an acclaimed novel and that aims itself fair and square at Mr Blair's 'trendy' New Britain. And, invariably, there will be a great deal of people associated with it – all of whom previously had a good deal of credibility – suddenly Losing It Big Time. Last year's choice cut, for example, was *Mad Cows*, in which a veritable smorgasbord of previously immaculate reputations – among them Anna Friel, Joanna Lumley, Sophie Dahl, Kathy Lette, director Sarah Sugarman – were roundly trashed, rather in the manner of that awesome machine that can reduce the lushest of luxury motors into a one-inch metal cube. This year's treat has got to be *Rancid Aluminium*, in which a gaggle of ace Brit faces – Tara Fitzgerald, Rhys Ifans, Sadie Frost, a Fiennes, Dani Behr, Nick Moran – are left with a good deal of egg on them. Bless!

The reviews for the film have been uniformly vile, but the one that interested me most pointed out that, as both Steven Berkoff and Keith Allen were in it, its dreadfulness was signalled well in advance and so anyone who parted with their money for a ticket expecting decent – as opposed to indecent – entertainment had only themselves to blame. The way this critic described it, the Allen/Berkoff alliance was a sort of Stalin–Hitler pact of bad acting and general hammery.

Now, I know that, while living the lotus-eating life down here in soft old Sussex, I've taken my eye off the ball a bit in recent years, but the last time I looked both Berkoff and Allen were bywords for raw, simmering sexuality, fierce integrity and, frankly incendiary talent. Now, apparently, they pack a punch somewhere between that of Mutt and Jeff, and Crystal Tips and Alistair. In short, they've Lost It. How'd that happen?

I think I know. It's because people want to lose it. This is a previously unexplored avenue, as credibility is popularly considered something that we cling to through thick and thin. As a lividly thin, pale, credible young thing (moi) wrote in *The Face* back in – aaiiieeee! – 1984: 'Credibility has replaced paying one's dues as the official credentials needed before a career in the communications industry can get off the launch pad. When you are rich and famous, you can do without it – though it hurts you so! – and once it is gone you will just have to live with the loss. Like virginity or a contact lens, once you lose your credibility you won't get it back, at least not in this life.'

But was I happy? Well, yes, but not as happy as I am now that I'm a portly old hack with about as much cred as a hostess trolley. I was talented, too; why, looking back at my second collection, *Sex and Sensibility*, I think there's a case for saying that between the years of 1983 and 1992 I was the best critic and essayist in this country, which probably means THE WORLD. Those were the days when I could change Kim Philby's mind about giving another interview to the West; when Radio 4 called me 'the cleverest woman in Britain'.

And did I enjoy it? No. Couldn't handle it. Used to get actually physically sick before I wrote; I was thinking too much, you see. Nowadays I only get sick when I drink too much, which is a much better deal.

There is a real, sensual kick that comes with Losing It, which I'm sure Messrs Berkoff and Allen have discovered for themselves and which explains why they are pursuing their goal so thoroughly. You're not meant to say it, though. You can leave your children, dump your spouse and put your parents out to grass on a sex farm, and still get away with it, in reasonably Bohemian circles. But if you – happily! – admit to betraying your talent, there's the most ridiculous amount of wailing, teeth-gnashing and finger-pointing.

It's mean to say it, of course, but the types who go in for this sort of moralising – oh what you could have been! – are always the types who never had any talent themselves in the first place, and so can't believe you had the gall to throw yours away. Think of poor Salieri, beseeching God to give the Gift to him and not to that moronic, dirty-minded 'creature' Mozart. Or of the hotel waiter who turned up at George Best's suite door bearing two bottles of Moët on ice: Best was back in Belfast to open a supermarket, for which he'd been paid £20,000 in cash, which now lay scattered across the king-size bed; his latest squeeze was the current Miss World, Mary Stavin, who was sat at the dressing table wearing two wisps of oyster silk and fixing her hair. The waiter took it all in – the Miss World, the £20,000, the champagne – and uttered the heartfelt cry, 'Oh, George, where did it all go wrong?'

Likewise, Laurence Olivier told Vivien Leigh, 'I am sick of the myth of the Glorious Couple', and promptly retired to Brighton with Joan Plowright, a woman as plain as her name, to commute every day to the Royal Court in London, taking a great delight in wearing his sober suit and hat, carrying an umbrella and briefcase, and passing for normal. Making films as bad as Harold Robbins's *The Betsy* was the ultimate luxury for him, not hardship – he was cocking a snook at that final sacred cow, his talent. The same happened to Richard Burton when he dumped the goddesses for a BBC PR girl and threw himself into a welter of bad films. It's like climbing Everest, destroying your talent; you do it because it's there.

If you've got it, flaunt it; if it ain't broke, break it. After a few years, there's something a bit precious about having too much talent, something a bit up yourself. Far better to throw it on the fire and join the hoi polloi. This, I am sure, was the reasoning behind the decision of those Titan talents Keith Allen and Steven Berkoff to make a film as bad as *Rancid Aluminium*. As one who has gone before them into the kingdom of mediocrity and found it a right laugh, I salute them.

5 FEBRUARY 2000

My friend's pregnant again. Fifth time in six years, all by the same man, and she's already chosen her next abortionist. Last time, it took 50 minutes from anaesthetic to home-time, and she felt so chirpy afterwards that she walked home and called me as she passed an Italian deli to see if I wanted anything. She is also half of the most devoted couple I know: six years, never a cross word that's not easily solved with a pen and thesaurus, and marriage on the cards. They go on holiday one hell of a lot – and I'm speaking as someone who took five last year. They've been together longer than anyone I know. Why? 'Because we don't have children. I know it sounds odd, but it's like every abortion brings us closer.'

'Don't you ever feel sort of weird, not even when you see really adorable babies in prams? Don't you ever feel sorry you had the last abortion, say?' Predictably, having turned 40 and buried my mother, I can't think of anything I'd like more than another baby. Women!

'No, but I'll tell you one thing for sure: there isn't a day that passes that I don't see at least one child who makes me thank God I've had four abortions, and vow to have four more, if I have to. When did all children start acting as if they're auditioning for *The Exorcist*?'

'What about X?' X is her boyfriend, a mature dreamboat with no apparent horn-buds or cloven hooves. 'Doesn't he ever feel regretful?'

'Don't be silly! I told you, X has three grown-up children from his first marriage. He said they're the reason it broke up. He was mad about his wife, then the children ruined everything. He says he's not in a hurry to lose another woman he loves that way.' Her pretty face clouded. 'I was feeling a bit wavery, actually. Then we went to Barbados. There were loads of families there. It was horrible, all these couples sitting there for hours, not speaking a word to each other, and the kids, like little jailers, demanding things non-stop. It was incredible to think that these people had originally been drawn together through attraction and sex. X just smiled at me sort of sadly and said, "See?"'

She shuddered. 'And I remembered that thing Sharon Stone said when reporters wouldn't stop asking if she was pregnant: "Climb out of my uterus, will ya?"' My friend shook her head. 'It seems to me that when you have a relationship it's private; it's your business. But the moment you're pregnant, suddenly everybody thinks it's their business. It's public. And everyone knows that public relationships never last.'

She's got a point. It's like the whole world, led by the media, has become one big interfering mother-in-law, forever coming forward and putting their oar in. We have all but abolished socialised childcare and the nanny state, but the organs of right-wing opinion have decided that women's bodies, once they have conceived, are nevertheless public property.

The fact that having children is a real laugh – I still think back to the infanthood of my second son as the happiest days of my life – has been totally lost in the static of censure. Everyone's got an opinion, especially those who don't have a womb. I wouldn't trust any of them, especially that alleged 'feminist', Dr Michel Odent, who recently suggested that men should stay out of the delivery room. Yeah, so male doctors feel free to deprive the putative mother of the painkilling drugs that the Odent tendency consider so wicked! This is the same Odent, don't forget, who last year suggested that women should devote themselves utterly to their children for the first few years after birth, while encouraging their husbands to pursue sex with other women! Funny, I didn't know that that was being a feminist; I thought it was being a Frenchman.

Women who work damage their children, says *Panorama*. Women who have affairs damage their children, says the *Guardian*. Women who drink even one glass of wine damage their children, say the doctors. Women who use technology to defer childbirth until they are settled and solvent damage their children, says the *Mail* in a fascinating about-face from a newspaper that previously prized social responsibility and self-reliance above all else, and spent decades demonising 'natural' teenage single mothers. (The *Mail* is extremely keen on Bad Mothers, which must be why, after calling me 'The Worst Mother In Britain' last year, it is now paying me £2 per word – must be those Wages Of Sin you hear about.)

On the other hand, says the equally strident evidence, simply by being born, children damage their mothers. Mothers are twice as likely to be depressed as non-mothers, and were recently discovered to be far less optimistic about the future. In a final, ironic twist, it appears that Mother Nature – since time immemorial the final authority to which the Family Values brigade resort – actually programmes women sexually to shut down on their husbands four years after the first child has been produced, and to stray elsewhere. If that doesn't happen, a third child will finish a marriage more often than not, anyway. DNA testing, meanwhile, has revealed that one in ten children is sending the card to the wrong man on Father's Day.

But if the organs of the silent majority – *Panorama*, the *Mail* and the rest – really want women to start enthusiastically replenishing and caring for the nation's stock once more, I suggest they call a moratorium on the Bad Mother issue. Otherwise, the number of very young women asking to be sterilised will continue to rise and rise. The fact that having a baby in the house is, under the right circumstances, about as much fun as you can have while someone's throwing up on you is being lost in the maelstrom of wagging fingers.

You won't get girls to behave like adults – to reproduce – simply by treating them like children, scolding them and lecturing them, over and over, until they decide to shut down out of sheer mulish stubbornness. Having a baby, at the end of the day, remains a young woman's own personal decision. No newspaper or government, no matter how mad and reactionary, would ever dare suggest a programme of mass rape, or even financial reward, as the monumentally sexist French did just after the war in order to replenish the stock.

If we don't stop making young women of child-bearing age feel that motherhood is a permanent test that they will never measure up to, these women will simply stop reproducing. There are, after all, so many other things for women to do these days. In seeking to guide the cream of child-bearing women into the ways of righteousness, we will instead have killed the goose that lays that shiniest of golden eggs: the future.

12 FEBRUARY 2000

As time goes on, and as I see more of this country, I often get the feeling that it is less of a 'land' than it used to be, and far more of a collection of small countries just waiting to break away. Perhaps the idea of devolution for Wales, Scotland and Northern Ireland has made each part of England think about its special-ness, too; perhaps it is a fear of being blanded out into one, big, soulless Euro-portion by Brussels that makes us cleave to local custom. And perhaps this is why commentators are having trouble finding the 'real' England; perhaps there isn't going to be one for much longer, but just the North, and the South, and the West, and the East.

What exactly does a pig farmer in Cornwall have in common with an estate agent in Cheshire or a night-club dancer in Hammersmith, anyway? Vitally, and unlike almost every other nation, Britain does not have a collective chip on its shoulder holding it together; we had it all, and we let it go. Far from being a so-called 'young' country, we are probably the most mature country there is, for good or ill; we don't go around panicking about being dissed like France or the US, and we look back in languor and amazement at our glorious past. It's not the worst way to be at all – but it does mean we lack a set of grievances to rally around.

I'm not immune from this. As I get older, I find that, more and more, I yearn to hear the accent of my calf country, the south-west of England. More than any other, we are the people of England that have never spoken yet, and still do not, unless you count the 'Ooo-arr-Ambrosiar!' advert. (Growing up, my only West Country role model was Cadbury's Caramel bunny.)

For years as a London-dweller I kidded myself that *The Archers* was set in the South-west, but my Sunday-morning fix went the way of all flesh when I could block out no longer the fact that the Aldridges were always 'popping into Birmingham' to see a ballet. I always forget how rarely the West Country accent is heard in the media until I go back and am surrounded by its lapping, quizzical sinuousness. I'm amazed when people find it odd or unattractive.

When my Dartington-educated friend recently accompanied me home for my mother's funeral, I noticed she was talking far less than usual, and this is a girl who could talk for England. She admitted she couldn't understand the Bristol accent, and had been terrified of responding to a question the wrong way ('Isn't it awful about Julie's mum?' – 'Mmm, yes, super!'). At first I thought this incredible; then I thought, well, where would she hear it?

The broadcasting media is alive with the buzz of Scots and the burble of Irish, but where is the West, or Birmingham, or Newcastle? It's not just that the West Country voices lack the 'authority' to read the news; anyone watching *Casualty* will be surprised to find that Nurse Lisa Duffin, played by Cathy Shipton, started life with a strong Bristol accent, which she was told to lose as viewers couldn't understand it. This would be insulting in any circumstances; considering *Casualty* is set and filmed in Bristol, it is downright surreal. Imagine the producers of *EastEnders* telling black or Asian characters to speak proper English because no one could understand them! It was I who first coined the word Capitalist (big C) to describe one who worships and fetishises London, and I was more than guilty of this myself during the Seventies and Eighties. But even then, when I went home to Bristol I was struck by the absolute lack of interest in London among even my liveliest and smartest Bristol friends. London was less than two hours on the train but might as well have been in Australia; they weren't frightened of it, but saw it as a place where people went who couldn't make it in Bristol! I got the impression that they considered London to be a city of whores – artistic, financial and sexual, more to be pitied than envied. I don't think they were far wrong.

If anything, it's got worse; London can't even create the thing it was synonymous with – pop music – any more. In the Sixties and Seventies, London either produced its own great pop groups – The Who, The Kinks, The Small Faces – or drew the best work from those provincials who moved there – The Beatles. When was the last great London sound? And how easily the wild northern boys are ruined by its siren song. The last albums by the once great Pulp and Oasis might just as well both have been called *London*, because that is surely what they're like: sound and fury, signifying nothing, all sucked dry.

'Perhaps you'll come home now?' – the neighbours still say that to me, even after 23 years away. For the first time, their question makes more sense than my answer. More and more, I see my whole flight from my home town to the capital as some sort of disorder, albeit one that plagues young people all over the world the moment hormones and ambition kick in. Politics and media in these islands are dominated by Scots who live in Islington and believe that every place in between doesn't matter a heap of beans; you're not telling me that's healthy.

I don't think I could ever go home for good, but I can carry my home with my voice: better Minnie Mouse from Ooo-Arr country than the Talking Clock lady and gent any day of the week. To people of the regions, the banal pronunciation that passes as the English norm conjures up all the glamour and glory of the drab couple in the weather house. After 23 years in the media, and to some extent the public eye, I'm still amazed that people are so amazed at the way I talk. How is a journalist 'meant' to talk – like a cosseted Oxbridge spawn whose Daddy was in the Cabinet and Mummy a minor aristo? Should I have realised while young that my accent was 'wrong', as Sue Lawley and Joan Bakewell did, and changed it for something more Sanderson?

Yes, I am from the western English working class. No, my name is not Lawson, Wyatt or Coren. Yes, I made it all by myself, with no old-school network and no trust-fund safety net. No, I have never had to wait for a parent to die or for a spouse to surrender worldly goods in a divorce court, because I made and spent my own first million by the endeavour of my own brain and hands (well, middle finger of right hand) before I was 35. Yes, I love my voice, because it speaks to me of all these things and of someone who is resourceful, unbowed, original and, above all, untamed. Would I swap it for a received pronunciation job, modulated and acceptable and like every other godawful boring journalist's voice? I'd rather have my tongue cut out.

19 FEBRUARY 2000

Of course people shouldn't be encouraged to say that specific groups of people are stupid or verging on the mentally subnormal. That is, they shouldn't say it due to race or gender. But when a group of people have chosen to be the way they are, those choices may well have been stupid.

I think it is fair to say, then, that violent criminals are stupider than most people; likewise Catholics, because they believe that they literally eat the body of Christ in a soggy wafer – not even a tasty Jammy Dodger! And I don't think that anyone who has spent more than 15 minutes in their company can deny that fashion people are the most remarkably stupid set of people on Earth. To believe that the way things look is more important than the way things are is as good a definition of cretinism as I have ever heard. That's why Naomi Campbell's periodic hissy fits about the 'racism' of fashion and beauty always ring so hollow – she has a point but, in a business built on making the fat, the old and the plain invisible, why should blackness be sacrosanct, or 'represented' in some way? There is no morality in modelling, except the way things look; if you accept this shamefully shallow set of rules, you cannot complain when your skin colour is not to someone's liking.

How predictable it was, then, that fashion should again embrace fur with such gusto: it looks good. That's why we like animals. And there is Naomi – who once swore that she'd rather go naked than wear fur – prancing down the catwalk in a mink. Poor Peta, the US anti-fur charity, but they should never have got mixed up with the fashionistas in the first place. Like I said, they're stupid – a perfect 10 isn't just their dress size, it's their IQ.

I'm afraid I've always been the little boy swinging on the lamppost when it comes to compassion in fashion, and have in the past taken first-rate pops at the rag trade's love affairs with Aids (that's Aids as affecting rich, white, 'artistic' men, of course, not the African women and children who make up 80 per cent of the victims) and breast cancer (just what a woman who's just had a double mastectomy needs to make her feel good about herself: Yasmin le Bon's perfect tits coming at her through a skin-tight FASHION TARGETS BREAST CANCER T-shirt). The point is that anything that can be fashionable must, by definition, become unfashionable. Of all the industries, fashion is the very personification of capitalism, because, unlike cars or computers, which you're meant to replace when they get old, you're meant to replace your clothes three times a year and chuck the old ones away, even though they are still perfectly serviceable. That is the whole point of fashion, and precisely why the Nineties thing about fashion people pretending to care about 'The Planet' was such a huge, brilliant joke.

So let us not castigate the likes of Puffy Combes, Tommy Hilfiger and John Galliano for draping their models in animal corpses (often with heads and paws left on), but rather give them three cheers for being so honest about the miserable, unimaginative business they tout their sad asses in. And three cheers, too, for those 'unspoilt' daughters of Albion, Karen Elson (brown-and-white striped mink jacket at Carolina Herrera) and Erin O'Connor (fluffy Tuscan lamb collar at Marc Jacobs) for proving that a down-to-earth, working-class funny face can be every bit as morally incontinent as the most stuck-up supermodel god-dess.

It's like being at public school, being in the rag trade: you get bullied at first, and then it's your turn to be a callous, sociopathic wretch. Last year, Elson was rejected by Dolce & Gabbana for being, at size 10, 'too fat'. The year before, she had been the toast of Milan. At 19, she was declared passé and superseded by 16-year-old Devon Aoki, the new favourite of Versace, Chanel, Yamamoto and Lagerfeld. Aoki looks perma-nently surprised, shocked by her good fortune. Hers is not a face that one can imagine ever expressing rebellion or contempt; neither are those of Audrey Marnay or Zora Star, two impression-able teenagers also being talked up by the designers and photographers who like their women young, dumb and grateful. These girls are, above all, passive, as the fashion writer Mimi Spencer put it after observing them up close: 'They look disconcertingly inexperienced – not merely in a sexual way, but in every sense imaginable. In magazines and on catwalks, they look like girls who have never opened a book, a can of soup, a door.'

It was disgusting to behold the recent spectacle of raddled old designer queens, all living like princes and as right-wing as kings, coming on like some Marxist scourge about how disgustingly over-paid supermodels are. 'Times are changing, and they have to realise that there is a world-wide economic crisis,' said a Fendi spokesman on why his house no longer wanted to employ supermodels. But none of the designers seems to have consid-ered the notion that the fashion houses themselves, as well as the supermodels, might think of charging less for their grossly inflated products.

If Claudia Schiffer is 'a joke, finished', what does Karl Lagerfeld think he is? If supermodels are so stupid, how come it's Christy Turlington and not Jean Paul Gaultier who has gone back to college? No, the supermodels' crime was not greed and temper – which are taken as proof of highly strung genius in male designers – but changing from malleable, mouldable girls into women who dared open their mouths and express opinions. Worst of all, they insulted the great god Fashion itself. 'It was a very dull point in fashion; people needed to gossip about us to make fashion more interesting,' said Turlington of the start of the supermodel feeding frenzy.

The supermodels saved their money and got out: Schiffer and Elle Macpherson into films, Crawford into being Cindy Inc., Christiansen into photography. Only Linda Evangelista – long hailed as the most 'professional' of the models, the 'chameleon', ever ready to change her hair colour at the whim of a bored designer – i.e., giving the impression that she was always the model, with the least fixed sense of herself – seems unable to move on. Last year on the catwalk, she seemed confused, and gave part of her fee back; in a US TV commercial for Visa, she intones blankly, 'I have no identity.' The perfect blank canvas with no other career to sustain or inspire her is a warning to all women who place their faith in fashion. Like the dead animals it parades on its catwalks, fashion is red in tooth and claw and, as in Nature, it is inevitably the bodies of women that are sucked dry and flung aside.

11 MARCH 2000

For some years now, I've been dreaming about Butlin's. Okay, so as first lines go it's nowhere near as lyrical as 'Last night I dreamed of Manderley', but it's the truth. Now, with my parents both dead, I find myself dreaming about Butlin's at least twice a week. I think it might be my Land Of Lost Content, but I wouldn't swear to it. I'm a happy sort of bunny, and I always believe that where I am is the best place to be. But if I had to say when I was the happiest I've ever been, I'd say it was during the four summer holidays my parents and I spent at Butlin's, Bognor Regis, in the late Sixties/early Seventies. For an imaginative, solitary, hedonistic, working-class girl child at that time, it was very heaven – truly, my very own empire of the senses. I'll tell you what: that old king wouldn't have said 'Bugger Bognor' from his deathbed if they'd had a Butlin's there then. He'd have risen from it, rolled up his trousers and entered the Knobbly Knees contest. Arriving at the front office, you checked in the Old You at the desk and went to find your chalet, where the limber, lithe and most definitely not shy New You, already having slipped into its sarong and sandals, would rise smiling from the single bed, sand falling from its silky thighs, to take your hand and lead you out into the shimmering surrealism that was Butlin's at its best.

Bob Lind's 'Elusive Butterfly' was often played during one of these holidays, and it is to the melancholy strains of this song that, in my dreams, I pad restlessly, vainly seeking my parents, through the deserted camp: through the echoey swimming pools with the parrots hanging from glass ceilings, past the abandoned crazy golf courses and through the Beachcomber Lounge, where the swimmers' legs move in eerie autonomy through the glass panels on the wall. But everything's in the wrong place now, and I can never find my way home again.

I went back there a few weeks ago. None of the fairground rides was open. Admittedly, it was February, but it also happened to be a scorching, sunny February day, as the majority of days in February were this year down here on the coast. And it was half-term! Would it have killed them to open up a few dodgems and turn the waltzer on? The once-beautiful indoor swimming pool now had no room for swimming at all, only for queuing wearily in order finally to use the water slides: 15 minutes of boredom in return for 15 seconds of fun.

Most of Butlin's is now a covered mini-mall of fast-food outlets and tacky gift shops. It's very hard to imagine exactly who would derive pleasure from such a visit, unless they had been held prisoner in a concrete bunker for the past 50 years. In the fast-food outlets, people queued for 20 minutes for a plate of chips. What's it going to be like in summer? And why is such food called 'fast' at all?

All in all, the decimation of my own little Shangri-La made me think of a phrase from the Joseph Heller novel, *Good As Gold* – 'crusading inertia'. Crusading inertia is best demonstrated, of course, by the 'revolutionary' replacement of human telephone operators by recorded ones telling you to push buttons after the tone: far from speeding things up and helping companies to work at maximum efficiency, automation has actually slowed down this part of life, not to mention been responsible for dangerously raising the blood pressure of millions. Look at traffic: there's now so much of it that it actually takes longer to get across London than it did 20 years ago. Before long, things will be so bad that it would have taken a shorter time in the heyday of the hansom cab.

Crusading inertia – by which I mean a frenzied determination to replace existing mechanisms with new ones, which invariably prove less satisfactory, but then cannot be changed back due to a combination of stinginess and pride – is everywhere. It's those

Virgin trains with ten types of ticket and an absolute inability to get anywhere on time. It's when businesses screw up, blithely explaining that 'the computers have crashed', as though the computers were Kings Of The Universe and thus naturally allowed to cause any length of inconvenience to we mere mortals without so much as an apology. Or those barcodes that don't work properly, so the checkout girl spends a good three minutes obsessively passing the object over and over the scanner until it looks like she's conducting an imaginary orchestra.

The biggest example of all must be e-mail, by which I remain distinctly underwhelmed. Both times when I attempted to speak to *Guardian* readers on its website, it took me the same time to receive and answer five e-mail questions as it would have done a dozen faxes. Nevertheless, a massive rush of my fans (80 per cent of whom I'd reckon were calling from work – crusading inertia in the marketplace) caused the sites to collapse; that wouldn't happen to a fax. Most misguided of all must be e-mail shopping. Whereas it would take most people less than an hour to pop out to Dixon's and pick up a simple computer accessory, it took a Mr Jon O'Neill 53 days – 53! – to attempt the same thing on-line, at which point he gave up and is still waiting for a refund for the item that never turned up.

If crusading inertia continues to pick up such sluggish speed, I can easily imagine us all in 20 years' time (surrounded by allegedly labour-saving technology but actually going to our graves far younger than our fathers), unable to make human contact, frustrated beyond recall by the sheer, bog-standard bovinity of machines, screaming ourselves into high blood pressure and heart attacks in our little padded cells – each life ending not with a bang, but with a piped version of *The Four Seasons*.

On an altogether cheerier note, the other day I was writing my next novel (*Rough Hands*, Orion Books, 2001, don't all rush at once), when a pun of such glittering, piquant perfection occurred to me that I had to get up and rush out into the garden simply because the force of my own cleverness forbade me to stay still. Sadly, I now believe that this pun is so gorgeous that it must have been thought of already. If this is so, could any reader supply me with details?

This is my pun: 'They married in Hastings and repented in Leicester.' Excuse me, I've just got to run outside again.

8 APRIL 2000

I'm always getting post that asks me to do weird things; things that would be so odd and out of character for me to do that, even though the sender invariably claims to be completely clued up about me and my work, I can't help but think that they've got me mixed up with some stonking old party girl such as Tara Palmer-Tomkinson or Melanie Phillips.

Getting asked to write for the *Erotic Review* was a good one. Have I or have I not repeated at least a dozen times in as many months that erotica is to porn what a crocheted cover is to a toilet roll: deeply naff and beloved only of a) self-pleasuring women who wish they liked real sex a whole lot more, and b) haggard seat-sniffing men who wish they could do it a whole lot more. I love the way erotica thinks it's better than porn – in much the same way as 'travellers' think they're better than tourists, but end up twice as loathed by the locals for being so presumptuous and tight – yet is as completely made up of clichés as the bored housewife, randy plumber and saucy schoolgirl of more honest smut. That is: ankles, buttocks, spanking, wisps of hair falling from a chignon, Victorian maids, the curtains blowing in the wind. (Sounds like an informal Wednesday night dinner party round my house, actually.)

Invitations to join a gym! Give a 'Masterclass' to a top advertising agency! (For no money. As if!) To take a course and become a successful writer! (Very funny.) Last week, I was asked to be on the radio show *In the Psychiatrist's Chair*, in the footsteps of all my heroes – those modest, mega-talented, gentle giants Steven Berkoff, Stephen Fry, Ken Russell and Barbara Cartland – even though my whole *raison d'être* in recent years has been to expose how the cult of psychiatry in general has brought us nothing but trouble, and how moaning micro-celebrities in particular should just SHUT UP and GET ON WITH IT. It does make you wonder what solar system these people have been in for the past 20 years.

Best of all, however, was an offer this week from a TV production company developing 'an exciting new series for Channel 4 about reconciliation through mediation. The purpose behind the series is to show how disagreements can be amicably resolved without loss of face and to the benefit of both parties involved in the debate. Mediation is pragmatic, it does not apportion blame, no sides are taken; mediators call this the win/win approach, because it is relatively quick and inexpensive, particularly compared to a court case, and circumvents the frustration and anger that long-running disputes can cause. As a way of illustrating the power of mediation, we are seeking the help of celebrities who are themselves involved in a long-running dispute, but are now interested in reconciliation. Each programme will focus on one dispute between two famous people. Both parties will talk about the dispute from their point of view [sic], they will then come together with a mediator to reconcile their differences, or at least reach a mutually agreeable truce.'

Of course, the point is that both *In the Psychiatrist's Chair* and this new one are exactly the sort of thing I delight in listening to/watching with my boyfriend, and shrieking, 'Ohmigod! How can people bear to do that to themselves in public!' It is a rule of thumb that the radio and TV programmes we most adore are those that we would run a mile not to be on, while we'd consider it a real feather in our cap to appear on those that bore us to tears. I, for one, won't be appearing in the Channel 4 series, because I believe in what Tennessee Williams said: 'Things are only ever black and white. The only people who think things are shades of grey are people who've had some of the black rub off on their souls.'

If this sort of sloppy thinking had been about 50 years ago, we wouldn't have had the Nuremberg Trials but the Nuremberg Mediations, and the Jews would have been encouraged to admit to their part in annoying Hitler. In short, I believe that mediation, like mercy, is the opposite of justice, not its beautiful assistant, as it is now being painted. Time and time again, mediation and reconciliation have been used as the lubricant of tyrants, helping them to slip out of all sorts of sticky corners.

The first known mediation, don't forget, was the Judgment of Solomon, which mooted that a baby be cut in half to keep two women – both claiming to be its mother – happy! It was only when the true mother backed down that Solomon handed the baby over to her, but in real life I'm afraid this rarely happens. In real life, it's the good guy who loses out from this sort of carry-on. In Chile and Argentina, the mothers of the Disappeared still wear black, because mediation and reconciliation have let the people who dropped trades unionists from helicopters and tortured three-year-old children in front of their parents get off scot free. Surely only the dimmest IRA groupie (hi, Tone!) hasn't cottoned on yet that the big-time M&R that was the Good Friday

Agreement was nothing more than a way for those brave butchers of Omagh to keep all their weapons while getting their goons out of jail. The Third Way is just a kid-gloved approach to letting business demoralise and exploit labour.

I'll never forget, also, the seminar organised by liberal Jews and Christians in an effort to reconcile with Muslims, which broke up early when the Muslims began to scream at the Jews and Christians about being blasphemers. Meanwhile, fathers are now routinely allowed to pay supervised visits to children whom they have raped, and I've lost count of the number of women killed in the process of being 'reconciled' with their violent partners. A few years ago, an Asian woman was actually killed in the very police station where she had fled for protection – when her husband came after her, the police put them in their 'domestic reconciliation unit' to talk it over. Ten minutes later, she was dead.

M&R represents all that is worst about the crusading inertia that so plagues us, the blundering zeal that has all but ruined the quality of everyday life here, in everything from rail privatisation to automated inquiries. In the realms of both the political and the personal, M&R is nothing more than yet another excuse for the nasty to walk all over the nice – even if they do coo, 'I hear what you're saying, I know where you're coming from', as they do it.

22 APRIL 2000

I know prejudice is a bad thing, and the last thing I'd want back in pubs and hotels are those signs that used to read 'No Blacks, No Irish, No Dogs'. But 'No Actors', as I believe was once a common sight? Mmm. Lead me to it. It's funny how other people who work in what are thought to be over-paid, parasitical occupations – estate agent, stockbroker, politician, hack – are routinely mocked and reviled. Yet I don't remember the last time I heard an Actor Joke – not since that old one about the out-of-work actor who comes home to find his wife raped and his dog dead. 'Your agent did it,' whimpers his wife. 'Oh, God!' says the actor. 'Did he leave a message?'

No, actors have done a damn good job presenting themselves as The People's Friend, and it's the best acting job any of them ever does. But the facts are somewhat different. Despite its outlaw credentials, acting is as conservative, selfish and reactionary a profession as you'll find; politically, they make prison officers look like social workers. The acting profession is snobbish (hence the continuing veneration of the useless Redgraves), racist (when did you last see a black actor playing anything but a mug or a thug?) and so sexist that women stop existing between the ages of 40 and 60, when they are allowed back in reduced numbers, so long as they play dotty old biddies.

Last week, one Jennifer Tuckett, a student at Cambridge, claimed that she had been kept out of the famous Footlights society by the boys' club that dominates drama there, and only allowed on stage when a young blonde stripped to her underwear was needed. 'Everything was so male-dominated and incredibly intimidating. There are about ten people on the Footlights committee; they all tend to be male. Women find it very intimidating, and friends tend to give their friends important roles.' Sadly, some might say that if a woman is determined to be an actor, Footlights are only doing the decent thing in giving her a taste of how her working life is going to be, like it or lump it; surely only a woman with either a skin thicker than a rhino's or else a masochistic streak a mile wide would choose to continue in such a profession. I never thought I'd have cause to agree with that big blethering perm-on-a-stick Michael Caine about anything, but he was totally right about this country's stuck-up thespians, as were Jane Horrocks, Bob Hoskins and Ray Winstone when they supported him. Though, of course, Caine himself, being an actor, is prey to all their vices; coming to fame during the heyday of British film-making, it didn't take him long to object to paying a decent level of tax and push off to America in order to stretch himself with such life-enhancing artefacts as *The Swarm IV*, *The Hand* and *Blame It on Rio*.

In fact, he is exactly the sort of actor – feet supposedly planted in the soil, hands grabbing at any fast buck floating by – who you'd expect to see in the new Barclays advert. In a brilliant example of our old friend socialism for the rich and capitalism for the poor, Barclays have paid Christ knows how much to a trio of actors – Anthony Hopkins, Tim Roth, Nick Moran, who have all made a great to-do about their alleged bucking of the system – to tout their slimy product while laying off workers and stranding clients by the hundreds of thousands. But then, allegedly left-wing British actors have always made me laugh – Roth and Gary Oldman come immediately to mind – because of their habit, during the reign of Mrs Thatcher, of leaving the country in a self-righteous strop about right-wing repression and then not moving to Cuba or Sweden, both of whose cinema is in good health and well subsidised by their governments. No, where did they go to escape Fatcher's Britain – why, Reagan's America, that famous bastion of freedom and equality! The new rash of British gangster films, wherein public-school directors exploit the real desperation and degradation of the working class for comic effect, are yet another expression of this vicious hypocrisy; see Vinnie Jones as a Cockney Uncle Tom, dropping his aitches and swallowing his pride for the glory of well-born Guy Ritchie.

It is refreshing, then, when an actor makes no pretence whatsoever of caring about the greater good, but simply follows his heart and his nose to the place where he will find the greatest wealth and ease possible on this planet. Step forward Anthony Hopkins, who has finished what he started with the Barclays ad by becoming an American citizen. I found it particularly touching that one of the people from his home town of Port Talbot who put the boot in was the local postmaster, Asghar Ali, an Asian, who spat, 'Sir Anthony is always harping on about his Welshness, but when the chips are down he goes away. To be honest, I think he is a hypocrite.'

No, not a hypocrite, Mr Ali, but an actor; a mercenary and a freebooter, if you want to be nasty about it, a citizen of the world if you buy their own brand. An Asian may easily become a Welshman within one generation, but an actor calls only the mirror home. A lifetime spent pretending that you are other people must surely distort your 'real' emotions, till such concepts as loyalty and integrity seem quite ... subjective, somehow, like pain and poverty in that Brecht lyric about Los Angeles doubling as heaven for the rich and hell for the poor.

As a child, I used to love films and film stars, but now find that the whole idea fills me with horror. Why? Why do we need to escape from our own lives so much that we will pay a few dozen people millions of dollars in order to waste their lives dressing up, spouting someone else's words and generally getting themselves well confused? Why do 'serious' actors such as Richard Gere, Winona Ryder and Sean Penn make TV commercials that cannot be shown in America? Are they ashamed of themselves? Why, if a woman shows her sex organs to one stranger, is she a prostitute, but if she shows them to millions, like Demi Moore and Sharon Stone, is she a superstar? Why are people paid a pittance for being real nurses, but a fortune for pretending to be nurses?

Ultimately, it is these and many other questions which will keep actors on the fronts of our newspapers and in the slipstreams of our subconscious; not, as they believe, for what they reveal to us about the human condition when they are practising their art, but for what they reveal when they are at their ease, or cutting that deal, or pulling up that skirt. They are our holy fools, and no money could ever be too much reward for the spectacles they make of themselves so that we may escape with at least a little dignity.

6 MAY 2000

Last week, writing about the Tony Martin case and different lengths of imprisonment being appropriate to different types of murder, liberal commentators repeated that old chestnut about how men guilty of 'desperate acts of domestic violence' ending in the death of the victim should not be punished as harshly as 'contract murders by professional killers'. I must say, what with two women each week in this country being killed by partners or ex-partners right now, I found this analysis offensive. There are few occasions when one even begins to understand what it must feel like to be a hated minority race in a country that recognises only the racially pure as having full civil rights, but reading, or hearing, the dismissal of domestic murder is definitely one of them.

Every week we hear that a man killed his wife for no more substantial reason than her 'nagging', or for smiling at another man, and each week some moronic bully gets off with a derisory sentence for such a crime. For any government to suggest that 'domestic' murderers will in future be treated with mercy seems to me as irresponsible as telling racist killers that they will be looked upon kindly simply because they let their feelings of rage and loathing, their emotional incontinence, get the better of them. For that is what we are talking about here; emotional incontinence – certainly not 'passion'.

Ah, passion! A rose between the teeth, a slap around the face, an adagio dance! Treat 'em mean and keep 'em keen! Like many stupid ideas about women, the *crime passionel* is French, and – like the also much-vaunted mistress/wife arrangement – was designed solely with the aim of making life easier for men at the expense of women. Are we truly to believe that such archaic notions have no connection with the chronic levels of sexual harassment and pornographic advertising that still exist in France, and which have created not a climate of enlightenment but one of bullying, hectoring oppression? Still, what can you expect from a country in which women didn't get the vote until 1945?

Yes, there certainly wasn't much for women in all that liberty, equality and fraternity floating about after the French revolution, and ever since then the human and civil rights of women have remained a blind spot with men who should know better. The list of otherwise intelligent, radical men who have talked about women in a style somewhere between Hitler and Al Murray the Pub Landlord is always surprising. Solzhenitsyn, writing with great disapproval of all the poor guys he found in the gulags imprisoned for 'trivial' crimes such as rape; Stokely Carmichael, telling women that their place in the black revolution was 'prone'.

Now, for your delectation, at London's Almeida Theatre, Tariq Ali, Howard Brenton and Andy de la Tour bring you *Snogging Ken*, a rigorous dissection of New Labour's blackguarding of the

Livingstone mayoral campaign. And who's behind it? – Blair, Brown, Mandelson? Nah – women! A pair of 'Blair Babes', as Andy de la Tour referred to them in a recent plug for the show. And what means do they use to bring the great man down? Typical woman's trick – lying about sex. Treacherous bitches. Men's need to believe in female perfidy seems to be the last prejudice to die, and is all present and incorrect even in men who would run screaming if you accused them of any sort of bigotry. And what starts with the type of mentality that believes you can never trust a woman ends up in the treatment of domestic murder as less serious than 'real' murder. And, with the exception of those cases where the perpetrator was in fear for his or her life, this reinforces the medieval message that when a woman sleeps with a man, she becomes his property and may be disposed of as he sees fit.

Those who believe most strongly in the brotherhood of man often give the impression that, by its very nature, it excludes women. John Mortimer, that floridly humanitarian old ham, once said something along the lines of 'My life is so challenging because I'll be writing a play in the morning and defending a wife-murderer in the afternoon.' He wouldn't have boasted about defending a race murderer, would he? Yet an average-size black man has far more chance of defending himself against an average-size white man than an average-size woman does.

Around the time Mortimer said this, the actress Jane Asher was appearing in one of his TV series, and I was shocked to pick up the paper soon after and see that he was currently defending a man who had killed his wife because she danced with another man at a party – she was called Jane Asher, too. And it struck me then how symbolic this was: the famous, middle-class Jane Asher, free to go about her business without fear of male murderousness – whom John Mortimer knew, and referred to in glowing terms – and this unknown, working-class Jane Asher, killed by one of her own class, only to have the cream of the legal élite rally around to defend a husband who did his level best to portray his wife as a strumpet. Mortimer, as a barrister, operates on the cab-rank principle. There are plenty of others who don't have that excuse.

Surely the whole point of being a liberal is being able to empathise, to put yourself in the other man's shoes? Yet when it comes to the domestic murder of women by men, the killer's brogues always seem far more easy for the liberal to slip on than the stilettos of the victim. It's a puzzlement.

With reference to my recent diatribe against those sad souls who hawk their wares in the bazaars of Thespus, I receive a letter from Emma Thompson, who is obviously a somewhat god-like being, despite the gallons of poison I have poured on her name in the past. Not a word of reprimand, but a wonderful anti-actor joke for me to add to my list:

'Some scientists were doing tests on dogs to see how like their owners they were. They took a mathematician's dog, an architect's dog and an actor's dog. Starting with the mathematician's dog, they put it into the first cubicle with a pile of bones. The dog looked at the bones, sorted them into three neat piles of two, four and six and then went and sat in the corner. Next, they sent in the architect's dog. It looked at the bones, and patted them into a nice geometrical shape, and went and sat in the corner. Then they sent in the actor's dog. It looked at the bones, ate them all, fucked the other two dogs and asked if it could go home early.'

And the words 'Kenneth Branagh' never even crossed our minds, did they?

3 JUNE 2000

If ever – after a particularly vicious stoning to death of an adulteress in Saudi Arabia, or an amputation of a shoplifter's hands in Afghanistan – anyone in the West dares to put up their hand and murmur in a teeny-weeny voice that, um, aren't Islamic countries a bit nasty to anyone who dares step beyond moral perimeters that most intelligent 12-year-olds could handle, there's always some media mullah who will bob up and tell us that, actually, pure Islam is so humane, so sweet-natured, so all-round pretty-in-the-pink, that it makes what passes for human rights in the West look like a bad hair day for the Spanish Inquisition.

Forget what's happening in those countries that merely call themselves Islamic – that's nothing to do with Islam. In fact, rumour has it that Rafsanjani was once a Methodist lay preacher in Shoeburyness, and so it is to the cruel Christianity of John Wesley that we owe the intemperate human rights record of Iran. Now, real Islam . . . for women, especially, a true Islamic state would be something between the Body Shop, Benidorm and Girton College. You'll get some Islamic feminist banging on about how the veil 'frees' the women who wear it (what, even on a sweltering hot day, when they're dying for a dip in the briney?). The speaker invariably won't be wearing a veil herself, of course; she'll be plastered in Pan-Stik and staggering under the weight of her 'do. But she'll go on to praise arranged marriages as having a far higher success rate than love matches – failing to mention, natch, that she herself is enjoying a full and happy married life with a twice-divorced Bondi Beach bum called Bruce. Either that, or a weedy Oxbridge academic who habitually walks six paces behind her. These Muslim humanists always bet on the fact that few Westerners ever bother to read the Koran. If you do, you'll find just as much nonsense and intolerance as you would in the Bible. But you just know that, if you asked a media mullah or Islamic feminist to explain a particularly choice bit, they will still find a way out – 'Oh, you made that up! Bloody Islamophobic meejah! You had that printed up at one of them joke shops at the end of the pier, where you can have a newspaper printed up with your own headlines, such as FRED SMITH SHAGS MADONNA!' (Though I suppose they'll have to stop doing this now, in case Guy Ritchie gives them what for. Incidentally, with a stepfather who's a Sir and a sister who's a Tabitha, how do you suppose he got that scar? Fell off his pony and landed on his silver spoon?)

Anyway, I find these people fascinating and, in some warped way, even admirable. Most voluble fantasists get a restraining order clamped on them at least, and many thousands are under lock and key even as we speak. But other fantasists are convincing enough not just to be able to wander around freely, but to have people take them completely seriously and, even better, to have TV researchers throw money at them to repeat their fantasies over and over again. It isn't just Islamic feminists, of course; that other great friend of women, Barbara Cartland, was Walter Mitty in a wig, Billy Liar in a ballgown, and made a very nice living out of it indeed, thank you. Her particular fantasy, of course, was that she was the epitome of femininity, though she was in reality a woman totally driven and obsessed by her career and her own importance. Despite her ceaseless yapping against the evils of feminism and the absolute desirability of women being passive and pliant at all times, she routinely scared seven shades out of every male journalist who crossed her path, speaking to them with an astounding rudeness that most of my mild-mannered little feminist friends would be hard pressed to match, even with a nasty case of PMS. (Another possible fantasy: if Barbara Cartland's books really were such humdinger bestsellers, why did they never feature in the book charts? Perhaps her publisher could explain it to me. This is not a dig – I'm just puzzled.)

The current focus for this country's fantasists is, of course, the wretched Dome, which continues to make supposedly clever men look nothing short of mad. You only have to read the collected quotations of Mandelson, Heseltine, Falconer and all, droning over and over again that the Dome was/is/will be the equivalent of the Taj Mahal, the Sistine Chapel, Einstein's kitchen and Hollywood in the Thirties – as opposed to what it is: a very inefficient and over-priced theme park – to know that, in one sense, the Dome is probably the most impressive building ever, in that it has acted as a bona fide bullshit detector on a massive scale. Anyone who has ever been connected with it will, till the end of their days, wear a giant invisible F, and any further bright ideas of theirs will be dead in the water.

So far as I can see, there is only one decent way out of this predicament, a grand, postmodern variation on going into the library with a loaded revolver. Let everyone involved in the conception, design, promotion and perpetuation of the Dome be removed from their tasteful Queen Anne piles and/or BoBo chic west London penthouses, and caged within their creation for the rest of their natural lives. Let them be subjected twenty-four-seven to the scorn and ridicule of the British people, and let them be haunted by the ghosts of all those who died (in various ways – physically, spiritually, educationally) for lack of resources while the obscene billions swilled into this monument to the inhumanity of politicians. There, that's my fantasy out.

17 JUNE 2000

I don't know if you saw the *Observer* last weekend, but there were the most gorgeous photos in the colour supplement of Will Self, his three children and his wife, the journalist Deborah Orr. Taking a tip from Tony Blair, perhaps, this was a serious re-branding: no more the junkie stud, instead the funky dad. Rugged Will, blonde Debs, sun-kissed boy and girl kiddies, and gorgeous, bouncing baby – they resembled what an advert for Sunny Delight might look like if Sunny Delight decided to aim itself at people who holiday in Kerala and know what 'frottage' means.

I felt there was something odd about these photos, and I kept gazing at them looking for clues. It took two days of puzzling over them before I tumbled: though he looked as certifiably, teeth-grindingly sexy as ever, I was free. For the first time in ten years, I didn't fancy Will Self!

To get the full clout of this, you've got to understand what Will Self represented, sexually, in the Nineties. Despite his drug and alcohol intake, to us London media babes he was a sexual icon packing the oomph of Jimi Hendrix, Robbie Williams and Gordon Brown all rolled into one. Every man wanted to be him and every woman wanted to have him. They usually did, too. At one time, I had three different friends whom he slept with for the first time on the same day. To add insult to injury, they all then proceeded to ring me up and tell me that they were having a passionate affair with him, he was The One, it was true love – the whole works. I soon put those bitches right, let me tell you – in a caring way, of course, as Dame Edna would say. So it was horribly vulgar and predictable for me to fall for Will, like saying your favourite film is *Casablanca* or your favourite Opal Fruit is strawberry. For years, I just looked at him across crowded rooms – you couldn't miss him; he was so tall and prehistoric-looking – until one night he followed my husband and me home, and showed us how to smoke crack. I'll never forget what a thrill it was being bossed about by him – now cut a hole in the Evian bottle, now stick the straw in there; like some depraved *Blue Peter* presenter – and I'll never forget how he looked when it hit him: slumped on my black leather sofa, with just one big juicy tear coursing down his left cheekbone. I was lost.

Sad, sad, sad; I took to calling his home when I knew he was out, just to hear his voice on the answerphone – sometimes, and this is really weird, I'd call his answerphone from my bedroom when he was sitting drinking vodka in my front room. The reality of him seemed too much to grasp; I was happier with the unreal thing. I was so chronically embarrassed by the predictability of my crush that I even took to inventing false crushes to put people off the trail. But I'm sure I didn't convince anyone. It's the name-dropping that does it, I always think. The search-engine of my mind was primed, and from that moment any word typed in, from AZTEC to ZEBRA, would have come up with one answer: WILL SELF. I had a truly amazing capability to turn any subject of conversation around to him – even with my parents, who, of course, didn't know him from Adam. My mum would be talking about the dog's flatulence problem – and I could turn it on a sixpence right round to Will. No problem.

After a couple of years, I felt I had to tell someone, so I went to my best friend's school at 10 in the morning, saying that I was her aunt and that there had been a death in the family. I dragged her to the Groucho, and told her everything while she sat there in her school uniform with her mouth open, the two of us looking like some corny Hogarthian print about innocence and corruption, as Jeffrey Bernard told me later. Three hours later, I staggered from the bar into the foyer where I walked slap-bang into Will, who gave me the biggest hug and the saddest smile I've ever seen. Somehow, I walked out the door and round the corner into Old Compton Street, where I fainted, and I'm not the type who faints. When I woke up, I burst into tears. In the taxi on the way home, I realised I was becoming a mentalist. Truly, this is the nearest I think I've ever been to going nuts.

So perhaps a life without crushes won't be such a bad thing, and no one can say that it's not about time. I did notice while on holiday with my boyfriend's mum last month that, though the Corsican men were well fit, I wasn't interested in any of them. I thought this was really good of me, and I told Mrs Raven about my lack of reaction, thinking I'd get praise. Instead, she laughed scornfully and said, 'I should hope not, at your age!' That hurt. So at least I'll be able to do dignified now. But, on the other hand, being a crushee is one of the few ways I can access my essential self, and it's not as if there are so many that I can afford to lose them.

I've always had crushes on people, really big bastards of crushes. I still remember the first crush I had, when I was four, on my friend Joy (an unexceptional lump, as I recall, whose miserable aspect chronically contradicted her given name), whom I would prevent from leaving my house by lying across the threshold and crying. When I was ten, I had to stop watching *Dad's Army* because I had crushes on three of them – the spiv, the toff and the virgin – and found it too confusing. One reason I've always enjoyed the prospect of falling in love and getting married is because the dull routine of marriage lends itself so perfectly to the agony of the illicit crush. I got through the sexual side of my first marriage – for six years! – by pretending that my husband was my friend Peter York. And people say I don't have any imagination! For those of you outside the slimy boundaries of Mediaville who can't conjure up either image, let's just say it was a lot like pretending Arthur Mullard was George Sanders.

My second husband was a really popular guy – which was great, because he had loads of friends whom I could conceive huge crushes on. And often they had lovely girlfriends, whom I could get gay crushes on, too! The *Modern Review*, my little magazine, provided endless crush fodder in the shape of young would-be writers – most of whom thought I was a stuck-up bitch because I wouldn't speak to them from one year to the next, lest my crush be detected. But still, Will loomed over my second marriage, lurked throughout my very enjoyable six months of lesbianism, and has seen considerable active service in my rich and strange inner life over the years since then.

And now? Nothing. I know it's a good thing, growing up, but I shall miss being crushed. Still, like Will himself, I'm taking it one day at a time.

24 JUNE 2000

I've been feeling a peculiar pang all week about C&A closing, though I can't have been inside one since I was 12. It was the sort of place my mother used to drag me round on a Saturday afternoon in the very early Seventies, looking for holiday clothes to wear on the annual Butlin's beano, and we'd invariably row because I wanted sludge-coloured midi-skirts from Chelsea Girl and she wanted me to wear acrylic turquoise minis. 'Why are you trying to make me dress like a child prostitute, Mother?' I would invariably hiss, to be answered by a resounding slap around the ear and a triumphant hiss of, 'Wait till I get thee 'ome!' Happy days.

My mother didn't want me to look like a child prostitute, of course; she only wanted me to carry on being Her Little Girl for a bit longer, a bit of a fool's errand once Marc Bolan, ambition and masturbation were in the frame. C&A was good at making little girls look very little, and the middle-aged look very middle-aged; it wasn't hot on the perennial teen look, and when it tried to do 'swinging', it ended up as the Panda Pops version of Coke. But nostalgia has a funny way of getting to you, and if I concentrate very hard I find I can bring myself to the verge of tears (not all the way – good Lord, let's keep a sense of proportion here) just thinking about those bri-nylon shirts with matching tie and hanky on men who smelled of Hai Karate; and those acrylic, Jacquard tunics on ladies called Audrey and Avril, blushing beneath their Max Factor Creme Puff as they danced slow with their next-door neighbour to 'Can't Take My Eyes Off You'. Those were innocent, heady days, after the Pill but before Aids, and it hit our parents for six. And it was C&A that dressed them for their brief shining place in the sun.

I don't care that C&A is Dutch; look at William of Orange. The point is that it, like he, made us more English. My blood runs cold when I try to imagine what they're going to put in our big C&A building in Brighton. When Liberty closed here – okay, Liberty is a crap shop, but it had a brilliant Muji concession and carried Rifat Ozbek and English Eccentrics – they built a Gap for Kids (which my friend Emma always says sounds really obscene) over the whole three floors! We already have at least half a dozen American coffee shops within two minutes' walk of each other, one of them on the site of a fantastic toy shop. Isn't it weird how the flight from perceived dullness ends up installing a much more profound and insidious type of monotony?

I yearn for decent dullness, properly done; no half-measures and no cut corners. *Two Way Family Favourites*. A Sunday roast, even on a blinding hot day in July, followed by Bartlett pears and Ideal Milk. The torpor and dread of Sunday afternoon, with no shops open. The classic serial on BBC 1, and tinned salmon for tea. *Sing Something Simple* and packing your satchel and wanting to die, right here, right now. And what have we got instead? Non-stop sex on TV, a ciabatta in every oven and a population who don't understand why they're not as happy as they used to be. It's because things aren't dull, that's why.

The fact is that English dullness is actually far more interesting, attractive and affecting than American know-how or European *savoir-faire*. I can't imagine any country but England producing Alan Bennett, for instance, and any country that can't produce Alan Bennett is no country I'd want to salute the flag of. And it was our very lack of know-how and *savoir faire* that made him possible. Bennett himself has a lovely, sad story about how, as a bright, working-class lad, he felt impatient with his parents' provincialism. Eager to please him, they set about sophisticating themselves, and when he came back home from university his mother announced, 'We've found an alcoholic drink we like. It's called bitter lemon.' Later, they learned to like wine, by which time Bennett was grown up and appreciated the purity and sweetness of their initial unworldliness: 'All I wanted was for them to be the way they had been. But by then of course it was too late.'

For dullness is such a delicate flower – so easy to destroy, so impossible to recapture. I experienced the Bitter Lemon Effect with my own parents. When I was growing up, I was a right royal predictable pain in the ass on social matters, virulently in favour of sex, drugs and horrible loud music, anti-religion, anti-capital punishment – the whole boring works. But I thought I was Che Guevara. I would rant on at my parents about their provincialism, their dullness – and though at the time I thought it was water off a duck's back, they were actually mad enough to take some of it on board.

When I'd go home to visit them in the Eighties, my mother would wheel out some new, daring social attitude: 'He's gay, of course,' she said casually over ginger nuts one day of her new hairdresser. 'I've met his partner. Lovely couple.' 'She's got a toyboy,' she'd shrug of her married friend. 'Each to his own, I say.' This Bedlam came to a head over faggots and peas one Sunday, when my father casually announced that he no longer believed in God! I moped over my Instant Whip, remembering what the neighbourhood had been like before it became bloody Liberty Hall: clandestine affairs, twitching curtains, vicious gossip, closed minds – brilliant, dirty fun, in fact, like Peyton Place-on-Avon. And now, here they were, letting it all hang out. In fact, I can just imagine my parents laughing themselves rigid (if they weren't already) at that awful Keith Chegwin smutfest the other night, which my worldly friends and I found so appalling. They were thoroughly 'with it' by the end – they thought the Lottery was better than Premium Bonds, the car-boot sale superior to the bring-and-buy, and pounds and pence better than shillings – so it was left to Muggins here to mourn the arcane glory of the thrupenny bit and the half-crown.

But just you wait and see. I believe that dullness will rise again, and triumph. On the Internet, for instance, you can spend many happy hours gazing at cornfields in Iowa, streets in Scunthorpe or long stretches of many a motorway. The most mesmerising song of the year so far is the mighty Black Box Recorder's 'The

English Motorway System' – 'The English motorway system is beautiful and strange/ It's been there for ever, it's never going to change/ It eliminates all diversions, it eliminates all emotions/ All you've got to do to stay alive is drive.' This is the voice of a generation in search of their birthright; not rioting, but queueing.

1 JULY 2000

Yay! That Tony Parsons novel, *Man and Boy*, has just dropped out of the paperback charts; after what seems like about eight years and three billion copies sold, the fruit of my much-despised first husband's brain will not be mocking me any longer whenever I step into WH Smith for a quick copy of *The Fur and Feather*. Let's face it, my last two novels stiffed so badly you could have done your ironing on them; then along comes Shorty, with a book that makes Jilly Cooper look like a prime example of vanity publishing.

I bought it the other day, at last, and found it strong stuff – Patience Strong, that is. No, really, having read the book, I can honestly report that it is not in any way autobiographical – the errant mother, Gina, is slender, beautiful and decent, while the long-suffering hero, Harry, is attractive to women, good in the sack and has all his own hair. So that rules me and Parsons right out.

I'm actually very glad for Tony, because he really did want it so badly. (Oh and, um, because I, too, had a million-selling number-one novel, *Ambition*, when I was 29. And it was my first novel. Which does, I think, have the edge on getting the glory with your fifth novel, when you're 49, as Tone has.) I'm only cross at myself; to think I swanned out and dumped the guy 16 years ago, leaving our bungalow in Billericay with nothing but a bottle of amyl nitrate, a G-string, a bust of Lenin and an attitude, in order to elope with my exotic Jewish lover to some millionaire's space-age pad in Hampstead! Why, if I'd stayed, I could be living the sweet life right now. But ... yep, remembering that face and that voice from the last *Late Review*, I guess it was but a small price to pay.

Ever since then it's been daggers drawn with every new dawn, and I suppose that, to those people who've had what is called an 'amicable divorce' (I love that; like 'friendly fire'), it seems a bit sad. I don't agree. I think that some people are meant to be our enemies from the start, but there's some sort of spanner in the works that makes us believe they're our nearest and dearest instead. When love turns to hate, it isn't really anything to get upset about; it's just that the truth will out. It's Nature's way of saying 'sorry' for all the sappy things she made you do and say when you thought you were 'in love'. But now you're deep in hate, and the fun really starts.

The awful truth is that most people are much more fun as enemies than they were as friends and/or lovers. Hatred brings out the artiste in individuals, whereas when we're in love we're all the same – one big blissed-out mess, like junkies are one and the same. If someone published your love letters, you'd want to crawl away and die, because, no matter how smart you are, they'd be some sort of variation of what Jeremy Thorpe famously wrote to Norman Scott: 'Bunnies can and will go to France!' When you hate someone, though, you're totally yourself, hard, clean and glinting; you are, in fact, everything they loved you for in the first place.

No matter how much sob sisters agonise about putting the

romance back into a relationship, the fact remains that it is easier to put mercury back into the thermometer. The only responsible sex education for children would be the words THINGS CHANGE. Sex, with the same person, simply stops feeling like ANYTHING after a while; that is the plain and awful truth. When it comes to sex, novelty counts for so much that the straightest, simplest act of missionary intercourse with a new partner feels one thousand times dirtier, and therefore better, than the most protracted and perverted of acts with a familiar one. This is what the sexperts cannot get around; this is why the divorce rate keeps rising. Hatred brings the sparkle back: puts a spring in your step and a mote in your eye. How could I have been that stupid? When we fall out of love with someone, it gives us such a window of opportunity to look at ourselves and our delusions.

Perhaps this is why I feel so pleased when a nice new feud is getting started; it's sort of a cross between mild sexual excitement and the feeling you get when the plane finally leaves the runway. And, like sex, I prefer it with men but I certainly don't rule women out, though it pains me to think of men gloating and thinking 'Catfight!' Still, if a broad wants some, she can certainly have some; the latest contender was one Deborah Bosley, a jealous old trout who wants desperately to be a writer, but whose professional peak actually was as a waitress (sorry, Debs, 'head waitress') at the Groucho Club, a post she left in order to shack up with a man old enough to be her granddad, Richard Ingrams. Recently she wrote a nasty letter to a newspaper about me, and I responded in kind.

Things were just getting warm when the dirty spoilsport wrote a piece for the current *New Statesman* detailing her 'isolation, boredom, loneliness and long death of spirit' as the kept woman of Ingrams in deepest Berkshire, a place not to her liking. She is also, she claims, becoming an alcoholic: 'Boredom and loneliness don't seem nearly so bad the other side of two bottles of wine a night.'

Don't you just hate it when people do that? Did no one inform this woman of the rules? Deborah, dear, don't make yourself look so pathetic, spineless and idle; that's my job. Our feud was shaping up so well, and now you've gone and ruined it by showing yourself not to be a worthy opponent, but instead a rather sad and confused mousewife who would make me feel a rotten bully if I were to stomp on you again. Now all you make me want to do is make you cups of tea and give you good advice. Along the lines of – there's this thing called earning your own living, Deborah, and, if you do it properly, you can live where you want. And you don't have to screw a man who looks like Victor Meldrew in order to keep a roof over your head.

Ah well, I know my next *bête noire* is out there somewhere, filing their teeth and combing their feet and waiting for the call. I shall struggle on till then, but lack of a loathe object does cause life to lose a little of its zap and zest. Still, I shall comfort myself with the knowledge that there are no friends – only enemies we have yet to make.

15 JULY 2000

By the time you read this, I will be in Torquay. Okay, as great first lines go, it's not 'Hale knew, before he had been in Brighton three hours, that they meant to murder him'. If I'd written that I was in Montenegro, or Arizona, the phrase would have a sort of Gothic grandeur; it's the 'Torquay' that robs it of its doomed glory. But sometimes doomed glory is a bore, and niceness is all you want or need.

I like everything about Torquay, and the first brilliant thing about it is the drive there from Brighton. Just as I didn't start going abroad until 1995, I didn't start being driven on motorways until a couple of years later. Just as well, really; both my husbands were blessed with short and filthy tempers, and I'm sure that any attempt at motoring would have brought our ill-starred unions to even faster and nastier ends. But then I had the good luck to take up with a young man of unparalleled patience and good humour, and we began to take motoring trips. Now I love them, with the zeal of a very late convert.

I like everything about driving: the maps, the service stations, the beautiful, long, sexy motorways, where the rushing of cars from the arterial roads makes you feel like Raquel Welch in *Fantastic Voyage*, all of us corpuscles streaming into the white-hot body politic of modern Britain. Motorways makes me feel oceanic and very loving towards mankind in a way that oceans themselves never do; all of us, rushing about our all-important business that we will one day discover wasn't important at all, moving frantically away from our deaths, we imagine, when of course every move we make, in any direction, brings us closer to them – how can you not love a crazy little species like that? We're just so cute!

On a motorway, I feel very impatient with green ideals, which would see us condemned to eke out our lives in one little patch, never pushing on here and there for fear of spoiling the ecology. It's a nice life for a tree, but no life for a human in all our restless and complex perfection.

In cars, I like to look at other people, and see them completely unselfconscious and secure as they are in no other area of life. For many people, confined by the drudgery of boring work and dull marriages, driving is the only time they are truly alone, in limbo, answerable to and belonging to no one. It is the only time they may experience anything like silence, as the demands and longer hours of being an ever-better parent and an ever-harder worker eat into our lives; the arrival of the mobile phone and its babbling captives has effectively rendered the train, once such a blessed retreat from ceaseless jabbering, into a regular little talkathon, but if it's your car you can keep your own phone turned off. We hear a lot about road rage, but I bet you anything that if cars were banned tomorrow, the murder rate would double as the last bastion of solitude was taken away from millions of over-worked, under-loved people. Road rage is not about roads at all, but about the rage in the rest of our lives; only in our cars do we feel free enough to express it.

Such is my love of motoring that, the other day, I cracked my boyfriend up – so much so that he had to pull over until he stopped laughing – by inquiring with genuine interest and excitement: 'So, which is your favourite colour traffic light – red, green or the orangey one?' But I was really interested.

Growing up, ours was the only family that didn't have a car (when I typed that sentence then, look you, I accidentally typed 'didn't have a care' instead, and as Freudian slips go that's a pretty good one). Instead, we went on holiday by train, and I can't help thinking this had a good deal to do with the incredible happiness of our family holidays. There can be no doubt that it is preferable to transport children in trains rather than cars; if the little darlings don't have somewhere they can stretch their legs and run about inside a vehicle, I find, their behaviour becomes so bad that it is a great temptation to let them stretch their legs and run about outside the vehicle. Like on the motorway.

Cars seem to me a very adult pleasure, like sex and drugs; and, like them, are not really appropriate for children. The sight of the modern child ferried from door to door, from home to school, day in, day out, is one of the most depressing of recent times, completely robbing children of the chance to explore and mature. Similarly, the commuter sitting in his car for two hours when a train could get him to work in 50 minutes makes no sense at all.

But though it may not be the most efficient form of transport known to man, driving can be fantastically pleasurable, something those on both sides of the current petrol price row seem to have forgotten. To the *Daily Mail*, the car is a grim necessity; to the government, it's an unnecessary menace. I suggest they both lighten up and sit down to watch the old English flick *Genevieve* together, which will surely give them a bit of perspective.

Like sex and drugs, cars are neither 'good' nor 'bad'; they are merely as good or bad as the people using them. At the moment, bad motorists seem to get away with far too much. The test should be made harder and the licence re-applied for every five years. If anyone is found driving under the influence of alcohol, their car keys should be taken away on the spot and never returned. If someone actually kills someone through careless driving, they should be dealt with the same as any other murderer. But most motorists are not irresponsible monsters; wincing under the accusations of spreading pollution, asthma and all manner of air-borne evil, they could actually use a little more Me time.

'Is Your Journey Really Necessary?' asked billboards beside the roads of Britain during the war and after, encouraging drivers not to waste petrol. What I'm proposing is a motoring culture in which driving is done as a pleasure, and in fact where only the unnecessary journeys are undertaken – every drive a wanted drive. We have worried ourselves out of guilt-free drinking, smoking and eating; it would be a shame if our anhedonia grew so all-consuming that the simple pleasure of driving towards somewhere nice on a sunny day with someone you love was also put beyond the pale.

29 JULY 2000

Isn't science wonderful? They put a man on the moon and now they've put caffeine in a lipstick. Hard Candy, for the hefty sum of £13.50, will flog you slugabeds LipAchino, Latte Lip or Café O Lip. Not just caffeine, but St John's Wort, the 'herbal Prozac', too, which you'll find in Tony & Tina's Mood Balance Lipstick. Hmm . . . call me an unreconstructed, killjoy feminist if you like, but I must say it strikes me as distinctly sad and suspect that women are striding into the 21st century eating cosmetics. Bread and circuses are off indefinitely, but let them eat lipstick.

The perfect lipstick has always been presented as the final frontier for female-friendly science; you would think we didn't ever die of cancers, the way all those hundreds of thousands of scientists are slaving away torturing animals day and night, supposedly to answer the insistent demand of the Eternal Woman for a perfect red with no blue in it, or for the ultimate beige that doesn't make you look as if you've got a blood disease. Who can forget the parties in the streets, the rejoicing world-wide, when in the Nineties those friendly men in white coats finally presented a waiting world with a lipstick that stayed on all day and never needed retouching? Thereby enabling women to save, oh, at least two minutes a day – that's 14 minutes a week! Lovely: an extra 14 minutes in which to wait for buses, give up on trains and get stuck at airports.

Phrases such as 'saving time' and 'time-saving' have always puzzled me. You can't 'save' time as you could pennies in a jar – five minutes here, a quarter of an hour there, and stick them all together until you've got enough for a week in the Bahamas. You can't store time; like vitamin C or orgasms, it needs replenishing each new day. If you are eight minutes idle, they'll find something else for you to do.

Fifty years ago, the mass availability of time – and labour-saving appliances in the household – was meant to herald an age when women, in particular, would trip-trop languidly around from coffee morning to bistro luncheon to dinner-dance. But now, even women who don't work (and, yes, I am going to stick to the old definition of 'work' meaning paid employment, because if we did not make that differentiation then anyone, man or woman, with children who was sacked from their job could not be described as out of work, and the government could do all sorts of crafty tricks with unemployment figures and benefits) are rushing around like mad things, stopping only to find the time, mysteriously, to fill in long magazine surveys about how they're so stressed and overworked that they feel like topping themselves.

The obvious answer to this dilemma, which no one ever seems to consider, is to simply STOP DOING SO MUCH – get your existing children adopted, have your womb taken out, start reading books instead of filling in those magazine surveys, and a year from now you will be totally on top of your game.

People simply do too much, except for those who do too little. Every time you do too much, you're taking that away from someone with very little to do already, so, in fact, you're not being good and clever, you're being nasty. Not to mention sucking up to the boss-man, who, of course, will dump you without a moment's thought when you become surplus to his requirements. There's something really creepy about people who 'love' their work, and really class-traitorous, too.

How many of you oldsters out there remember the auto-biographical Patti Smith single 'Piss Factory' ('scuse French), in which our young-blood heroine went to work in said factory and worked a bit too hard, in fact, until the union representative on the factory floor had to take her to one side and ask her to slow down as it was showing the rest of them up. Naturally, Patti, being a rebel, didn't listen and carried on churning it out, until the other women cornered her one lunchtime and stuck her head down a toilet. At the time, of course, I thought this was the most tragic and unfair thing I had ever heard. Now, I think the little sneak totally deserved it.

For years, I was the busiest bee in town, until I realised that this merely made every booby I married feel that he could coast by on writing one shopping list and one thank-you letter a week, while Baby here churned it out and brought home the Baco-Bits. Now I take it easy – and I make no bones about it, either. Whenever I am commissioned to write a piece, I never play eager, but ask immediately what is 'the least possible words by the latest possible time' I can do. At first, people laughed, thinking I was mucking about, but they soon realised that I was serious and, let me tell you, they know who's boss now. And, if I should somehow finish my work before time, I'll sit on it until the last possible minute. Because I know for a fact that the more work you do, the more you'll get dropped on to you.

There is something hideously unsexy about busy, efficient or 'driven' people. As for 'thrusting', as used in the context of work, well, what are they trying to overcompensate for? (Just think of poor Ian Beale in *EastEnders*.) Imagine how bad in bed those men who are always in a hurry must be; those mobile drones with their phones on the train, wanting everything done last week.

And the sort of strange woman who finds such men attractive! They obviously looked a bit too long at Adam Chance in *Crossroads* and never got over it. Chances are that, if you are 'busy, busy, busy' (and, obviously, I'm talking here about white-collar workers, not nurses or people looking after their old parents), you are actually thick, thick, thick, because you haven't got the wit to skive, skive, skive or delegate, delegate, delegate.

Busy people often act like martyrs, but the fact is that they are tremendous egoists; they believe – or at least they want the onlooker to believe – that if they let up for one minute the world will end. I don't for a moment believe that about myself or anybody, and indeed the fact is that most people would do their jobs better if they did them less, not more. Don't make that deadline; take the long way home. When you see two queues, stand in the longer one and daydream. And look, Chicken Licken, the sky still won't fall down.

5 AUGUST 2000

When I was young, I was very partisan. Everything, with me, was for or against – *Blue Peter* vs *Magpie*, Bowie vs Bolan. I put a lot of it down to growing up in a city with two football teams. If you've got one (Brighton, say, or Torquay), then you're united, and if you've got loads (London), they kind of cancel each other out. But if it's the either/or example of Bristol City and Bristol Rovers (and, similarly, in Manchester, Liverpool and Glasgow), it encourages an antagonistic mentality. At my junior school, knowing the lyrics to 'The Red, Red Robin' (City) when you should have known the lyrics to 'Goodnight, Irene' was the difference between living your life as a social pariah and living it as a sidekick of the gods. (It says so much about the superiority of Bristol Rovers that only they had the imagination to take their anthem from the old blues legend Leadbelly.) On the home front, and until I was at least ten years old, I thought that 'Capitalist!' was literally a swear word, such was the vehemence with which my dad yelled it at the TV screen. On many a night I was awoken from my childish truckle bed to be carried downstairs to watch the latest victories of the Viet Cong. Thus I grew up unable not to feel strongly about the slightest of Issues, and could be driven to white-knuckle rage by those bovine types who would say, when asked to choose between, for example, spring and autumn, 'Oh, you can't really choose, can you, because it's like comparing apples and oranges.' But why can't you compare apples and oranges – why can apples be compared only with other apples?

By 18, my lack of ability to see the other chap's POV had me marching behind an SWP banner against the National Front and penning vicious pieces in the *NME* about the rash of nihilist punks, such as Howard Devoto (I know this is getting boring now, but hang on in there), who refused to nail their colours to the mast with self-adoring songs such as 'Shot by Both Sides'. Shot by both sides? As if anyone would bother. My fiercely partisan view of the world lasted until I was well into my thirties. When I was courting my ex-girlfriend, I once broke up with her – though admittedly only for a day – when she refused to agree with me that if Adolf Hitler had lived he should have been put to death. It was an incredibly hedonistic, pleasurable affair, too, so you can imagine how strange and surreal it must have seemed, suddenly interrupting our idyllic sunny afternoon sessions with bouts of interrogation about her preferred method of punishment for the world's major dead war criminals. But now, in my forties, I actually appear to have started seeing both sides of loads of arguments. Take the proposed repeal on public sex for homosexuals. No one wants to be on the same side as a bunch of joyless *Daily Mail* curtain-twitchers, but doesn't demanding the right to use public conveniences for one's private pleasure seem rather selfish, almost crypto-Thatcherite? There is no such thing as society, just my own spontaneous sexual fancies. Most of us manage to wait until we get home. Why not gay men? Then there's the euro, and imperial measures. I certainly don't want to live in a world of bland euro-portions, where high streets from Hounslow to Hamburg to The Hague all look and sound the same, but I can't help thinking that the very people who are asking us to get hot under the collar (measured in inches, natch) about our national identity and sovereignty are the very same people – the *Daily Mail* again, Mrs T, the *Spectator* – who have spent the past 50 years crawling so far up the fundament of the US that only the soles of their feet are now visible. It seems highly unlikely that the EU could wreak anything like the havoc on the political, social and cultural life of this country that the US has done, so why all the panic and purity suddenly? Similarly, the sight of the G8 summit, at a cost of £500 million – including, for some reason, a £4 million replica of Bill Clinton's home in Arkansas – was repellent but, on the other hand, what sort of message about independence and putting their own house in order does it send to the developing world if we keep treating it like a ditzy wife who has run up a huge credit-card bill, pranged the company car and still expects to get away with it scot free? These countries did, after all, clamour for independence and autonomy, which seems hardly compatible with such indulgence. Then there's economic immigration – and before you get your recycled Biros out, I'm obviously not referring to people who flee in fear for their lives, but rather to those people who come here in pursuit of a better lifestyle. No one wants to see people dying in the backs of vans – but what is the long-term effect on the already weak developing world if its fittest, brightest and most able people are welcomed into the West as yet more fodder for our many-mawed corporate monster? Surely it would be far better for everyone if those people with skills stayed at home and used them for the betterment of their own struggling countries. Yet I know that, if I was one of these same people, I would be over here like a shot. This is, after all is said and done, the best country out of a bad bunch, and I would certainly never want to live anywhere else. So it seems a bit phoney of me to be against any sort of immigration. (Just as phoney, in fact, as those knee-jerk liberals who are always running England down, but then, when it comes to immigration, seem to change their minds completely and maintain that a man's life isn't worth living unless he can live it on this sceptred isle.) The immediate effect on my day-to-day life of seeing both sides of an argument is that I feel a good deal more relaxed and tranquil, but also, if the truth be told, only half alive. That's not to say I'm not happier. It's just that I do miss the adrenalin rush that fierce, blinding hatred of the other side invariably provided, and I'm sure that's why a lot of people go in for hate on a regular basis. Hate, like love, stirs up certain pleasurable chemicals in us that become addictive. Meanwhile, I'm going to kick back and enjoy the summer scraps from my vantage point, and dream of the day when I'm back in the fray once more.

12 AUGUST 2000

I once had a very dear friend whose dancing was described as 'stiff in all the wrong places'. This Government, in contrast, is liberal in all the wrong places. If you are a sick person waiting for an operation, an old person waiting for a decent pension rise or an unemployed person hoping for a little dignity – you're joking, aren't you? If, however, you are a psychopathic Irish murderer of either denomination, General Pinochet or a paedophile with an average of 300 offences against children by the time you're finally caught (as the average paedophile has), you can expect to be chucked under the chin and sent along home with an ominous, 'And don't do it again!' Watching the Maze murderers trot off to get their 'compensation', never has that old *Private Eye* line about misplaced clemency rung truer: MURDER NOW AND WIN A FORD FIESTA!

Why do governments, establishments and judicial systems of every complexion do all they can to let nasty people get away with things – be they the IMF or a kinky headmaster – while pouring contempt on the meek, the poor and the law-abiding? I've been thinking about this for a long time, and I've come to the conclusion that civilised 'soft' men – that is, men who push pens, make laws and wear white collars for a living – in a horrible primeval part of their minds, still believe that they should be uncivilised 'hard' men; men who go around causing havoc, hurt and mayhem wherever they can. They obviously can't chuck it all in and run off to enact a career of evil themselves, but when they are called upon by the people to deal with such types, their innate sympathy and self-loathing show through in the way that they do not come down on them with the full force of the law but rather bend over backwards to excuse any old wife murderer, child molester, mad bomber or Fascist dictator. Forge a banknote or sell some drugs, however, and they'll clap you away for life; your crimes weren't 'manly' enough, you see.

Of course, I don't go along with mad old Mugabe in believing that this Government is made up exclusively of effeminate homosexuals, but you must admit that it has a higher proportion of Softies than any in recent memory – even our rampantly heterosexual leader always took the female parts in school plays, and was known by jealous classmates at various points in his education as both 'Emily' and 'Miranda'. And as we know from the work of artists as varied as Genet, Pasolini and Isherwood, there's nothing like being a Softie oneself to make one admire the thug, the brute and the bully. This sad syndrome is currently a great force in popular culture, as well as in politics. The sorry spectacle of public-schoolboys making films about how well dressed, witty and cool working-class sociopaths are continues with the forthcoming *Snatch*, the latest film by Guy Ritchie, whose mother is a Lady.

In the recent controversy over the naming of paedophiles, it was interesting to see how the Government and its most virulent critics on both left and right combined to speak as one logical, male, middle-class voice to quell the fears (and, covertly, mock the efforts) of a supposedly illogical, mostly female, massively working-class mob. Suddenly, people who have shown nothing but contempt for and mistrust of the police were lecturing the *News of the World* and its readers to 'let the police and professionals deal with it'. Is this the same 'inherently racist' police force that 'bungled' the Stephen Lawrence case, or is it another lot?

The fact is that the contempt shown to anxious parents is part and parcel of the contempt shown to the working class of this country over the past 20 years. For, make no mistake, it is working-class children who are the victims of abduction, assault by strangers and murder; the rest live their lives in a cradle-to-rave bubble of play-dates and people-movers. The lonely death of a raped child in England is in no way less 'political' than that of an African child by starvation; both are about the triumph of brute force over beauty and innocence. A sensible socialist should have no more scruples about watching the execution of a child murderer than she should have about watching the execution of the heads of the world banks. Not only have the working classes been stripped of their rights at work and in unemployment, they are not even allowed to be fully informed in order to protect their one precious thing – their children – to the best of their abilities.

We are told by liberals in law, media and government that we mustn't back any laws that might make paedophiles 'more' dangerous; we must, it seems, speak soothingly to them, not make any sudden moves and wind them three times a day after meals. But no one ever seems to care about making decent, law-abiding people meaner and nastier, which successive governments' failure to punish evil adequately certainly has done. Seeing how this Government seems tirelessly determined to punish virtue and reward violence has, I'm afraid, turned even me from a rather docile and squeamish individual into a full-on red-mist mentalist. Not a day now goes by when I do not imagine what it would feel like physically to injure a member of the current regime. For instance, I cannot see murderers swagger from the Maze, their victims' bodies still lost and unburied, without wanting to shut Peter Mandelson's treacherous hand, which signed the documents that freed them, in a car door, or hear about British bankrolling of yet another bunch of filthy foreign gangsters without feeling a compulsion to put Robin Cook's beard in a mangle and turn it until his eyes pop. On hearing that Lord Irvine had spent £1,528 of public money on two heated towel rails in the same week as the majestic 15p rise for pensioners was announced, I had a brief but pleasing fantasy of tying him, naked, to those same towel rails – one at the front, one at the back – and leaving him like that until his skin came off in strips. And who, on hearing Paul Boateng's quite repulsively posh and priggish voice assuring us that working-class parents have absolutely no need to be informed of active paedophiles in their communities, can honestly say that it would be much of a loss if one day soon he was left to rot in a muddy field somewhere?

See what I mean? But it's not my fault that society made me like this. Don't make me any angrier, I'm warning you, or I might go underground. At least while I'm writing here, you can keep an eye on me.

26 AUGUST 2000

My old alma mater (a strange phrase that, and one I always imagine eliciting the response, 'I'm not your mother, and don't call me Alma!'), the *NME*, recently compiled a list of the Top 30 most miserable albums, inspired by similar lists in both Nick Hornby's *High Fidelity* and David Eggers's *A Heartbreaking Work of Staggering Genius*. The American Seventies pop group Big Star topped the list with the horribly maudlin *Sister Lovers*. Big Star are, incidentally, the fave rave of no less than Gordon Brown, which doesn't bode very well for his marriage, as I've never met a woman who could stand more than two minutes of them.

Anyway, all the usual suspects were there – Kurt Cobain, Nick Drake, Ian Curtis, Billie Holliday, Gram Parsons, Jeff Buckley – all of them dead, while the rest would be better off that way, to judge from the weeping and whining on show. Surprisingly to some people, the Smiths were nowhere to be seen, which backs up my theory that there was never anything slightly depressing about them, and that Morrissey was just having a laugh. Would that *NME*'s editor, Ben Knowles, had similar access to his funny bone: 'Music can be the most incredibly positive and uplifting experience – but I wouldn't advise listening to too many of them in one sitting.' (Thank you, Amos Starkadder.) To most women, such doomsaying is a complete and utter mystery, albeit a laughable one, as is the male attraction to depressing pop music; only four of the 30 records were by women, too. When gals get drunk, they want to dance to 'I Will Survive' and 'Dancing Queen'; when men get drunk, they want to hug the stereo and listen to Joy Division. 'Last night a DJ saved my life!' goes a happy female disco hit from the Eighties; men would rather listen to John Peel spinning The Sulking Scabs singing 'I Love You (But You're Dead)' and make it worse.

This is because, as I've said before, women largely lack the self-pity gene. Maybe it was bred out of them because their lives are so much tougher than men's (periods, childbirth, low pay, breast cancer, the menopause, some of them having to have sex with David Baddiel) that Nature realised that the addition of self-pity to this sorry stew would mean that the female population might commit ritual suicide on their 12th birthdays rather than tramp on through this vale of tears.

Whatever the reasons, it was very sweetly summed up when the *NME*, in a follow-up to its chart, asked nine young recording artistes what their favourite sad songs were. While the eight men asked chose appealing-sounding songs such as 'Tractor Rape Chain' and 'Buzzards and Dreadful Crows', the one little lady involved, Kathryn Williams, chose 'Astral Weeks' by Van Morrison, because 'it just takes you somewhere else. If you're feeling a bit drowsy or down, it just perks you up. It makes you feel like you've been sitting in the sun all day.'

Isn't that adorable? The self-pity gene of this particular young woman was obviously just so inactive that she automatically turned the question inside out in her mind and changed it to 'What record makes you feel happy?', simply because, like most women, she couldn't see any point in making a drama out of a crisis.

Whole musical genres have been built around male self-pity, which is often the flip side of narcissism – the blues (quite justifiable, what with slavery), folk, heavy metal and rap. This last is peculiarly vile and depressing in its puffed-up, queeny melodrama – if Eminem felt any more sorry for himself, he'd explode. Rap, which is massively male, is the wet blanket thrown on the black female joyfulness and optimism of dance and soul. With the black-on-black killing of young men at epidemic proportions in the US, rap is also more proof, if it were needed, that, despite what stupid old Lenny Bruce said about using it so much that it lost its sting, the word 'Nigger' will always represent ignorance and loathing. Only now, it is self-loathing, too – leading, in turn, to more male self-pity, while black women look on the bright side and continue to climb the ladder of education and work.

To judge by the way British boys are performing at school, they have also been listening to the siren song of self-pity on their Walkmans. 'Aww, shucks – if the system isn't going to be utterly weighted against girls like it was for the first 40 years of secondary school exams, I ain't gonna play! I'm gonna listen to my Eminem records, feel sorry for myself, never do my homework and, hey, I'll still be king of the world, because that nice David Blunkett is so worried about girls coming top for one lousy year that he'll soon have switched things around – less course-work, less poncy fiction-reading – so that boys are on top again!' Take into account, also, that well into the Seventies even grammar schools – those allegedly honourable centres of excellence – habitually adjusted the marks of boys and girls so that three-quarters of their pupils would not be female, and you have to ask yourself whether girls being on top academically may simply be the natural order of things, and one of the reasons God made men so big and strong. There's always going to be a demand for bin-men, navvies and strong-men at the circus – I don't know what Blunkett's getting in such a state about.

But male self-pity is not always funny; sometimes, it serves as an excuse for the most loathsome sorts of behaviour. A handy catch-all cliché that the ivory-tower-dwellers among us have been dishing up in an attempt to turn popular feeling against those appalling oiks in Paulsgrove (my God, I bet none of them has even read one Julian Barnes novel!) is, 'The abused, in turn, abuse.' This is, rather, one of the silliest and most easily disproved of modern myths. Some 90 per cent of abused children are women; some 90 per cent of child abusers are men. If it was really true that 'the abused abuse', then 90 per cent of all child abusers would be women, wouldn't they?

But no – even in this arena, women who have suffered sexual abuse as children seem infinitely more likely to make a conscious effort to stop the cycle of monstrousness, and not to inflict it on anyone else. Too many alleged male victims of molestation, though, cannot see beyond their own pain, and seem determined to make others suffer. The recent self-pity displayed by certain paedophiles has been awesome in its lack of self-awareness. But then, self-pity has always been the ecstasy of the worthless. So put down that Radiohead record RIGHT NOW – yes, you! You never know where it will end.

2 SEPTEMBER 2000

Yippee skippee! According to doctors at Edinburgh University, we may well be looking at a safe, effective and commercially available male Pill some time over the next five years. Why, then, does my heart not skip a beat in sheer molten gratitude, as the men in white coats believe the hearts of all sexually active women across the nation should?

Lots of reasons, actually; let's start with the ignoble, demeaning cliché. Are women, who are notoriously better at remembering things than men, really going to gamble with their hard-won controlled fertility on the backs of a breed who can barely remember one birthday and one anniversary a year, let alone to take a pill more than 200 times during it? And, at the risk of sounding like an Anthony Trollope novel, Do You Really Trust Him? I know well from talking to my younger friends that these days it is often the male half of a couple who yearns to hear the patter of tiny trainers, while the distaff side desires nothing more than to concentrate on her career before she comes anywhere near having that greasy stuff smeared on her stomach so they can give her a scan. Take one broody man, one woman with an irrational prejudice against abortion, stir in the male Pill and *voilà!* – a liar's charter.

Not only does the male Pill hold the possibility of making your man into a liar, don't you think that, even supposing he remembers to take it and you remain childless, it makes him a bit of a daddy, too? Your daddy, that is: there is something rather unwholesomely I can't-handle-this-nasty-contraception-thing-look-after-me-please about handing responsibility for your sexuality over to someone else.

And it works both ways: not only does he become The Boss,

but you become a Good Girl, rather more so than is good for any romantic relationship. If you're handing over contraception duties to him, your husband/boyfriend's going to trust you a touch too much; if there's no chance of anybody but him picking them apples, they're going to start looking not half as juicy. This is not to say that actively attempting to make your spouse jealous is anything but pathetic.

But on the other hand, what he imagines you getting up to on your nights off is nothing to do with you. Many studies show that the stronger the suspicion that his gal is not altogether dead from the waist down where other men are concerned, the more your average man makes a big effort to be good in bed. The old chestnut 'Treat 'em mean and keep 'em keen', always the fastest way to become catnip to boys, mutates into 'Keep 'em sure and be a bore' when we imagine a male Pill.

Then there's the fact that I like a quiet life, as I'm sure you do. After two marriages of (to paraphrase 'Living Doll') screaming, squawking, keening, sulking hysterics, I am now lucky enough to be going steady with a young man of almost unbelievable sweet temper. Long exposure to such sunniness has rendered me, too, extremely easygoing and barely recognisable as my uptight Eighties self, and I have no desire to return to this tormented state. One of the main reasons for marital discord is, I believe, the mad, modern desire to share everything, from household tasks to bank accounts. The key to domestic harmony, on the other hand, is to divide everything, so that each has his job and doesn't interfere with the other one. Hence I would no more dream of letting my boyfriend drive my fertility than I would dream of trying to drive his car. Stick to what you're best at, and happiness will result.

Let's face it, romantic relationships are full of arguments just waiting to happen, and sharing rather than dividing tasks is the quickest way to end up in a whirlwind of resentment and martyrdom; it also leaves women wide open to that eternal dirty dig of 'nagging'. And there's worse. If you get pregnant through your own miscalculations or poor memory skills, you're going to breathe a quick 'Ooo! Stupid cow' before booking that lunchtime termination. If he gets you pregnant through his own inefficiency or idleness, the potential for relationship-wrecking fights is limitless. You're not going to forgive him quickly, if at all.

Then again, it's political. Women fought and died and worried their brains in order to help you gain control of your one and only body. Are you really happy to hand yours over to a man, no matter how benign, just because bothering with contraception is a 'drag'? Yeah, voting's pretty annoying, innit, having to drag yourself down to the polling station – I know, why not let your husband vote for you, too? Then you'll have even more time to spend at the hairdresser. As politicians are always telling us, you can't have rights without responsibilities. If this is so, it's very likely that the reverse is true, too. Let a man share responsibility for your reproductive system, and before long he is going to feel that he has rights over it; in short, he is going to become one of those men you hear of in America who burst into the operating room just before aforementioned lunchtime abortion and start screaming scary crap about it being his ickle baby, too!

My last reason for being sceptical about a male Pill is the most embarrassing, and the hardest to put across without sounding as though I have swallowed one too many Black Lace books, but bear with me. I actually like the idea of aggressive, rampaging sperm, and of my duty as a healthy, modern, selfish woman to evade and frustrate them at every turn. Day in and day out, the sexually active woman who refuses to obey Nature's diktat that she become a walking incubator once a year for 20 years scores a near triumph against the tyranny of biology; if the man's firing blanks to begin with, it does rob us of our victory somewhat. In the eternal battle between sperm and ovum, I want to be Bette Davis, walking all over the opposition in Fuck-Me shoes; I don't want to be Jennifer Aniston, muddling meekly through with a lot of help from her friends. And while I may be an extreme case, I feel that for a lot of women the merest likelihood of conception makes sex more exciting; I've only known one girl who was married to a man who had a vasectomy, and whereas before she had been perfectly faithful to him, within three weeks she had run off with an imperfect stranger she met at a party. Mind you, the dumped hubster was a sexually repellent premature ejaculator, so that might have had some bearing on it.

Phew, that's better. But to get back to basics, I would suggest that if a woman is so loath to organise something as fundamental as her own fertility, it could be a sign that she isn't that interested in sex anyway – 'He wants it so much, let him arrange it!' – in which case, perhaps you simply shouldn't be doing it at all. Now there is a revolutionary thought.

23 SEPTEMBER 2000

Babies: are they the New Baguettes (Fendi, not Pret à Manger), the New Sex or the New Salvation? Whatever, the Glossips (glossy gossip magazines: *Hello!*, *OK!* and *Now*) decided that something was in the air last week when all three starred on their front covers not a wedding, a scrummy chocolate bar – or even both – but babies. In the week following the terminally tarnished nuptials of Turner-Bovey Inc., the babies acted as tiny John the Baptists, supposedly cleansing the cash-for-most-profound-moments racket of its tacky taste – though why selling the first pictures of your infant is better than selling your marriage, which at least involves two consenting, if not quite sentient, adults, I'll never understand. And exactly what is the difference between being poor and making your child beg on the street and being worth millions and selling photographs of your children for another half a mill – as Iman and Bowie and Catherine and Michael have just done in *Hello!* and *OK!*, respectively, if not respectably – except that, if you're rich, you've really got no excuse?

Babies are currently the best way to launder whatever you feel is a bit lacking in sparkle in your life. They will launder your money, your sordid past, your boring present, and make sure you come up smelling of Eau de Bonnepointe. We are more or less immune to the cooing of a thousand blonde TV presenter girls, but there is something peculiarly repulsive about middle-aged showbiz millionaires with exciting, squalid pasts (and I say this as someone with an exciting, squalid past myself) wearing sick on their shoulders as if it were the George Cross and expecting to be taken to the heart of Middle England/Middle America/the Middle Ages. I'm talking about David Bowie, who regularly took his own weight in cocaine (admittedly, not difficult in the Seventies), insisted that another woman shared the wedding night bed with him and his poor first wife, and said things such as, 'Everyone's bisexual, man', and, 'What this country needs is a really strong fascist leader.' Now he says of his marriage and fatherhood, in the midst of an 18-page photo-spread, 'There's a joy and contentment that's almost palpable to both of us; overnight, our lives have been enriched beyond belief.' And Michael Douglas – he of the substance abuse and sex addiction, whose wife once found him in bed with her best friend – now simpers in the middle of a 21-page feature (mine's bigger than yours, Limey!) that 'I'm the official burper!' (Of the baby, one hopes.)

Of course, no one would turn down the chance of shacking up with Iman or Catherine Zeta Jones, and goodness knows I'm not condemning dumping spouses and moving on in one's life – what, me, the *Daily Mail*'s official Worst Mother in Britain? But there is something vile about men such as Bowie and Douglas, who are forever drawing attention to their own alleged integrity and liberal politics, not only cashing in on their private lives, but proclaiming them with such gluttonous gloating. Why should we give them any more credibility than we do to the Turner-Boveys? Yet, regardless of these grabfests, we undoubtedly will continue to read about Bowie's dedication to his art and Douglas's anti-Hollywood stance.

To my mind, you can't really blame a Turner or a Bovey for selling their souls: they are creatures only of and for the marketplace, with no resonance or responsibility in our culture. (No teenager ever sat sobbing in her bedroom, 'Oh, I hate my life – only Anthea Turner understands me!') On the other hand, the sex and drugs counterculture that both Bowie and Douglas enjoyed and exploited so flagrantly was, on balance, a far better thing than the joyless repression it replaced. But it did undoubt-edly create many casualties. And it is these people – the single mother on methadone, the Bowie casualty nodding out in a toilet somewhere, still convinced that the Starman will save him – that I can't help but think of when I see these huge spreads of ex-counterculture icons enjoying all the spoils that mainstream success, monogamy and jogging bring. More than anything, it's the same creepy feeling that hearing John Peel's *Home Truths* gives me. I know we're meant to genuflect before his portrait as though he was a hairy Queen Mother, but I find it filthily objectionable that someone who grew rich and respected from preaching the Sixties mantra 'if it feels good, do it!' can, when it suits them, come over so cosy and domestic that it would have Nigella Lawson reaching for the crack-pipe. Like his friend Bowie and their contemporary Douglas, Peel advocated ceaseless shagging and substance abuse as the road to the palace of wisdom. Yet because they had money, and lots of it, they managed to survive the Seventies and thrive in the decades that followed. For the young working class swept away by this message, however, the road of excess led to madness, alienation and incarceration.

I don't blame Peel, Bowie and Douglas for changing their minds. But I do blame them for rubbing our collective noses in the fact that the rich and famous can walk on the wild side and still return to the domestic fold when it suits them, whereas the young and poor need only stray off the straight and narrow once to be trapped in a cul-de-sac of sorrow.

And the third magazine, *Now*? Well, that featured babies, too – but not the beloved bartered little bundles of joy who have already proved so profitable to reformed roués and their young trophy wives. No, *Now* featured grim shots of Meg Mathews and Patsy Kensit pushing prams, with the headline 'Poor babies: Victims of the rock'n'roll lifestyle'. It was amazingly consistent, if nothing else. Though a million miles and pounds removed from some inner-city sink estate, Meg and Patsy got the blame simply by sticking around. Their globe-trotting husbands, on the other hand, were painted as the innocent victims. Patriarchy invariably finds a way of making all the nicest things in life into a stick with which to beat women: food (you'll get fat), alcohol (you'll get infertile), sex (you'll be a slag). Now, apparently, it even uses babies to beat their mothers with, while celebrating the spawning of old, rich men, regardless of their promiscuous pasts. Like Angela Bowie and Diandra Douglas, who have been effectively written out of their husbands' shiny new lives, the message to Meg and Patsy is clear: go on, clear off, and leave the field clear for your famous husbands to get married to someone younger, cleaner, fresher, with no stretch marks on their minds or bodies. Just like we wanted poor Paula Yates to. But, somehow, I think girls today are made of sterner stuff.

30 SEPTEMBER 2000

And the cant just keeps on coming – last weekend, the death of Paula Yates continued to push wars, famine and the fallout from Big Brother Bernie Ecclestone off the front pages of the nation's newspapers. If one is of a conspiracist set of mind, one might imagine that Paula had been sleeping with the president (sorry, prime minister), perhaps – as her great heroine Marilyn Monroe had done in her day – and that, when she threatened, in a last desperate midnight phone call to make their affair public, MI5 were sent in to do their stuff with a vodka bottle and a hypodermic. Just in time for the party conference.

What's that, you say? It's a load of old codswallop? Well, yes, if you want to nitpick. But it's certainly no more ludicrous than the rest of the swill that has been written about this woman since her death. The one truly alarming thing that Yates's death did reveal to me was not about the madness of modern society, but rather about the silliness of serious newspapers. It revealed, rather shockingly, that the broadsheet press is now home to even more Sob Sisters than the traditionally mocked tabloids. Come on down, Muriel, Justine, Jane, Deborah, Yvonne. The byline was different, but the sob remained the same: Paula Yates Died For Our Sins; Paula Yates, Innocent Victim Of A Feeding-Frenzied Media; Tragic Paula, Broken Butterfly On The Wheel Of

Misogyny. Paula, We Hardly Knew You! What Are We Doing? What Does It Mean? Where Are We Going? Where Have We Been? What's It All About, Alfie! Muriel Gray, whom I can only hope has since been sedated, went so far as to write of Yates that she was the most powerful British female role model of our age – a role model, in a country that contains Barbara Castle, Dr Sheila Cassidy and Kate Moss. A role model whose currency was blowjobs and breast enhancement. In the words of the great Jim Royle: Arse.

I'll put my cards on the table here. I met Paula when we were both 17, and we loathed each other from the word go. I came back to my desk at the *NME* one afternoon, and she was sitting on it, legs wide apart, no knickers, screeching at the top of her voice about sex. I was, without doubt, a stuck-up little madam, but I'd never seen anything so gross in my life.

I've read many times since that Paula was a part of 'the London punk scene', but this wasn't true at all; she never went to the Roxy or the Vortex, and she didn't know any of the groups – The Clash, Sex Pistols, The Jam or even, God help her, The Damned. I actually knew the groupies of the time, and they were intelligent, hard-working young women of working-class extraction, with names such as Sue and Tracey and Debbie, who were (and punk was unique in this, as far as I know) respected by the bands as mates and equals who just happened to get a lot of shagging done. None of these girls would have dreamed of giving any musician a blowjob 20 minutes after meeting him (and especially not Bob Geldof – Jesus!); that was sad, tacky, Sixties free-love shit.

Touchingly, Paula couldn't even be a groupie properly. She was too needy, too clammy. No wonder the other Boomtown Rats called her 'The Limpet'; as Queen Groupie titles go, it's hardly 'The Mouth' or 'Platinum Pussy', is it?

She envied me my cred; I envied her her confidence. We never stopped loathing each other. Our last point of contact was when a mutual friend tried to make peace, and she spat at him, 'Don't talk about that woman to me, because it's like talking to the Jews about Hitler' – a remark, it must be said, that in its sheer self-importance and tastelessness was typical of Paula. Nevertheless, our lives ran parallel. We both got married at 19 to stroppy, bossy horrors, and had children. In 1995, we both left our husbands for rather more exciting young lovers. I remember being in bed with my girlfriend at Blakes Hotel when I heard that Paula and Michael Hutchence had just been ambushed by the paparazzi coming out of a hotel – not as classy a one as Blakes, though – a few streets away; I remember feeling really clever that I was 'invisible', and that I could commit adultery without paying the price of public ridicule and reprimand. Eight weeks later, my lady love and I were splashed all over the tabloid press and my mother was crying inconsolably down the phone, on top of nursing my dad through the cancer that would soon kill him. Served me right.

We both lost custody of our children to bitter, self-righteous men, and suffered further media bullying about our suitability as mothers. We both took up with younger men, though mine turned out to be a total gem and hers turned out to be a parade of junkies, jokes and kiss-and-sellers. We both bought houses by the seaside, but, whereas I turned my back on London, Paula hung on in there, falling out of her dress at pap-infested parties and premieres. Keeping one foot in this arena meant, inevitably, that Paula would fret about her fading beauty, which was not a problem for me. Though I was a beautiful young woman, my looks were only ever the icing on the cake – writing was what really mattered. A good writer, when she could be bothered, Paula neglected her craft in favour of frocks and famous men;

she expected to have an easy ride through life because she was blonde and fluffy.

For a reputedly smart woman, why didn't she realise that being blonde and fluffy is no basis on which to build a life, and that Baby Doll turns to Baby Jane pretty damned quick if held a beat too long? F. Scott Fitzgerald wrote of poor mad, dead Zelda, 'Too late, she realised that work is the only dignity.' Paula, with her fantasies of being a perfect Fifties homemaker, never realised this.

No doubt having learned from our initial rejection and belated recognition of Monroe as a comrade in the sex war, we are always ready to claim any woman as a 'sister' when she dies young. But there is a happy medium between being catty and being over-emotional. Paula was not Marilyn, and she was certainly not the Princess of Wales; she had no resonance or significance for society as a whole, just to the people who loved her, which was surely enough. Let her be remembered, then, as a person, and by those who knew her; not as a symbol, a syndrome or a modern malaise by the Sob Sisters, however sympathetic, who didn't. Let her go.

14 OCTOBER 2000

I have always had a low opinion of my critics, but last weekend's shower, who decided that I was 'jealous' of poor Paula Yates, left me cackling with glee. God, yes, how could I not have seen it all these years – forget Dorothy Parker in her prime or Ava Gardner at her peak: what I really, REALLY wanted all along was to be a suicidal, silicone-breasted, bleached-blonde, 40-year-old mother of four, adulterous spawn of Hughie Green and a Bluebell Girl, with a dead boyfriend, an even deader career and a habit of being sick into her handbag at public parties. What a deluded fool I've been. I'll try to rectify matters now that you've drawn it to my attention. Shall I start by cultivating a heroin habit, or by making myself unemployable? I'll reach that state of grace that is Pauladom by any means possible.

A few days before, in this same newspaper, Charlotte Raven was accused of being 'jealous' of Nigella Lawson simply for stating the obvious: that someone who spends so much time creating such an ostentatiously 'perfect' life is obviously dealing with a good many demons. If anything, it was a new way of understanding and empathising with the Nigella Phenomenon, rather than writing her off as some sort of souped-up Proust'n'pashmina Stepford Wife. Apart from anything else, our combined critics are using the wrong word – they mean 'envious'. If we were 'jealous' of Paula and Nigella, it would mean we coveted them sexually. And who'd dare say such a thing of such flagrantly heterosexual gals as Miss Raven and myself?

I've noticed for a while now that when men criticise other men, not even the most immature observer will turn round and lisp, 'Oooh, you're jealous, Tom Bower – you're jealous of Richard Branson cos he's such a dish! And as for you, Michael Crick, stop being jealous of Jeffrey Archer, because he's such a better writer than you!' When a woman criticises another, however, the geek chorus is always on hand to prolong the myth that the only reason one woman could find another not to her taste would be because she envied her. It's a pathetic point of view, and one more suitable for readers of the *Daily Star*, frankly.

I don't think women are generally envious of other women. If they were, Jennifer Lopez wouldn't invariably be voted most beautiful woman in the world by other women. If we were uniformly green-eyed bitches, wouldn't we choose someone a bit more mundane, such as Meg Ryan or Sandra Bullock? The antipathy to *Big Brother*'s Melanie was read by some social critics as female antipathy to attractive women, but women despised Mel for one reason and one reason only – she was, personality-wise, a truly amazing combination of man-pleaser and control-freak, a hard double-punch to pull off, but one of spectacular awfulness when achieved. What sort of woman goes around letting men snog her, and then saying, 'You really shouldn't have done that', as though she was somewhere else at the time? Surely this is no way for a grown-up female to conduct herself – but then, Mel was rather odd, in that she was a 28-year-old woman who dressed like a teenager and lived with her mother.

Besides, Mel was never beautiful – she was 'attractive', a thin gruel when placed beside actual beauty, Claire the Florist. And didn't Mel herself realise this, to judge by her hostile body language when the luscious giggler first bounced through the door of the *Big Brother* house! In my experience, it's your 'attractive' women who can be most obsessed with the pecking order, as Mel proved. Beautiful girls and plain girls have pretty much sorted where they stand by the time they're 18, and cut their cloth accordingly, but the merely attractive girl spends her life feeling superior to the plain ones and inferior to the beautiful ones, and it can make her a bit of a bitch. Mind you, I don't say that disapprovingly – a touch of bitchiness can be the finishing touch in a woman, rendering pleasingly tart what might otherwise be wishy-washily bland.

Reading Patrick Jephson's 'exposé' of Diana, I could not believe the way some of the broadsheet harpies picked up on her tendency to swear, have affairs and laugh at dirty jokes as proof of her basic worthlessness. If we applied this strict no-sex-we're-saints criteria to men, everyone from Gandhi to Geldof would be out of the running as any sort of of hero. My favourite Diana moment has to be that much tutted-over time when she crept up behind the Legge-Bourke woman and whispered silkily, 'So sorry about the baby!' Frankly, if someone has a double-barrelled name and thinks that being accused of having an abortion is anything to get upset about, they deserve what they get.

Here, unusually, I think we did see in Diana's critics a touch of genuine girl-on-girl envy, albeit by a bunch of women who are motivated by a bourgeois form of class envy – 'If Charles had chosen me, little Lesley from Cheam, I'd have been a much better princess than that stuck-up bitch!' – as much as anything.

So, generally, women are not jealous of each other: how could the fashion rags sell as well if they were? Women don't buy them to look at the dreadful clothes, but rather to look at the beautiful models. Men are more envious of beautiful women than women are – envious generally, as well as jealous specifically, of any they may personally be in love with. This one's thick, that one's a gold-digger, the other one's a 'ho. When Eminem disses Christina Aguilera in that lisping little voice, say, I can't help but think of a drag queen made bitter by a real woman's breasts. And how do you explain the far greater ratio of male-to-female sex changes than female-to-male ones? Venus envy.

You can't blame men for envying women; I just wish they'd be more honest about it, instead of covering it up with macho and strut. It's only natural to like us more. For instance, off the top of my head, I can think of a dozen women who are so pretty that they make me want to stand up and cheer whenever I see a photo of them – Mariella Frostrup, Tamzin Outhwaite, Martine McCutcheon, Famke Janssen, Halle Berry, Natalie (though not Nicole) Appleton, Tyra Banks, Kylie (still), Kate Moss, Frankie Rayder, Amanda Burton and Emmanuelle Béart – but I'd have to think long and hard before I could compile a list of men who make me feel the same way. Yet I think I know enough about myself by now to know that I am at least 95 per cent heterosexual. This is why lesbianism makes so much more sense than male homosexuality. I find it far easier to appreciate the way that the loathsome Peter Stringfellow feels about women than I can understand the way the glorious George Michael feels about men. To be crude about it, you could call it the Scrotum Factor. I mean, who the hell can look at a scrotum and think, 'Wow!'?

21 OCTOBER 2000

Domestic violence has never been more fashionable, not to say radio-friendly. You can't go anywhere without hearing Eminem's queeny, hissy-fit whine – for a man who hates fags, he does a lovely job of sounding like a sitcom parody of one. As I think I've said before (this is a special service for my train-spotting readers who like to keep tabs on the number of times I use a particular line), when I hear Marshall Mathers III (in Eminem's real name, we get a delicious insight into what a nerd he really is) going on about Christina Aguilera and what a 'little bitch' she is, I am reminded of nothing so much as a silicone-breasted drag queen jealous of a real woman's breasts.

Aguilera claims that she initially attracted Mathers's wrath by saying that domestic violence was a bad thing. Wow, yes, what a bitch! You can't blame old Marshall for being mad at her, though. He has, after all, been given the impression by his female fans that nothing presses their buttons half as much as the idea of women being raped and murdered. The over-educated novelist Zadie Smith drools on about him like an overheated eight-year-old with a Ricky Martin fixation; Daphne and Celeste dream of marrying him – though, oddly, for two young women who are excited by such a threatening performer, they were reduced to tears earlier this year when a few plastic bottles were thrown at them at a pop festival. Rape and murder of women – good; throwing plastic bottles at them – bad. Is this what they call pretzel logic?

Mind you, this bilge came after a decade of shameful nonsense from the music press, which, being nerdy white boys par excellence, saw in rap music a quick, convenient way to feel well hard. There has always been the odd song about the advisability of killing one's 'woman' ('Delilah', 'Hey Joe', 'Where the Wild Roses Grow'), but with the development of gangsta rap in the late Eighties, the wholesale rape, torture and killing of women became almost mandatory. Not so much moon and June, as slice and dice. Suddenly, gently raised boys called Ben and Tim discovered the 'bitch slap', and their guilt about being white could be forgotten.

As it ever was, from Elvis to the Police, it is the whiter-than-white Eminem who has taken a music of black origin and had the greatest success with it. But, as black musicians seek to escape the straitjacket of violence, Eminem shows no sign of growing up. His most notorious song details the murder and disposal of his wife, Kim, and features their daughter, Haley, singing babyishly over the litany of abuse as her father explains how he is about to throw her mother's body in the river. If Eminem had been singing about killing a black man, say, and throwing his body in the river, would Zadie Smith still be wetting herself over him? And if not, why not? Why is it 'black humour' to sing about killing a white woman, but a horrible sin if the fictional victim is a black man? And, to confuse matters, what if Kim had been black? Would the song have then still been acceptable (she's still a bitch, after all) or not (oops, but she's from an ethnic minority)?

The point I am trying to make is not that domestic violence is 'worse' than racial violence, but that they are equally bad. It makes no moral sense to laugh at and excuse one and to revile the other. There are certainly more sexual hate crimes than racial hate crimes: two women a week in the UK are murdered by their partners; men who kill their wives are routinely let off with a pat on the head and a suspended sentence. If the white killers of black people were treated so lightly, there would quite rightly be riots. The judges who consider wife-murder a mere trifle didn't need Eminem to get them into such a filthy state, but it does demonstrate that, far from being 'rebel' music, a youth culture that finds domestic violence funny and cool is merely echoing the dominant and ultraconservative values of the Establishment.

The same Establishment, let us not forget, ennobled Sean Connery, who once said, 'To slap a woman is not the cruellest thing you can do to her.' (Imagine if he had suggested the same treatment for uppity immigrants – do you think he would have got that gong?) Then there was the highly respected lady novelist, recently created a life peer, who said she 'cheered' when, in *The Archers*, a vicious male character struck his girlfriend – she was, opined the Lady, 'unbearably smug' and thus deserved it. And don't let's forget the woman who owns the River Café, who said that her favourite way to spend an evening in was with something eggy on a tray 'and something fascinating on TV, like the O. J. trial', as if it were some superior soap. Would she have said the same about the trial of the policemen who beat up Rodney King – that it was a great accompaniment to a quiet supper? And Rodney King didn't even die.

Simpson was a wife-beater long known to the LAPD. Like all

wife-beaters, he was a sad little man made momentarily powerful by superior strength. When a man hits a woman – and I speak from personal experience – he seeks to blot out his own totally understandable lack of self-esteem in a moment of dominance. For that short period of seeing abject fear on the face of another person, he becomes John Wayne. And, like John Wayne, he is often full of righteous, if not justified anger: she did this, she didn't do that, she deserves it. When a man hits a woman, he seeks to remove her identity; she becomes an object, a child, something to be 'dealt' with. What he does instead is remove his own, and in raising his hand instantly negates all the centuries of civilisation and privilege that have been his, thereby becoming a beast. Despite whatever self-righteous alibi he may have been serving himself, he knows this, and his self-esteem plummets even lower, calling for yet another fix of fear inflicting. And so it goes on.

Worldwide, domestic violence causes more deaths of women aged 15–44 than cancer, malaria, traffic accidents and war. A quarter of women in this country will experience violence from a partner at some point in their lives. Domestic violence often starts or escalates during pregnancy. What a piece of work is Man. There are three times as many animal shelters in the US as there are refuges for battered women and their children. Think about that next time you hum along to 'Smack My Bitch Up'.

28 OCTOBER 2000

I don't know if any of you remember that fantastic bit in the film *Jackie Brown* where Bridget Fonda, playing a sexy slacker, is warned by her boyfriend as she lights up the nth joint of the day and surfs channels, 'That stuff's gonna rob you of your ambition.' Bridget giggles: 'Not if your ambition is to get high and watch TV!'

It was a great answer, and I thought of it the other day when the usual suspects were banging on about us endangering our poor ickle kiddies by stuffing them full of junk food and leaving them to fester on the sofa. When columnists use 'us' in this context, of course, they mean 'the working class', but they can't say that because they're meant to be liberals and it would sound snooty. So they cover themselves in communal guilt while covertly making the best of this fine opportunity to give the proles a good kicking; yes, the paedophile protests in Portsmouth have died down, but here's another window of contempt for oiks that every good closet-patrician can access.

I'm not so sure, myself; having grown up working class, it's struck me as I've moved up the social ladder how much more right about lots of things they instinctively are than their so-called betters – who don't even come out of full-time education until their mid-twenties and spend the rest of their lives exploiting the contacts they made during it and their family connections, rather than truly making their own way in the world. If you took away their cleaners and nannies, I doubt whether these people could cope for a weekend nearly as well as numerous single parents I've known living in garden-free council flats. And yes, I am aware of how self-righteous that sounds and, no, I don't give a toss.

Nigella Lawson and her fragrant ilk are currently berating the working-class women of Britain for condemning their kids to a life of corpulence and couch-potatory; excitable Health Minister Yvette Cooper has even more of her elastic in a twang, declaring that today's children 'may' not live as long as their parents. But Bridget's answer rings once more in my ears; why should working-class children want to be fit? And why should they want to live until they are 90?

Should they be fit for the soul-destroying call-centre McJobs which will be their main source of income now that traditional industry has been destroyed? Should they want to stay fit into middle-age so that they can experience being told that they are too old to hire at 55, as they have seen happen to their grandparents? And should they want to live to be old so that they can receive a 75p a week rise in their pension, find that DO NOT RESUSCITATE is written on their hospital records and wait five years for a hip operation before dying on a trolley in the corridor of some filthy hospital? Is it any wonder that the working class often do not appear to have the same attachment to longevity as the middle class, but would rather enjoy the here and now?

Maybe they have it right, like dogs eating grass to then attain the desired effect of making themselves sick after ingesting poison. Because whatever our class, the fact remains that those of us who do not die of heart disease brought on by a sedentary lifestyle, will probably die of cancer, brought on by Christ knows what. In the past two years, I have seen both my parents die; my father, who was extremely fit and sporty, slowly and painfully from a type of cancer and my mother, who was extremely self-indulgent, from a heart attack in the time it took me to leave the room and make her a cup of tea. And I sure as hell know how I'd like to go. 'Five portions of fruit and veg a day!' we chant like children afraid of the dark, convinced that this bizarre counting ritual will in some way help us.

Alternatively, you could eat, drink and be chubby, because we're all going to die anyway. 'Gimme a pig's foot and a bottle of beer,' sang Bessie Smith, and her delight in the swinish pleasures of gluttony reflected a *joie de vivre* that just wouldn't be the same if we changed it to an apple and a bottle of Evian. Health is often what we obsess about the most when we lack those things which make life truly transcendent: politics, sex, God.

Those who place too much emphasis on healthy eating display a fear of both life, in all its messiness, and death, in all its inevitability. And I've got to say that the muesli-munching middle classes, last time I looked, didn't even throw up half as many appealing physical specimens as the junk-crunching proles, from where we recruit our best examples of beauty and athleticism: Moss, Campbell, Lewis, Beckham.

Middle-class parents may stuff their children full of fruit and veg, but they abuse them in a hundred ways completely unknown to the innocent, coronary-courting sink-estate mum, by hot-housing them academically until suicide seems a welcome option (middle-class young men aged between 18 and 25 have never killed themselves as much, often just before or after an 'important' exam), by making them appear in self-serving TV programmes as dinky accessories to their parents' fab lifestyle, and worst of all by waving their horrible hairy scrotums in tiny children's faces in the name of (yeah, right) 'growing up with a healthy attitude to sex'.

Among all of last week's breast-beating about the beastly proles killing their kiddies with calories, no one so much as raised an eyebrow at an excerpt from John Mortimer's forthcoming autobiography, printed in a Sunday paper: 'I was 62 when my daughter Rosie was born. When she was very young we were having a bath together (a fact which would lead to our immediate arrest if known to the social workers) and she suddenly said, "I don't love you, Dad."

'"That's very sad," I told her.

'"Yes," Rosie admitted, "it's sad but it is interesting."'

Such is the arrogance of the middle classes that it obviously never occurred to Mortimer that his daughter had ceased to love him because, let's face it, to be trapped in a confined space with a naked, wet, 62-year-old John Mortimer must be so unpleasant that it would feel to a small child exactly like a punishment, one that must be outlawed somewhere in the Geneva Convention – he's a lawyer, he should know. I've often thought it would be fun to be a lesbian, but such an early experience would make it practically compulsory. No, there's definitely worse things I could do than fill my teen angel up with carbos; praise the Lord and pass the chip pan.

4 NOVEMBER 2000

If there's one thing I hate it's UnBooks – all those nasty, market-driven gimmicky little bits of fluff such as Craig Brown's *Little Book of Crap*, Sada Walkington's *Babe's Bible* and, um, Julie Burchill's *Diana*, if you're going to be a cat about it. Whereas a real book is a glorious pustule of pain and pleasure, bursting forth with a life of its own, an UnBook is nothing more than an extended magazine article, plumped up and puffed out by publisher and hack in cahoots to part the punter from his money.

Mind you, there's an exception to every rule, and one of my prized possessions is *The Complete Naff Guide*, published by Arrow Books in 1983. Comprising hundreds of hilarious lists of all things naff, one of my favourites is the following, which I've edited for reasons of space:

Naff parasexual activity:

Riding.

Watching wrestling on TV.

Dancing on own in self-adoring way in discotheque.

Walking around in the nude.

Walking in Wales.

Climbing mountains.

Playing squash.

Being a schoolmaster.

Having a massage in the afternoon from a tattooed Turk.

See anything missing there? How about cooking, decorating and gardening? Of course, this was the innocent Eighties, when we were all sure – from my thoroughly respectable working-class parents to my profoundly reprobate media mates – that leisure time was solely designed for the extreme usage of sex and alcohol. If you'd have told us that within ten years British people would be working longer hours with less job security than anyone else in Europe, yet still the minute they walked in the front door would not reach for the Scotch bottle but for the secateurs, stencils or saffron, we'd have – well, we wouldn't have said anything, because we'd have been in a sex-and-drink stupor.

The New Domesticity – is it parasexual, or what? Cooking – all that kneading and whipping and rising. Gardening – all that poking and prodding and planting seeds down on your knees. And as for decorating – sweating and sawing and pushing things in where they've no chance of fitting, splashing paint and paste all over the show. If they still made *Carry On* films, they wouldn't be set in holiday camps and hospitals, as they used to be, but in TV studios concerned with the making of cooking, gardening and decorating programmes. *Double* your *entendre* and take it away!

Of course there's always been TV drudges, but we never felt the need to fancy them before. No one drooled on about Percy Thrower and Fanny Cradock, even though their names seemed to beg for a verbal groping. Yet this island is full of boobies who claim to fancy Charlie Dimmock and Alan Titchmarsh, Carol Smillie and Handy Andy, Nigella Lawson and Jamie Oliver. (Okay, scratch that last one. Not fancying Jamie Oliver would be as perverse as not fancying a golden Labrador puppy, and I certainly don't intend to rock the boat on this one.) It's because we're putting our sex-emotions where our nesting-emotions should be, and vice versa, and everything's got horribly skewed. I recently read poor dear Roy Strong describing a vile-sounding gardening book (*A Gentle Plea for Chaos*, by Mirabel Osler) thus: 'This is gardening as a tempestuous, angry love affair.' I'm sorry, but that's just plain barking.

I once heard a comic say how sad and strange it is that when we're home-bound teenagers and have nowhere to have sex in the warm and dry, we want it all the time. But the minute we get our own home and warm, dry rooms in which to Do It, we don't want to Do It at all. The New Domesticity is the buzz of clamorous denial that desire is dead: Oh, I'd love to have wild dirty sex with you, but I've got to ice this cake/rag-roll this wall/prune these roses.

When did all this rushing about like Keystone Kops start? I bet they don't do it in Italy. Nor in the past, that other sun-kissed foreign country, either. When my parents got home from work, and I from school, we were more than happy to laze fustily around the imitation-log gas fire and gaze raptly at 'colour TV' eating fish and chips from newspaper. Walking the dog around the block was the only reason we would ever see fit to stir our stumps. As a child, it was the most restful and secure home life I can imagine. If my mother had been constantly in the kitchen, or my father in the garden, or the pair of them running wildly around the house re-decorating it, I wouldn't have liked that at all. I'd have thought there was something wrong with their marriage. And I'd have been right.

One of the great things about going steady with someone is the endless hours you can spend with them doing absolutely nothing; like a lot of other things about love, from baby voices to nipple-sucking, it takes you right back there to a pre-work state of grace. The minute you feel the need to look for diversion, the magic has gone. And you might as well start dividing up your records now, because whether it takes six months or six years, your love is on the way out.

Pulp's greatest and saddest song, 'Live Bed Show', says it best: 'She doesn't have to go to work/But she doesn't want to stay in bed/Cos It's changed from something wonderful/To something else instead.' People seem to have totally lost the ability to do nothing; perhaps that's why we're addicted to *The Royle Family* – we think we're laughing at them, but we're really envying their comatose comfort. Frightened by the insecurity of the jobs market, perhaps, it is almost as if we feel that Da Big Boss Man can see us even when we're at home, and we feel we've got to prove to him that our work ethic goes right to the bone.

To put a twist on that really dumb cliché about how 'people who love animals don't like people', I would say that there is a good case to be made that people who bang on a bit too much about 'beautiful homes' and 'happy families' don't actually like people, in all their difficult, messy glory. In the past, it was the tyrannical Mr Barrett-type paterfamilias who sought to bend and break his family to his will in the name of domestic harmony. Now it comes smelling of vanilla, nutmeg and varnish. But it's still a con. 'Home' is where the people we love are. And once they're gone, no cooking smells, stencilled borders or roses around the door will make it home again. It's time we stopped kidding ourselves otherwise, put down our mindless implements, stopped our endless fidgeting and enjoyed our loved ones while we can.

9 DECEMBER 2000

I don't normally feel the need to return to the scene of a hate-crime – once I've dissed 'em, they stay dissed – but in John Lennon's case, I will make an exception. John Lennon! Even his name makes me feel nauseous. Was one human being, with the possible exception of Jeffrey Archer, ever such an all-weather compendium of lies, boasts and eye-watering phoneyness? It's actually quite hard to think of a person you can't stand one damned thing about – even Jeffrey Archer's good for a cheap laugh – but Lennon takes the booby prize every time. I would have let the old geezer rest in pieces if there hadn't been this recent flurry of sentimental activity around his remains. The *Beatles Anthology* book comes out and cretins queue all night for it. That album gets to number one. George Michael, whose once-sharp brain must surely have been well bleached by the bright brazen sun of La-La Land, buys Lennon's piano, partly 'to keep it out of tiny hands in Tokyo' and partly because 'Imagine' was – ahem – the greatest song ever written, casting a giant shadow over today's bonsai bands. Liam Gallagher, Mr Brains Trust himself, names his kiddie after his all-time hero, while, in a Putative Project of truly sumptuous grotesquerie, plans for Yoko Ono and Michael Jackson to bring a *Yellow Submarine* musical to the West End stage in 2002 are announced.

To cap it all, any swot lucky enough to be blessed with BBC Choice can tonight experience 'an evening of programmes dedicated to one of the greatest singer-songwriters and one of the most influential political artists of modern times'. Yes, be still my beating heart as the Professional Widow introduces such toe-tapping classics as 'Instant Karma', 'Power to the People' and 'No. 9 Dream' (bet you can't whistle that one). There's also an ass-sucking documentary, *Gimme Some Truth*, in which (according to a reverent BBC press release) 'an American fan turns up on Lennon's doorstep saying that he needs to talk to him because he believes that Lennon's lyrics were written specifically for him. He is invited into the house for something to eat.' For some reason, this piece of writing made me hoot with laughter, so I just wanted to share it with you. And, as the cherry on top, there's a long, lingering look at the 'Lennon Shrine' in New York's Central Park, containing interviews with 'the thousands of people who make a pilgrimage to the shrine on the anniversary of his death'. And every one of them nuttier than his killer, Mark Chapman, I'll be bound.

Lennon; what a phoney! For a start – working-class hero? My arse. The Marianne Faithfull cover version was more heartfelt! Lennon was about as working class as a Wilmslow dentist, unlike Paul, George, and Ringo. That's why the tosser was at art school in the early Fifties, for Pete's sake! (And, on the subject of Petes, who was it insisted that the original Beatles drummer, Pete Best, be sacked because he was too good-looking and all the girls screamed at him? Right first time.)

Someone once said that pop stars must be either sexy or profound; when you get the pair, you've hit the jackpot. Lennon was neither. 'Imagine''s lyrics could have come out of a stoned fortune cookie or maudlin Christmas cracker, and generally appeal to vicious go-getters who'd sell their best pet to a torture lab if the price was right. But more seriously, he wasn't sexy in the least – he was hideous, even when young. Those piggy little eyes, that thin, curtain-twitching little mouth, the voice a tight whine of ill-temper – ugh! If he was anything like as unattractive, whiny and boring as a child as he was as an adult, I'm not surprised his mother – Julia, by all accounts an attractive, intelligent, high-spirited woman who must have felt she'd given birth to a switched baby – ran away and left him with his Aunt Mimi. (See that early giveaway as to his manicured roots, by the way; working-class people never refer to their mother's sister as 'Aunt'; she is invariably 'Auntie'.)

The young adult Lennon was an appealing chap, too: this is the man, remember, who, in front of a packed dressing room, shouted 'Queer Jew' in response to Brian Epstein fussing, 'Now what shall I call this autobiography of mine?' He was crap during the Beatles – everyone knows that Paul wrote 99 per cent of all the decent songs – and crap after the Beatles. He was always the weakest link. I'll take the spirit and soul of Ringo's 'Back Off Boogaloo' and 'It Don't Come Easy' over the smug platitudes of 'Woman' or 'Starting Over', any day.

Ah, the Yoko years! Move over Romeo and Juliet, Dante and Beatrice and Jimmy and Janette Krankie, and let this pair of lovers show you how it's really done! In reality, of course, their alliance was a fetid mess of domestic violence, drug addiction and mutual adultery – hey, if I'd wanted that, I could have got it at home. After the initial provincial excitement of copping off with a 'Jap', as Lennon so frequently referred to his lady love, I think it fair to say that there wasn't even a great deal of physical attraction – on either side – and who can blame either one?

16 DECEMBER 2000

My friend Joanne Good drives what I sometimes think must be the best morning radio show in the country. Broadcasting as Breakfast Live in Brighton, six days a week from 6 to 9 a.m., on BBC Southern Counties Radio ('serving Surrey, Sussex and north-east Hampshire' – I don't know why, but the specificness of that 'north-east Hampshire' always makes me laugh), she is tireless and shameless, with the personality of a hydraulic pump crossed with a go-go girl, even at that time of morning. She jumps from topic to totally unrelated topic – from the Panzer Mansion, the Brighton mansion that was full of midgets between the wars, to the girly Seventies habit of writing pop stars' names on one's rough book at school – with all the enthusiasm of a nine-year-old let loose in Claire's Accessories.

To make things bittersweet, Joanne has an enemy, one 'E. Thompson', who despises her so much that she will not even do her the courtesy of writing to her on a nice piece of notepaper, and instead sends her harsh missives on the back of cancelled cheques and various other paper waste. Rose Red to Joanne's Snow White, 'E. Thompson' is like Anne Robinson with PMT, and seems obsessed with raining on Joanne's parade by correcting her grammar, picking on her pronunciation and generally letting her know what a silly girl she is. Because Joanne is so used to being popular, she reads these letters with a voice full of disbelief and doubt, almost as if she thinks it is one of her friends having a laugh. And then, never missing a beat, she is immediately back to her old bouncy self, uninhibitedly scampering up and down the keyboard of her mind like a cartoon kitten trying to play the piano. Forget the endless sea, sodomy and members of Supergrass that make Brighton such a joy; Joanne's radio show alone is all the reason you need to move here.

But there is a downside to Joanne. Not one, but two people inhabit her body. She was, and still is, an actress – if you watched *Crossroads* in the early Eighties, you'll remember her as Carole Sands, the waifish blonde beauty who worked as a mechanic at the motel garage, predating Kylie Minogue's Charlene by at least half a decade. These days, it's *Casualty* and panto, but to hear her go on you'd think it was Chekhov and Pinter. Alongside Joanne the Broadcaster, who is down to earth, vivid and witty as you could wish, there lives Joanne the Luvvie, who is frankly unbearable. Last week, discussing her forthcoming appearance in *Cinderella* alongside Julian Clary and a huge pumpkin, she compared acting to 'being in the trenches during the First World War, and about to go over the top'. For once, she wasn't joking.

Actors have always been preposterous people, but such military metaphors take their folly to new heights of deliciousness. Who can forget Liz Hurley stating that she would never date 'a civilian' (i.e. a non-actor), because they wouldn't be able to deal with the pressure? (The pressure of being caked in make-up and having their photo taken, this must be.) Then there are people who should know better encouraging thesps to think of themselves as warriors – Richard Eyre, talking about Jason Robards in the *Guardian* last week, gushed that, 'like a campaign veteran, he speaks of the music of *Long Day's Journey* in the tones of a man who loves the smell of napalm in the morning'. Ew!

Surely the word 'punter' would be a better choice than civilian? Being an actor is far more like being a prostitute than a soldier: you get hired for the way you look, and you show private parts of your body to strangers, which I've never heard was the way to make it big in the SAS – the Navy, maybe. I've never got an answer from even the most know-all of my regular detractors/

correspondents, so I'll ask the question again – when Demi Moore shows her breasts on film or Sharon Stone her vagina, what, exactly, makes them artistes and not sex industry workers, albeit highly astute, excellently paid sex industry workers? I'm not being snotty; I'm genuinely interested.

As with prostitutes, the money actors get for their goods goes down as they age past their peak of physical perfection. Just look at Arnie, down from $20m to $15m a picture, with a promise of only $8m if the next one lays an egg. Also, one feels a good deal more contempt for well-bred and educated types – your Vanessas and Emmas, who lower themselves to it – than for the cheap and cheerful Martines and Patsys, who might otherwise be wasting their beauty in Woolworths. Of course, some men go to prostitutes not for sex but to hear them tell their sad story – take a bow, Melanie Griffith, whose films no one has been to see for a decade but whose tale of woe, broadcast daily on the Internet, has made her hot once more.

There are exceptions to every rule – Kathy Burke, Rachel Weisz and Jude Law, for example, are the very models of dignity, restraint and perception, both as people and as artistes – but, generally, actors are horrifically silly. So, are they actors because they're silly, or silly because they're actors? Whatever, 'stress' – that great mantra alibi of the silly at work – has been adopted by actors as by no other group of workers; not nurses, not teachers, not people who work for Marco Pierre White. Remember Stephen Fry running out on his colleagues on that first night and sending a bleating letter to the papers about the stress and strain he was under? Yeah, like the secret police came in the middle of the night, forced him out of bed at gunpoint and made him do all those acting jobs and commercials that earned him so many millions of pounds. Just what is so stressful about a prolonged, incredibly well-paying game of Let's Pretend?

They're still at it. 'It was a nightmare,' says *Cold Feet*'s John Thompson of filming three TV shows. 'I was becoming a multiple personality!' As Larry Olivier said to Dustin Hoffman after the latter had been agonising over how to play a scene, 'Ever thought of acting, dear boy?'

Lots of actors like to play up their social conscience; many even claim to be socialists ('socialist actor' must rate with 'friendly fire' as one of the best oxymorons of all time). Without fail, they talk about what hard work play-acting is, with not a thought to what an insult such jabber is to miners, fire fighters and the like, or even to people with profoundly boring jobs. The fact is that being an actor, or a writer, or a footballer, or anything you enjoy, is not a pain, it's a privilege. If it does cause you so much stress, maybe that's because you're not very good at it. (It is interesting that those, such as Hurley and Fry, who moan the most about how hard acting is are indeed spectacularly bad at it.) Perhaps stress is just Mother Nature's way of telling us that we're crap at our jobs and should try something new.

23 DECEMBER 2000

A few weeks ago, I read a feature in the *Daily Mail* by Paul Burrell, the former butler to the late Princess of Wales – 'My rock,' she called him. Burrell has been as loyal and devoted a friend to the Princess since her death as he was during her life, and I'm sure what he wrote – 'What would the Royals buy for Christmas?' – was intended to be a soft-focus, sepia-tinted glimpse of a much-missed fascinator at a nostalgic time of year. I must say, though, that, in the picture it painted of the deluxe isolation of the Windsors, and especially of the vulnerable and fragile girl who became their brood mare par excellence, I found this romp through the royal wish-list easily as chilling as any treacherous Highgrove phone conversation transcript or bland Buck Pal message of sympathy. With the media currently wetting itself over Prince William, it wouldn't hurt for a minute to remember his mother, without whom he wouldn't have ended up looking like that. Not with Camilla Parker Bowles as a mum.

Each Christmas, Burrell would help the Princess locate, wrap and dispatch more than 200 presents. Featuring heavily among these would be aromatherapy kits – which, for me, have come to symbolise the fragrant solitude of the modern civil sex war, as bored housewives and career girls too good for the miserable men on offer wallow in candle-lit limbo in aromatherapy baths called such things as Sensuality and Afterglow while their putative suitors download barnyard porn in their locked studies. Then there would come the Smythson address books, in hand-bound goatskin, £195, in which the Princess and her circle might carefully write the personal details of all those close friends whose husbands and wives they would one day sleep with, if they hadn't already.

I find it particularly poignant that she was apparently a collector of Halcyon Days enamel boxes; all that clutter, to soften that harsh, blaring life – £85 for a poxing empty tin box! You can see why the firm has got four royal warrants, for its products' extortionate hollowness echoes the Windsor way. To obscure her loneliness even further, here comes her army of Herond hand-painted china animals, from £55 for a tiny 'frog prince' to £4,000 for a limited-edition giraffe. 'Each year, I would ensure that the latest edition was carefully wrapped and placed inside the Princess's stocking, which I had filled on Wills's and

Harry's behalf,' reports Burrell, and what a wealth of estrangement and loss there is in this good servant's innocent testimony.

Diana would, according to Burrell, turn to Turnbull & Asser for bespoke shirts, ties and dressing gowns for her faithless husband and stolen sons – I mention this only because the appropriateness of the name of this hawker of haberdashery to the ruling classes is so delightful. (Almost as gorgeous as my husband's divorce lawyers, Hart & Loveless!) From J. Floris would come scented candles, fragrances and vaporising oils – the Princess was particularly fond of Seasonal Spice at this time of year, doubtless to drown out the pong of paranoia, the stink of betrayal and the whiff of cordite coming off Balmoral. Price's candles – a dozen for £6.90 – would provide the lighting at every royal dining table, ensuring that daylight was not let in upon the magic and, even more important, that the hated face of the spouse opposite could be mutated – after a few tots of The King's Ginger Liqueur, available only from Berry Bros & Rudd of St James's – into the welcoming features of the beloved.

From the General Trading Company – 'an Aladdin's Cave for those in Sloane Ranger territory' – Diana would buy those tragic cushions whose mottoes became so horribly apt with the unfurling of her miserable life. I'M A LUXURY FEW CAN AFFORD – GOOD GIRLS GO TO HEAVEN; BAD GIRLS GO EVERYWHERE – THOSE WHO SAY THAT MONEY CAN'T BUY YOU HAPPINESS DON'T KNOW WHERE TO SHOP. She would also pick up china sweet dishes, no doubt for her fellow bulimics to display their poison of choice. And she might grab a monogrammed washbag for her husband from Eximious, By Appointment to the Prince of Wales, in which he might keep those all-important unguents for removing the stench of his adultery.

Silver monogrammed key chains (£40 upwards) make a perfect

gift for men and women alike, apparently, and are so much more appropriate than the cufflinks saying 'Gladys' and 'Fred' which the ever-sensitive Prince Charles wore to dinner on the first night of his honeymoon, only to be amazed when his unreasonable, hysterical wife showed distress at his continuing devotion to his mistress. (In an interesting insight into the cesspit that is the Parker Bowles mind, isn't it attractive how the very idea of working-class names, attached to such obviously classy pieces of ass as herself and Chas, struck her as being such a hoot?)

Much is made of Diana's 'lonely' Christmases in later years, but I bet they seemed like heaven after being locked up with the Addams Family all those years. She did have family, after all – sisters and a brother who would have been happy to have her. But what people who are trapped in the tradition of the family Christmas fail to realise is that, once you have made good your escape, voluntary or otherwise, the prospect of living through the whole dreary panto again, this time with another set of personality disorders and ancient grudges, is not an especially attractive one.

There is a lot of cant talked about The Family at Christmas, with those such as myself – preparing to face my first Christmas as an orphan – the focus of pity and concern from those who will be enmeshed in the bosom of theirs. But far from each family becoming a Holy Family at this time of year, it seems to my jaded outsider's eyes that, with a few lucky exceptions, most families become royal families, waving expensive geegaws at each other to divert attention from each other's dismay at having to play the same old tired roles – harassed housewife, bluff paterfamilias, exasperated adult children – that we spend the rest of the year struggling so valiantly to escape. Though I loved my parents to bits, the prospect of my first Christmas spent as a free agent – no one's daughter, mother or wife – seems incredibly exciting and exotic, and not a little overdue. So don't all you family types feel too sorry for us solitaires. In return, we'll try not to feel too sorry for you, stuck with your families this Christmas, when you'd far rather be with those you love.

30 DECEMBER 2000

Resolution. Even the word I don't like. It sounds like revolution, then sneaks away with a weasly ssss. And, of course, it's the opposite of revolution – it won't change anything. Sure, it'll make you feel like the hero of your own story, but isn't that a bit of a sad desire to start with?

Attach the word to New Year's, of course, and you've got a recipe for true cretinism. Is there still anyone over the age of 12 who makes New Year's resolutions? If I've learned anything from 41 years of being on this planet, it's that uttering the words 'I'm never going to (insert pet vice here) again' makes you look about as worldly as Tom Kitten. Yes, you will, and yes, your words will come back to haunt you, making your defeat all the more poignant. Then you'll end up saying, 'Well, I'm strong enough now to give in to temptation just the once', and before you know it you're doing tricks for bottle tops in Cardboard City.

I am of the opinion that interfering in people's self-destructiveness, or even in their mild hell-raising, actually makes the situation far worse. The three great addiction stories of the year were those of Robbie Williams, Daniella Westbrook and Will Self, and the various fates of these famous addicts carried an interesting lesson. Self has taken many cures for heroin addiction, administered both by himself and by alleged professionals.

But despite a lot of hypocritical cant from Mr Dictionary-Swallower over the years, he had never been truly drug-free for more than five minutes in the past 30 years or so until earlier this year: suddenly, while wrapping a huge slab of dope in a perfume-drenched cloth in order to take it to America to get him through a reading tour, he got this overview of himself and looked down at this forty-something father of three indulging in this terminally undignified activity. That was what got him clean, he swears; not the expensive therapy or the self-loathing, but the sheer inappropriateness of it all.

The simple difference between Self, who did give up, and Williams and Westbrook, both of whom fall off the wagon more often than cheap sound systems, is that Self was almost twice their age and had therefore done loads more drugs. There comes a day when intoxication, like anything else, becomes boring, and a clean-up undertaken under these circumstances would seem to stand a whole lot more chance of sticking than one that is tried because society doesn't approve or you might get the sack from a soap opera. Vitally, Westbrook and Williams are young and beautiful – she still looks better with just the one nostril than most of us do with two – and there is nothing like being young and beautiful to make you feel immortal.

Over Christmas and the New Year, all of our shabby double standards about intoxication come into play. As we reel from party to party, well fed and employed, we are meant to heed the words of the Homeless Tsar – and in this case how appropriate that title is, tsars being a byword for treating oppressed people very badly in a cold climate – and not give as much as a spare 50p piece to the poor youngster on the blanket outside the bank in case he or she spends it all on drink! But if being homeless at Christmas or the New Year doesn't deserve a drink, what does? Wouldn't it be funny, though totally understandable, if those who live on the streets looked at us and pitied us for our inability to be happy without getting smashed, despite all the comforts we have? While reminding us that every junkie started out on a puff of marijuana and therefore we can't be trusted to try it without being punished by law (and at the same time condemning the nanny state), the curtain-twitching Tory press will contrive both to egg us on and to rein us in where drink is concerned, this year as all others.

Do these hacks actually get paid for reminding us to drink one glass of water for every glass of alcohol? Does everyone not know by now that this is wise? And does anyone actually do it? But if you think about it, the Alternate Glass Of Water theory is to the liver what the Marquess of Queensbury rules are to fighting: that is, it doesn't actually protect the body in the long run, but just enables it to take punishment for longer without switching off, as it would if left to itself while being drowned in alcohol or hit around the head. In both cases, something that is obviously very bad for people is encouraged by 'sensible' precautions, which simply add up to more profits for drinks manufacturers and boxing promoters alike.

Having said that, I certainly plan to spend another happy New Year insensible with drink, because that's the kind of crazy guy I am. But I do so in the knowledge that I am as much a drug abuser as the sweet-faced junkie in the street, and, like him – but unlike your self-deluding 'sensible' drinker – I won't be boring friends with tales of my hangovers or swearing never to do it again. Once you're hooked, you're hooked, and then all that matters is carrying off your addiction with a certain self-aware dignity until such time as it becomes that worst of all things, a bore, to you. Then, and only then, can you really think seriously about getting and staying clean.

If old Alanis Morissette was here, I bet she'd say that this next thing was ironic, but nevertheless: it is sad and strange that even though we may behave bestially when intoxicated, what separates us from our animal friends is the knowledge that we are all going to die. And if that isn't the scariest, creepiest thing you've ever heard, then you're a cooler customer than me, Gunga Din. Mankind drinks and drugs himself insensible because he knows he's not around for long, and that, not some highfalutin heraldry, is what elevates us above the rest of the natural world. 'By making a beast of himself man forgets the pain of being human,' said no less than Sam Beckett.

So, next time you see some disgusting drunk – be he suited and booted and reeling home from the City, or sitting on the pavement with piles and a pet rat called Satan – just think: maybe the reason he's like that is because he's simply more sensitive than sensible, social-drinking, Chardonnay-sipping you. Maybe you're the brute, and that's why he's there and you're here, reading the *Guardian* like a civilised human being. Happy New Year!